I have had the great privilege of seei and through Rebecca's life. Her own incredible personal healing was the spark that ignited this intense fire and desire to help encourage the body of Christ to better understand and minister divine healing. I have personally been inspired by watching Rebecca practice what she shares throughout this book. She has seen many, many people healed in this wonderful journey and I believe *HOPE: A Practical Guide to Praying for Healing* will be a game changer for all who read it.

JASON CHIN
Founder of Love Says Go Ministries (Basel, Switzerland)
Author of *Love Says Go*

The question of "Does God still heal today?" has plagued many of us as believers. In her book, *HOPE,* Rebecca comes alongside us like a world-class coach with practical tools grounded in biblical truth to answer that question and reorient our thinking about healing. Rebecca and *HOPE* give us permission to be ourselves and to be on our own journey. By the end of the book, you will feel like a runner with your feet planted at your starting block, ready to begin the great race that God has before you. I highly recommend this resource as a practical, powerful, and potential igniting tool.

KRISTEN D'ARPA
Founder of i Go Glocal and Kristen D'Arpa Ministries
Author of *Kingdom Culture School of Ministry* curriculum

This fresh and compelling book reflects the author's desire to take Scripture seriously and at face value, as well as her desire to bear honest witness to her own experience of God's redeeming and healing love. As you journey with the author through the Word and through her own restoration, you may come to see God and yourself in a radically new way, which, as the author points out, could just transform your whole life!

DR. GERALD WRIGHT
Professor of Intercultural Studies, Palm Beach Atlantic University

HOPE: A Practical Guide to Healing is not a book—but an invitation. This book is for those who want more of God, are not satisfied with one more sermon, book, or lecture on propositional truth or are fed up with spiritual life meetings promising five ways, guaranteed or money back, to revive one's soul. Additionally, this book is for those who see the power of God to heal, so prevalent in the Gospels and book of Acts, but wonder why we see little today. This is an honest book and has the feel of a friendly conversation with Ribnick in Starbucks. Be careful: As you again think of God's love and the power of the kingdom of God amongst us, perhaps you, like Rebecca, will be forever changed.

DR. ROBERT DUFFETT
Former president of Eastern University (Philadelphia, Pennsylvania)

I love this book! *HOPE* is not a theory on healing but rather a handbook of how healing can become a normal part of your life. Rebecca tackles the hard questions that all of us have had concerning healing. She sets a solid biblical foundation and then fills the pages with personal testimonies of God's healing power at work today. Rebecca is a model of what God wants to do in you and through you! As you read this book, may your faith be ignited and may you be activated into a lifestyle of miracles.

BECKY BABCOCK
Director of Escuela Sobrenatural and Escuela de Formación Extrema
(Buenos Aires, Argentina)

I am grateful to Rebecca Ribnick for writing *HOPE: A Practical Guide to Praying for Healing.* Not only has she walked a serious healing journey herself, she is fighting for others to receive healing as well. In *HOPE,* Rebecca has taken serious theological concepts and brought new life to them through a strong knowledge and understanding of God's Word. *HOPE* provides a refreshing vantage point for every person to walk in God's healing.

PASTOR KRISTI GRANER
Founder and director of Dare to Believe Ministry

In Acts 1, Luke writes about what Jesus began both to do and teach. This book reveals a proper understanding of the Scriptures concerning healing and miracles. It is also filled with the practical application of these precious truths. As I read it, I was gripped by the reality of the author's own personal journey and was amazed by her resolve to see Jesus' healing grace released through her life. It has inspired me and I believe it will do the same for you to release God's love, compassion, and healing.

JEFF COLLINS
International minister, founder of Jeff Collins Ministry
Ministries of Vision International

It has been an honor and privilege to know Rebecca and watch her not just write this book but live this message. *HOPE* is very comprehensive, yet highly personal and engaging. This book will motivate you to see Jesus' love and power flow through you to impact the surrounding world.

PAUL RAPLEY
International minister, founder of Paul Rapley Ministries
Medically healed of cancer, supernaturally healed of numerous pains

HOPE

a practical
guide to
praying for
healing

REBECCA RIBNICK

HOPE: A PRACTICAL GUIDE TO PRAYING FOR HEALING
Copyright © 2018 Rebecca Ribnick

ISBN-13: 978-1-7328934-0-5

Edited by Lauren Stinton
Cover Design by Georgia Dahler Designs
Layout by Jonathan McGraw

Printed in the United States of America

• • •

To Mom and Dad.
Your tenacity kept me alive.
Your encouragement kept me going.
And your support means health and
freedom for countless others.
It was worth it.
It was all worth it.

• • •

CONTENTS

Foreword 11

Introduction 15

01: The Question of Beginnings 17

02: The Question of Who He Is 31

03: The Question of Who We Are 47

04: The Question of Will: Part 1 63

05: The Question of Will: Part 2 77

06: The Question of Cost and Kingdom Come...........89

07: The Question of Origin....................................105

08: The Question of Punishment and Lessons............121

09: The Question of Gifting...................................143

10: The Question of Failure...................................159

11: The Question Without an Answer......................175

12: The Questions That Limit Us............................191

13: The Question of How: Part 1 213

14: The Question of How: Part 2 231

15: The Question of Increase 247

16: The Question of Endings (and New Beginnings)..........267

Acknowledgments..285

Testimonies 287

Bibliography and Suggested Resources..................289

FOREWORD

...

The young woman stood smiling at the front of the crowded room. "All right," she said. "Now that we've learned, we're going to do."

A stranger to me previously, Rebecca had just spent an hour explaining the New Testament's teaching on the subject of divine healing. As a biblical scholar, I found nothing objectionable; her explanation was concise and accurate. I believed that our God does heal. I just had never seen it happen personally. That's why I had come.

"God particularly wants to heal backs, knees, and other joints tonight," she continued. "Are there people here who would like healing in those areas?"

Although I had intended just to observe at this meeting, at this point I thought, *Why not?* A group of seven or eight of us somewhat hesitantly got to our feet. My right knee, which for some years doctors had told me required surgical replacement (a "total knee," as they called it), objected to my change of position, as always. I first injured the knee in a judo match in college, then absentmindedly slammed a car door on it some years later, then had it give way entirely while I pumped my bike up a precipitous incline. When we approached such tests of our conditioning, my brother always sang out, "Hills are our friends!" Well, not for me, not that day. Afterward I made things work the best I could, but lately even standing to teach my classes had become dauntingly painful. Constricted by the knee's growing limitations, my life was shrinking more and more. The time for the surgery could not be far off.

"Okay, look around," Rebecca continued. "Do you see those who are standing? You who are still sitting are going to be the ones doing the praying. Don't worry; I'll be here if you need me. Please gather around those who are already standing. Distribute yourselves so that several people can pray for each one who is expressing a need."

Next to me, my wife, Cathy, arose and moved away to join a group surrounding a woman ten feet away. For the next few minutes, the room filled with the sounds of shuffling feet and chairs being shoved aside to facilitate movement. Clusters of people were now scattered around the room's perimeter and crisscrossing the interior. No one was near me, however, except for the young man I had noticed earlier in the row ahead of me. He was unknown to me, although I had been attending this church for more than ten years. I later learned that he was a friend of Rebecca's, already familiar with the practice of healing prayer.

"Go ahead. You know what to do. I've explained everything you need to know. Please interview the person you are praying for, learn about their situation, and go to prayer. I will be moving around the room to answer any questions." Rebecca edged to the far side of the room.

The young man in the row in front of me had stood waiting. Now as Rebecca began to move about and as a murmur of low conversation and prayer formed a backdrop, he turned to face me with a friendly smile. Contrary to Rebecca's instructions, however, he didn't begin to interview me, nor did he pray. He simply stated, "God has healed your knee."

What? I hadn't told anyone anything about the knee. How did he know? Then I became aware of an electric tingling extending a few inches north and south of my kneecap on the bad leg. As a scholar, I try to cultivate a practiced objectivity, and at this point it kicked in. I observed with no particular emotion that my right knee area continued to feel this tingling for ten minutes. While noting this alien sensation, I also watched and listened as people around the room rejoiced and exclaimed, "I don't hurt now! I can move without pain. Oh, praise God!" Others remained in quiet prayer. A few were like me, just watching, observers wondering what God was doing.

At length Rebecca ended the night with prayer and the group began to break up. Only a few people remained behind when Cathy and I left. Walking to the car, my knee felt somehow different, but the precise difference eluded me. I didn't say much but told Cathy that I thought something had happened during prayer. Arriving home, I descended from the entry level to the bedroom via the stairs, closely checking the knee's response. For some time, stairs had been especially painful, but that night I felt nothing. For the next several days, I continued to check the knee. More and more, my confidence grew that God had healed me. Because my knee had not felt normal for twenty years, it took some time to assess. As the realization settled upon me that I was no longer disabled, I could think of nothing else. I went about my routine in a kind of daze. God had touched me— me! Personally. Physically. Immediately.

This was the most profound spiritual experience of my life since my initial conversion to Christ as a high school senior. One thing was sure, I thought. I didn't need the various arguments for the existence of God anymore. Let the philosophers have them! Virtually all my knee's cartilage between the tibia and the femur had abraded through injury and wear. That was a physical fact. Now that cartilage seemed to be back, equally a fact. The utter reality of the supernatural repeatedly struck my awareness like a splash of cold water. It was literally something I could touch. God changed my life that night in Rebecca's hands-on seminar.

Soon I began myself to pray regularly for others to be healed, and God did amazing things. I am still seeing miracles as Cathy and I teach and minister healing and deliverance. I have seen cancer healed numerous times; I have seen backs and shoulders restored, ulcerative colitis disappear but for a small scar or two, diseased eyes healed, ears returned to full function after doctors have given up. Through me God has healed other people's knees. I have seen drug-resistant pneumonia clear in response to prayer. A young woman's damaged rib cage, the left side "permanently" twisted by a terrible accident that left her in continual agony, returned to its normal position under my hands in the name of Jesus. Healing: Again and again, I have seen it. I expect, by God's infinite mercy and grace, to keep seeing it.

As I have prayed and learned, I have also come to be great friends with Rebecca, the person who first showed me that healing is real and that God does it as we come to him in faith and expectation. As brother and sister in Christ, we continue to seek more from God. And naturally, as a professor, my reaction to something this big has been to read everything I could lay my hands on about divine healing. I have collected and absorbed many helpful books. You would likely recognize a number of the authors, because they are famous. But I can tell you that none of these books is better than the one you hold in your hand, and most are not as good. Don't believe me? Then try this: Begin to read the first chapter. I guarantee you will not put this book down until you look up, surprised, and realize you are in the third or fourth chapter. It reads well, and it reads true, because it was born in experience, and born in God.

DR. MICHAEL O. WISE
Scholar-in-Residence
University of Northwestern–St. Paul

INTRODUCTION

. . .

"You're so brave, baby girl."

I nod slowly, reassured by my mother's voice, even though I can't quite see her face. The pain does that; it makes everything else a blur.

Beads of sweat break out on my forehead as another wave of intense pain racks my body. I squeeze my eyes shut and tightly grasp my mom's hand. *Jesus,* I think, *I can't do this. It hurts too much. Just take me home.*

When the pain subsides, I open my eyes to see my mom's face. Comforting. Loving. Scared.

Okay, Jesus, I pray again. *Don't take me but help me. This pain is too much. This cross is too much for me to bear.*

. . .

I wish that were the only time this scene played out. It wasn't. Unfortunately for all of us, we relived this scene day after day, month after month. For sixteen years, I battled an incredibly painful and often debilitating disease. I believed God made me sick for some purpose I didn't or couldn't understand, so I suffered as nobly as I could, attempting to carry what I thought was my divinely assigned burden.

However, contrary to my own theological understanding of healing, miracles, and God's working today, Jesus radically healed me and rewrote my future. In a moment, he freed me from years of pain and illness.

This book is not about suffering, nor is it about surviving. This book is about healing. In all of the painful, soul-searching, question-asking, heart-wrenching messiness associated with sickness and disease, this book is about how God already chose to heal two thousand years ago and how we can apprehend that healing and see it here and now in our lives.

Jesus said that we would know a tree by its fruit (Matt. 7:17–20). For me, that looks like twelve years and counting of health. It also means witnessing countless miracles firsthand as I've learned more about healing. Through a stint on the mission field, three years of ministry school, and traveling around the world studying and teaching about healing, I've learned that Scripture instead of experience must set my expectation for how God will move in my life. I've learned that he's better than we think he is, and if it's not too good to be true, it's not the end of the story. Above all, I've learned that there is hope for things to change.

I can't promise healing, but I can promise hope. Not the kind of hope that is synonymous with "One day I wish . . ." No, I mean the confident expectation of coming good to your life.

What I didn't know lying in that bed all those years ago is now the drumbeat of my life: Jesus still heals.

1

THE QUESTION OF BEGINNINGS

...

This story begins not in far-off India or the remote African jungle but in a typical midwestern suburb, in a typical midwestern family. The protagonist is towheaded and shy, and as most children would, she tags along with her big sister, acting as both accomplice and accidental foil in their plans to antagonize their brother. Her daddy calls her his "sweet little girl," and in his warm embrace, she knows she is.

It isn't until this little girl is four or five years old that her parents begin to notice a problem. If their happy-natured child catches a cold, it quickly turns into bronchitis or pneumonia, and a day in bed becomes several in the hospital. The cycle repeats itself over and over, baffling doctors and leaving the girl in chronic pain.

The family is a kind, loving, Bible-believing Christian family. The parents regularly pray for a medical breakthrough and wisdom for the doctors. But nothing changes. Their little girl is often bedridden and continues to grow worse. Finally, a nurse at the children's hospital pulls the mother aside and bluntly tells her, "Your daughter isn't improving with our care," and suggests they consider alternative medicine. Willing to try anything, the parents pursue the nurse's recommendation.

Now thirteen and too weak to take even the few steps from the car to the doctor's office, the girl lies in her father's arms as he carries her into the building. To their great joy, inside they receive the first step in the breakthrough they so desperately seek: a diagnosis. The new doctor recognizes the autoimmune disease wreaking havoc on the girl's body and knows it is the underlying cause of numerous secondary illnesses. He prescribes a regimen of twice-weekly IVs consisting of a potent cocktail of vitamins and minerals to boost her weakened immune system, as well as a strict diet and closely guarded sleep schedule and exercise program. The rigorous course of treatment and highly disciplined lifestyle create a fragile balance within the girl's body that opens a whole new life to her. It isn't perfect—this life still consists of IVs that sting and cause her arm to ache, regular injections, countless pills, and only enough energy to be involved in school, church, and sports on a part-time basis, but this new balance is a measurable upgrade from the previous years spent in the tiny world that existed between her bed and the couch.

Though occasionally disheartened by her inability to join her friends in eating pizza, attending sleepovers, or playing a full game of basketball, the girl is pleased. This new life is far better than the years she was too sick to attend school or see her friends. A deep-seated conviction that her sickness somehow brings a unique glory to God helps her accept her circumstances. She believes her illness is her cross to bear, and so she bears it daily with little complaint. Friends, family, and other well-meaning Christians praise her resolve and hold her up as a model of faith in the midst of suffering.

The girl's positive attitude and strict life perimeters keep everything in balance throughout high school. When it comes time to discuss colleges, she chooses a school in southern Florida so she can spread her wings—and live in a climate that eases the dull ache that haunts her waking hours. Nervous about how her body will respond to the new routine, the girl is happily surprised when she makes it through her first year of college, followed by a second. God provides for her through caring friends, helpful professors, and school breaks at home consisting of IVs and sleep.

Yet she can't shake a sense of foreboding as she struggles to complete her sophomore year. She knows her reserve is empty, and there is no strength remaining to continue for another semester.

The summer between her sophomore and junior years of college, roughly sixteen years after this torment began, the girl shares her fears with a dear friend. This friend is the daughter of missionaries and grew up outside of Western culture. More important, she grew up outside of Western mindsets surrounding healing. The friend suggests the girl's physical illness could be spiritually related.

At first, the girl is offended. Instead of hearing a helpful suggestion, she hears the same accusation that was frequently brought against her throughout her lengthy diagnostic process—she's making it all up. Defensive and hurt, she tries to listen as her friend explains that things can be both physical and spiritual. The friend suggests they meet with her missionary mother, who regularly prays for inner healing with different individuals.

The girl goes home and thinks about the conversation. That night, trying unsuccessfully to sleep, she has a bad feeling so intense that it seems almost physical, as if something is sitting on her chest through the night. Realizing how desperate she is, she decides to schedule a time to pray with her friend's mother. She feels trapped in her own body, frustrated and afraid. She is certain that without a drastic change, she'll be forced to withdraw from college and return to her old routine of IVs and bed rest.

At the friend's house a few days later, the mother explains this strange new concept of inner healing and tells the girl what to expect. Skeptical but willing to try anything, the girl agrees and quietly bows her head and folds her hands, hoping against hope. Over the next several hours, her perseverance is rewarded in incredible ways. The great Counselor meets with her, bringing freedom and clarity to difficult areas of her life. Her anxiety dissipates as God gently replaces different hurts, painful memories, and heart wounds with his loving truth. She is amazed—she didn't know prayer could do this.

"I just don't feel like we're finished praying," the woman says when they stop for lunch. "Can you come back later today?"

The girl agrees and they set a time to continue where they left off. But to her surprise, the woman adds, "Don't let Satan stop you from coming back this evening."

The words startle the girl; she knows the devil is real and involved in the world, but she assumes it is only in the lives of those involved with the occult, or maybe it is something missionaries run into—but it definitely is not to be expected in suburban Midwest America.

Walking the girl to her car, the woman says again, "Don't let the devil stop you from returning tonight."

That statement, along with her sense of new and profound freedom, stick with the girl throughout the day. With a mixture of fear and anticipation, she returns to the friend's house that evening. During this second time of prayer, something wondrous happens. Jesus radically encounters her. To her complete surprise—and contrary to her understanding of how God interacts with people—Jesus shows her how he fights for her. It blows her mind. He reveals the source of her sickness and destroys it as she watches, removing the pain, the exhaustion, and all the endless hours of doctors' visits. It is a true miracle—the girl is fully healed.

Though the retelling of this story reads like a black-and-white encounter with God, it doesn't feel that way to the girl. At times, she is afraid she imagined it. She assumes visions or encounters with God are like those in the Bible—dramatic and involving something like writing on a wall or a blinding light from heaven that knocks you off your donkey. Only later does she learn that the majority of encounters with God are so small that they can be missed or mistaken for one's imagination. Also, even though she hated being sick, her understanding of how to live—her very identity—involved the illness. Without it, she doesn't know who she is.

Fortunately, Jesus heals the whole person. That night he healed her body and gave her a brand-new identity—she knows she is no longer the sick girl but is free to walk in the health, dreams, and abundant life he created for her. She remembers the advice she received from her friend's mother: Let time substantiate her healing before she talks about it with others, particularly those who are likely to question the validity of her encounter. Even though Jesus healed her in an instant, the process of learning what "healthy" looks and feels like in her everyday life ends up taking her years.

The morning after this encounter with Jesus, the girl still goes in for her scheduled IV, but as she watches the liquid steadily drip into her vein, she realizes it feels different. She knows this will be her final treatment. A smile spreads across her face as she catches the first glimpse of the full, healthy life ahead of her.

I can't help but smile and shake my head in amazement every time I tell this story. It's been twelve years since that wonderful day when Jesus dramatically and radically transformed my life. In a single moment, God removed something that had plagued me for over sixteen years, and he sparked a passion for healing within me that set in motion a wild, decade-long ride that sent me around the world and eventually back to school on the West Coast. Even more than a physical change, my healing was a direct encounter with the incredibly intimate and specific love God had for *me*, an encounter that forever marked me and recalibrated my understanding of just how good and personal my heavenly Father is.

I don't claim to have all the answers—far from it. What follows is intended only as an introduction to biblical healing (also called divine or miraculous healing). There's much more to experience, learn, and grow into on the subject. But what I can do is offer my own experience as someone who was surprised by God's healing power and—now—has lived twelve years and counting of a profoundly transformed life. As we go, you'll hear more of my adventures and what's kept me burning to see the full manifestation of God's kingdom here on earth.

STARTING OUT

Many people are surprised when they learn that my years of illness didn't lead me to pray for my own healing—not directly, anyway. There were moments when I cried out for relief or secretly wished for a miracle, but in many ways, my sickness and theology pacified my resistance to illness. I was resigned to my fate and lacked the physical and emotional energy necessary to do anything more than survive the day at hand. Sickness didn't spark my pursuit of biblical healing—my own miracle did.

Miraculous healings and the idea that something spiritual could affect me physically were entirely foreign to me before I was healed. In fact, I was ignorant of any relationship between the spiritual and physical that could influence my daily life and found the idea offensive. Nor had I ever personally witnessed God's miraculous power. After months of walking in my new health, I struggled to understand this concept and my own experience until one day, it felt like a certain passage of Scripture stood up and hit me on the head: "Before your very eyes Jesus Christ was clearly portrayed as crucified" (Gal. 3:1). Suddenly I saw that it was not a strange thing for the spiritual and physical worlds to be intertwined, but it was a normal part of our existence. The Holy Spirit opened my eyes to see that the very cornerstone of my faith, Christ crucified, is based on the fact that God did something physically that affected me spiritually. We are spirit, soul, and body, and each part of our triune nature impacts the others.

Being healed upended my theology of healing, but what took my body seconds to receive took my mind much, much longer. Reconciling my understanding of God with what happened that evening required wading through old mindsets and, to put it bluntly, some bad theology that kept me from seeing the truth about healing revealed in Scripture. It is my deep desire to see God's healing power on full display within the church. In this book, I want to remove some of the stumbling blocks and hurdles of offense that exist in the place between our experience and our understanding of biblical healing.

Wisdom dictates that we build a house upon a solid foundation, lest it be shaken and destroyed when the rain and floods come (see Matt. 7:24–27). And the rain and flood will come when we pursue healing, for the subject is irrevocably linked to the hardest moments and questions we face as humans. The Bible is always the first stop when studying doctrine or determining God's will for a given situation. So instead of jumping straight into a healing model that teaches us *how* to pray for healing, it's important that we lay a solid, scriptural foundation that teaches us *why* we pray and—even more important—who God is in light of the subject. To that end, this book is divided into three sections:

1. **The Basics:** And I mean the very basics. Not about healing, but about who God is and who we are in light of that revelation. It is essential that we get this down first, or we will approach God with uncertainty, and healing will become another way we try to earn our heavenly Father's affection.

2. **Healing Theology:** This is the largest section in the book and where we will dig into the heart of the matter: investigating the difficult topics and questions surrounding healing. These include:

    - Does God still heal miraculously?

    - Is it always God's will to heal?

    - Does God make us sick to teach us a lesson?

    - What is the origin of illness?

    - What is our role in healing?

    - What if someone isn't healed?

3. **Healing Prayer Model:** There are many ways to pray for healing (Jesus himself demonstrated several different methods), but in this book, we will walk through a simple prayer model that will get you started. This book also provides a few keys to hold on to before, during, and after you pray.

SET YOUR EXPECTATIONS HIGH

Have you ever gone to see a wildly popular movie, one everybody was raving about, but it ended up being a letdown because your expectations were too high? Improperly set expectations have the power to greatly impact our emotions and enjoyment. Expectations are tricky things; unmet expectations can be a considerable source of pain that leads us away from hope and toward the apparent safety of self-protection as we attempt to insulate our hearts from further pain. The result of unprocessed disappointment and unmet expectations is a life lived less bravely than our dreams require. Remembering our past pain, we limit what we dare hope for. We hedge our bets against future shortcomings instead of relying on our "God of hope" who desires to fill us with "all joy and peace" as we trust him, so we "may overflow with hope by the power of the Holy Spirit" (Rom. 15:13). Hope, the confident expectation of coming good, is a necessary ingredient for a healthy spiritual life.

In the same way that we tend to find whatever we're looking for and can't find what we don't look for, when we live with biblically sound expectations for God to work in and through our lives, we create the space for him to act. God wants to work through you more than you want him to work through you. In fact, God wants to encounter you more than you want to be encountered, and he wants to see you living in your amazing, uniquely designed destiny even more than you want to live in that destiny. His hope level for your life is off the charts. His expectations for your life are ridiculously high, and you do not disappoint him.

I want to live with the same level of hope that God has in every situation, regardless of what I'm facing. With that said, here are a few things I am fully expecting to occur as you read this book:

1. **God will encounter you.** God loves to encounter us with more of himself. Everyone who asks receives; those who seek find; and knocking garners an open door (Matt. 7:8). He's promised to be found by all who look for him (Jer. 29:13). In fact, it's impossible to ask for more of God and not receive more of him. He always responds to our call.

2. **You will get hungrier for more of God.** In the physical world, eating fills you up, but a funny thing happens in the realm of God's kingdom—the more we eat, the hungrier we get.[1] Each chapter and every testimony you'll read in this book are a fresh

---

1. I first heard this description of "kingdom appetite" explained by pastor and author Bill Johnson.

invitation into the limitless realm of intimately knowing our kind and loving God. The more we experience him and his goodness, the greater our desire will be to see his kingdom realities manifest in our lives. In the same way, doing the works of our heavenly Father only makes us hungrier to see more. The more spiritual "eating" we do, the hungrier for God we will become.

3. **Your heart will be set on fire.** There's a remarkable scene after the resurrection when Jesus joined a couple of his followers who were walking to Emmaus. For whatever reason, the men were kept from recognizing his identity. As they discussed their confusion regarding Jesus' crucifixion and inexplicably empty tomb, the still-unrecognized Jesus gave one of history's greatest Bible lessons, explaining the recent events in light of the Scriptures. Later that evening, after Jesus departed and they realized his true identity, the men made a profound statement in Luke 24:32: "Were not our hearts burning within us while he talked with us on the road and opened the Scriptures to us?" When biblical truth and the presence of God touch our lives, our hearts are set on fire.

   I can't anticipate every question, nor will this book answer all the critics' queries, but I believe that God's holy, empowering, igniting fire will fall on hungry hearts as they read this book. I pray this book will give you permission to pursue healing and that it will act as a match to hearts longing to be set on fire—it is fiery hearts that will set the world ablaze.

4. **People will be healed.** This may seem like a bold statement, but the longer I've studied divine healing, the more I am convinced of God's nature and desire to heal and the more confident I am of what he will do. God always backs up the teaching of his Word with a demonstration of his love and

power. That is how Jesus did things (see Matt. 4:23, 9:35). I'm not promising that everyone who reads this will be healed (though that's my prayer), but I do know that the keys presented here can lead to a lifestyle of expectancy and boldness that will see many people healed when you pray.

HOW TO WIN WITHOUT A FIGHT

Before we begin our investigation of God and healing, there's one last thing to mention: We are not transformed by trying harder. Isn't that wonderful, liberating news? Instead, we are transformed by the renewing of our minds (Rom. 12:2).[2] Nowhere does Scripture suggest that transformation comes through doing more or working harder, though that's often what we try. The Holy Spirit is at work leading us into all truth and teaching us to believe like Jesus does (John 16:13). Therefore, the question that leads to changed lives is not "How can I do that better?" but "What is a better belief?"

An apple tree naturally bears apples; it doesn't have to concentrate to avoid an orange or two appearing on its branches. Likewise, a lemon tree produces lemons. The very nature of the tree determines the fruit the tree will bear. Similarly, our root systems determine the fruit we will bear. As Christians, we are called to live lives that look like Jesus', who promised, "I am the vine; you are the branches. If you remain in me and I in you, you will bear much fruit" (John 15:5). If our lives don't match Jesus' in a given area—including healing—it signals an opportunity to upgrade our root systems (our beliefs). I pray that as you read this, your mind is continually renewed with scripturally sound beliefs that match those of Jesus, complete with similar fruit.

---

2. Pastor and author Steve Backlund was the first person I heard explain this concept. I highly recommend his great resources on the subject of renewing the mind.

CHAPTER KEYS

When I began my study of divine healing, my initial response was a painful mix of regret and sorrow over what I didn't know—how was it possible that I grew up in church, frequented Bible studies, and even attended a Christian university, yet I spent years suffering without anyone telling me about God's desire to heal or teaching me how to pursue healing? My initial sadness quickly melted into anger and offense. It was easier to be angry and offended over what I didn't know, sweeping it under a rug labeled "Doctrine I Don't Believe," than it was to embrace the reality of my own ignorance and the humility necessary to learn and grow.

You can't know what you've never been taught. Repositioning my own heart from offense to humility was an extremely important and often-repeated act that enabled me to see what I had missed for many years. If you are anything like me, it is possible offense may mark a few places of great opportunity for you as well. As you read this book, notice if and when offense creeps into your thoughts. Before we discuss healing, it is vital we recognize offense for what it is: a signal of where God wants to work in our lives. Otherwise, every time we are offended by what we don't know; what hasn't happened; or the physical, emotional, and mental pain surrounding the subject, we will shut down and miss the opportunity to step further into God's destiny for us—the lives we were created for. Our loving heavenly Father has incredible plans for you that include your walking in freedom and abundant life.

Americans have a strong cultural value for independence and making a way for oneself. We believe that through hard work and a little ingenuity, we can accomplish great things. This can-do spirit has led to many great innovations and ideas over the course of the last several centuries, while simultaneously placing great importance on doing things alone. My desire for this book is the exact opposite of this go-it-alone American individualism; I envision this book as part of a relay, not an individual race. Instead of running the same lap I have run—experiencing the trying, failing, questioning, frustration, and pain I experienced—I hope you can take the baton of my experience and keep going. Start a new lap.

MINISTRY

There's always more of God to know and experience. Few things make him happier than a desire to learn and grow in our knowledge, revelation, and relationship with him. He will transform our lives through the renewing of our minds until we naturally bear the good fruit he promised. And he will move mightily in and through us.

Father, thank you that you're continually revealing more of yourself to me and transforming me into the person you created me to be. Empower me by your Holy Spirit to grasp the depth, breadth, height, and length of your incredible love for me. Encounter me. Make me hungrier for you. Set me on fire. Enable me to learn humbly. Renew my mind with your truth until I hope, believe, and bear fruit like Jesus. May the sick be healed through my hands. In Jesus' mighty name I pray. Amen.

2

THE QUESTION OF WHO HE IS

...

The lunchtime rush is in full swing as I navigate the crowded café, searching for a place to eat my salad. Finding a table near the back, I sit down and promptly resume reading the book I began the night before. My food goes mostly untouched as I feast on story after story of God encounters and miracles. The author is a friend of mine—not a "super Christian" but an all-around regular guy. Yet time after time, God shows up and shows off in his life. As I read, I feel a growing desire for God to move similarly through my life.

God, I pray silently, *set me up with an opportunity to step out in faith today. And please make it obvious!*

"Excuse me. Is this seat taken?" A woman's voice breaks in on my thoughts.

I look up and can't believe what I see. "No, feel free," I manage to say, regaining my composure. I turn back to my book but to no avail—I can't ignore the forearm crutches the woman props against the table.

Finishing my lunch, I turn toward the woman and start a conversation. "Would you mind telling me what the crutches are for?"

"Not at all," she says and recounts an astonishing story that began with a slip on the ice that broke her neck and required multiple surgeries over the course of several years. She has metal rods and plates in her body to prevent paralysis. "I still need the crutches for support and have regular physical therapy, but only one other man in the world has walked after breaking his neck the same way." Her story is full of God moments, extraordinary coincidences, and just-at-the-right-time help.

"Wow. That is incredible," I say. I can feel my heart rate quicken, and butterflies swirl in my stomach in anticipation of my next few words. "I think this might be another one of those God moments you described. Is it okay if I pray for full healing in your neck?"

She consents, and right there in the noisy café, I pray for her. "I command all pain to go and full restoration to come in this neck and body in Jesus' name. Amen."

She seems surprised that my prayer lasted just a few seconds.

"How are you feeling?" I ask.

"That was very kind of you," she says in what feels like a brush-off. "I do feel peace, and you have so much love—" She stops speaking. Shock slowly spreads over her face as it dawns on her that she's turning just her neck, not her whole body, to speak to me. "I can't turn my neck this way! There's a metal bar right here that prevents it."

"God's healing you. Would you mind if I prayed again?" I place my hand on the spot she indicates. "Thank you for what you're doing. More, Lord."

"It feels all warm and like there's little bubbles all through my neck and back," she says, holding up her soda for emphasis. Her eyes fill with tears.

"That's amazing," I say, misty eyed. "Jesus has an incredible plan for your life. He loves you so much and just demonstrated his love to you."

We laugh and thank God together as the warm, bubbly feeling keeps working in her body. "I'm supposed to go to physical therapy right now," she tells me, still in shock. Fresh tears fill her eyes. "I can't wait to tell my husband."

• • •

Moments like the one in that café amaze me as God intervenes in the middle of normal life with a manifestation of his love and goodness. Healing is a physical manifestation of his unique and personal love, and it's what happens when his greater kingdom reality supersedes our current physical reality. Healing is literally heaven coming to earth.

For roughly sixteen years, I believed God sent my illness. I saw it as a cross to carry instead of an enemy to fight. I prayed to get through hard times, for God to sustain me, even for wisdom for the doctors treating me, but I do not recall a single time when I asked God for physical healing. I did not understand the true nature of God as a good Father. My lack of revelation about the very nature of his goodness kept me from hoping, praying, or expecting him to act out of that goodness toward me.

Two things are of paramount importance here: that we know, beyond a shadow of a doubt, God's nature as a kind, perfectly loving, and extraordinarily good Father, and that we validate our inherent need to personally encounter him as that Father. The foundation of our lives, the bedrock on which everything else is built, is knowing who he is and experiencing his love and goodness for ourselves. Experientially knowing and regularly encountering God's personal, unique, and perfect love for *me* is the key that unlocks the abundant life he created.

As John the Beloved wrote, "We know and rely on the love God has for us" (1 John 4:16). The goodness of God is the most significant takeaway from this book; everything else is secondary to personally knowing the love of God.

UNENDING GOODNESS

There's an amazing scene in Exodus where Moses asks to see God's glory. God replies, "I will cause all my goodness to pass in front of you" (Exod. 33:19). Moses looks for God's glory and finds his goodness, and in the process he learns it's impossible to encounter God apart from his goodness. God never takes a break from being good; he never changes his mind—whether you "deserve" to encounter his goodness or not. His goodness leads him to always act on our behalf and is so constant, so consistent, and so dependable that we can step out in faith solely on the revelation of his goodness and know he will never let us fall.

In fact, in the kingdom of God, we can never overestimate God's goodness and his desire to encounter us as our loving Father. Never. Graham Cooke, a noted Christian author and speaker, once contrasted the difference between worldly wisdom and heavenly wisdom. The first says, "If it's too good to be true, someone's about to get conned." But the second says, "If it's *not* too good to be true, it's not God." Think about it: The very foundation of Christianity is a too-good-to-be-true story if ever there was one. Our faith is based on the fact that God, out of his goodness, created us in his likeness and gave us authority over the earth; we promptly handed our authority over to Satan, but God's redemption plan was already in place. It was God's idea to become like us, die for us, be raised again, call us sons and daughters, and seat us in heavenly places with every spiritual blessing, so we could share in an inheritance with his Son. If that's not too good to be true, I don't know what is—and that's just the basic gospel message. When we are healed, four truths are impressed upon us simultaneously:

1. God is real.
2. God is personal.
3. God is powerful.
4. God is good.

These truths find footing in our hearts whether we are healed from cancer or a cold. God cannot remain an obscure, esoteric idea after we encounter him. There can be no question about his goodness, nor can we question his intensely personal kindness when he concerns himself with *our* pain. It is only a real, personally involved, powerful, and good God who takes away cancer, back pain, arthritis, hip pain, or anything else. It may offend our sensibilities that God is willing to heal something as "unimportant" as a hip when we consider the life-threatening issues facing our world like cancer or AIDS, but if it's important to you, it's important to God.

Children need to experience personal and specific love from their parents. It's not enough to know that Mom and Dad love people in general—I must know they love *me*. As a life-long Christian, I never thought to question God's existence or power or his love for the world in general, but I did occasionally wonder about his love and goodness for me. My own healing was the first time I experienced the too-good-to-be-true reality of life in the kingdom of God. God healed me, tangibly demonstrating his personal love and goodness for *me,* not the world at large. In a moment, he healed my body from years of illness and my heart from years of unspoken questions about my Father's love. My very identity changed from a girl who was special because of what she suffered to a girl who is special because of her Father's love. In a heartbeat, I became a uniquely loved and intimately known daughter instead of "the sick girl." God Almighty was closer, kinder, and more knowable than I ever imagined.

God is never separated from his nature, and he never changes. We are not big enough nor our actions grievous enough to effect a change in his character. He is fundamentally and unequivocally good. You can't get God without his goodness.

WANTING MORE

The years immediately following my healing were full of wonder and excitement. Every morning I got up before my roommates and prayed, "I've never done today healthy. How do we do it?" Each day was an adventure with endless possibilities never before available to me. It took me the next two years to relearn "normal." The strict discipline that had guided my life was no longer needed, and the possibility of milkshakes, staying up past eleven, and early morning surf sessions suddenly opened to me. I was like a little puppy running around experiencing life and my own personality for the first time. When I was asked to explain the drastic change, my eyes filled with tears, and I described the wonderful day when God's goodness touched my heart and body. Throughout my years of illness, I laughed at a joke or something funny but never just from the joy of living. Chronic emotional or physical pain robs us of our ability to "laugh at the days to come" (Prov. 31:25), but now I was able to play, live, and laugh simply because I was alive.

Wherever I went, I told the remarkable story of what God did for me, eager for everyone I met to experience my extremely good God for herself. After I received my bachelor's degree, my zeal for sharing God's goodness led me to accept an internship with a nonprofit in Southeast Asia, working with a group of missionaries. Yet as the years passed and life became "normal," a gnawing sense of hunger grew within me: I wanted more. I wanted to encounter God in all his goodness one more time.

When you're thirsty, your body is telling you it needs to be hydrated; you recognize this signal and respond by drinking water. This is one way the human body was designed to care for itself. If we ignore our thirst, we put ourselves in a dangerous position that can quickly become life threatening. In the same way, thirsting for an encounter with God is a spiritual signal. It tells us that we require a fresh touch of the love, kindness, and goodness of our heavenly Father. Trying to satisfy the desire for more of God by engaging only our minds, while ignoring the desperate cries of our hearts, is much like trying to quench thirst with coffee—your mouth may no longer be dry, but the real need isn't met.

When I returned to the States, I was a model of Christian industry, trying to drown out my thirst for a fresh encounter by drinking another cup of coffee. I attempted to bury my need for a fresh experience with God's goodness and personal love for me through discipline: I read and studied the Bible more, mentored more students, and volunteered more at my church, even telling others I was "three times the Lord's because he made me, redeemed me, and healed me." But then I would silently add, trying to convince myself, *And I don't deserve another thing from him. Others need what I've experienced.*

Spiritual disciplines are essential to a healthy Christian life, but they are the rules, not the game. Intimately knowing God is the purpose of our existence. I assumed I'd already experienced more than my fair share of God's goodness, and guilt over my desire for a fresh encounter racked my conscience. The things that once satisfied my hunger for God were slowly replaced by dissatisfaction and restlessness. With each passing week, the desire grew, and with it came a deep-seated frustration and an ever-increasing desperation to experience God's goodness again. Contrary to my best efforts, the hunger to encounter God consumed me—a hunger I didn't know how to satisfy.

Though I didn't realize it at the time, I was operating from a very faulty view of God that said he is limited in quantity or ability to give of himself. I thought I was good to go. Surely I had already received my allotted portion of God's goodness when I was healed, so I tried to run for years on that one encounter. I was like a bride who heard her bridegroom confess his love on their wedding day and ever after attempted to convince herself that that one moment was sufficient for secure, prolonged love.

Satan will not give us a desire for more of God. The origin of our desire for God is God himself. When we experience his goodness, we are given a taste for something we were created to crave. This craving to know and be known by God is written into the very core of who we are and can't be ignored or satisfied apart from him, and it cannot be managed by discipline. The desire to encounter God's goodness is an invitation into deeper places than we've ever before ventured. It is God drawing us closer to himself.

God longs to intimately know us as our Father and meet us in our pursuit of him. When we come near to him, he moves ever closer to us (Jas. 4:8). As important as it is to pursue God with our heads through Bible study, Scripture memorization, and time spent reading the Word, it cannot come at the cost of pursuing him with our hearts. Our time spent learning about him is always with the aim of growing closer to him. Our heady pursuits are designed to awaken a desire to experience the goodness and love of God for ourselves. We don't just study the Bible to learn about God but to encounter the God about whom we have learned. I tasted of his goodness when I was healed, and it left me craving more of him. And nothing apart from him could satisfy that craving.

WE LOVE BECAUSE HE FIRST LOVES

Two words mean "to know" in French. The first is *savoir*, which refers to knowing a fact or how to do something. You could say, "I *savoir* how to drive." The other "to know" word is *connaître*, which is used in the sense of experientially knowing a person or being familiar with something. You could say, "I *connaître* my mom." The difference is knowing with your head versus knowing experientially with your heart. For most of my life, my knowledge of God's love for me was *savoir* knowledge instead of a *connaître* knowing. God desires to take us far beyond learning about him or knowing his promises into a place where we encounter his love and experience his promises. As this happens, we are transformed into who we were created to be: a display of his image.

Similarly, Paul wrote about his longing to "know Christ" (Phil. 3:10). The word *know* in this verse is the Greek word *ginōskō*, which means experiential knowledge. The same word is even used as a euphemism for sexual intercourse—the highest level of experientially knowing a person.[3]

Growing in the personal, experiential knowledge of God's love is not a selfish pursuit. We are incapable of loving him without the love he first gives us (1 John 4:19). As we grow in our *connaître* knowing of the Father's love for us, we simultaneously grow in our capacity to love him in return. It's an intentional symbiotic relationship of great beauty. We benefit from the experiential knowledge of his love, and so does everyone around us.

I thought that nobly abstaining from experiencing God's specific and personal goodness meant there was more to go around—a conclusion contrary to God's omnipotent, omniscient, and omnipresent nature. Instead of eating the fresh bread available to me every day, I lived on starvation rations, effectively cutting myself off from my source of strength, transformation, and the Holy Spirit's empowerment to love God in the first place. God is all powerful, all knowing, and all present; he never runs out of himself or the love he has to give. It's impossible to steal God's love from another person, because there's never less of his love to go around.

---

3. James Strong, *The New Strong's Exhaustive Concordance of the Bible*, expanded ed. (Nashville: Thomas Nelson, 2010), word number 1097.

ENCOUNTER GOD

I took a scuba class in college. We spent the first several classes out of the water learning about the gear, the basics of diving, and the different sea life we might see. After the dry classroom work, we spent a few classes in the pool learning how to use the equipment and what to do if something went wrong or we suddenly lost the use of our regulators. Though slightly boring, all of this was extremely important. It would be dangerous to attempt a dive without these preliminary steps. At that point in the course, if someone had asked me if I knew *about* scuba diving, I could have answered, "Yes, I do." But no amount of diving in a pool, however deep, will ever replace the feeling of descending to the ocean floor.

An encounter with God moves us from the realm of an idea or concept to a personal experience. It's the difference between splashing on the surface and diving into the depths. I knew God conceptually all my life, but I tangibly encountered him when I was healed. He was more real, more loving, and closer than I ever imagined. Encounters are heart-based, felt experiences with the very person of God. Encounters are the relational part of our relationship with him, the place where love and intimacy are exchanged—not just conceptually but experientially. Encounters can come in times of prayer, worship, or studying the Bible, but they can also come in dreams, while driving, or even watching a movie. We can encounter the personal love of God any moment we stop and turn our affection to him or become aware of his presence, be it in worship or while washing dishes. Encounters are unique and highly personal, varying in nature from the dramatic to the subtle.

The Bible is laced with encounters; in fact, it's primarily a description of God encountering humanity and humans processing what they experienced. Some encounters cannot be missed and are overwhelming, while many are so subtle that only God's grace keeps us from walking past the opportunity. A great example of this is Moses and the burning bush. While we may think of it as one of the most dramatic, clear-cut encounters in the Bible, notice one little detail: Nothing occurred *until* Moses went out of his way to see why the bush wasn't consumed by fire.

> *Now Moses was tending the flock of Jethro his father-in-law, the priest of Midian, and he led the flock to the far side of the wilderness and came to Horeb, the mountain of God. There the angel of the LORD appeared to him in flames of fire from within a bush. Moses saw that though the bush was on fire it did not burn up. So Moses thought, "I will go over and see this strange sight—why the bush does not burn up."*
>
> *When the LORD saw that he had gone over to look, God called to him from within the bush, "Moses! Moses!"*

EXODUS 3:1-4

I love that God casually caught Moses' attention and used his natural curiosity to lead him into a place where he would encounter him. It even seems that God would have been okay if Moses had walked past what became one of the historical turning points in the Old Testament. As God is a master communicator, I strongly suspect that if Moses had missed this particular opportunity, God would have tried again. It is even possible that this wasn't the first time God called out to Moses; maybe the recorded encounter was just the first time Moses responded to the tug on his heart. Our encounters with God are often quite similar. God subtly woos and calls out to us, and we must go out of our way to respond to his invitations to intimacy.

Scripture is our judge for every encounter. The Bible sets safe boundaries, and God never acts contrarily to what he said and revealed in those pages. But when our pursuit of God centers on learning *about* him without encountering him, it's like the scuba diver who practices in a pool without ever venturing into the ocean. We could memorize facts and Greek root words until we're blue in the face, but all the knowing about God will never replace knowing God. Intensive Bible study is both necessary and highly profitable, but the Bible was always intended to draw us closer to the heart of the Father. Scripture and our theology are meant to bring us into deeper relationship with the author of the Bible himself. Theology that doesn't lead us into an encounter with God greatly minimizes the life-giving power available to us. Even healing and the gifts of the Holy Spirit are not an end unto themselves—they are also meant to bring us into deeper relationship with our loving God.

God is unchanging in nature; how he revealed himself to one person in Scripture is how he still is today. Every encounter shared in Scripture is an opportunity to learn about God and a demonstration of what's available in our relationship with him. That means what he's done for me is something he is willing to do for you. When David wrote, "Taste and see that the LORD is good" (Ps. 34:8), he wasn't just describing his personal time with God but inviting us into an available encounter with a tangibly knowable God. Imagine what would happen if our prayer times looked more like Jesus' or Peter's, or we expected God to speak to us like he did to those in the early church (see Mark 9:2–9; Acts 10:9–22). The idea of God interacting with us as he did with people in Scripture opens up limitless possibilities and creates expectancy for him to move in ways we never before dared dream.

God is better than we thought possible. Our loving heavenly Father desires to interact with us beyond the realm of the mind. If you've never encountered the love of God for yourself, hold on and dive in—this life is about to get far more exciting than you ever thought possible.

KNOWING OUR GOOD FATHER

I'm blessed to have an earthly father who loves me unconditionally. He is proud of me and would stop at nothing to see my life surpass his in every way. He's always provided for me, always accepted me, and always encouraged me. He isn't perfect, but he's been a great example of unconditional love in my life. Unfortunately, not all of us had wonderful fathers. Merely the word *father* can trigger negative emotions and fears in many of us, and it can be far too easy to project our experiences with earthly fathers onto our heavenly Father, assuming he will be angry, absent, or uninterested. The result is that many people find it very hard to relate to God as a good Father.

We cannot afford to let our past experiences dictate our future relationship with God. Instead, we have to look to Scripture to see God's true character and nature. God is not the best human we can imagine; he is something entirely different. The very best dad on his very best day pales in comparison to our heavenly Papa (see Matt. 7:11). God is the very definition of good. He is the father who stands still, staring at the horizon and waiting for his child (Luke 15:20). He is the one who vows to satisfy our hunger and thirst with every good thing (Ps. 107:9). He is the one who saw us in dire need and pain and said, "I will take their place." God is both intensely good and highly personal. He is the best Dad we could ever know, and we are his children.

CHAPTER KEYS

Healing is not a safe subject. For every question answered, several others rise to take its place. There is much we don't know. But one thing we can and must know with absolute certainty before praying for healing is the fiercely personal and good nature of our adoring heavenly Father. We need to know this conceptually from our study of Scripture as well as experientially from personally encountering his love. We need to know this because facts and situations will lie; they will scream at us from a limited earthly perspective, tempting us to lessen our expectation of God's goodness and question his motives. But we cannot lower our understanding of God's nature to match the least common denominator of our pain. Instead, we need to allow the revelation of God's extreme goodness and love to set our expectation and hope level.

Jesus paid the necessary price to bring us into an extremely personal relationship with our Father—something truly amazing, not a hang-on-and-hope-for-heaven life. This desire we feel to know God is God-given. Encountering this love for ourselves enables us to love him in return. His goodness is never overestimated. There is no end to him, nor is there a limited amount of his love. We are not stealing from someone else when we encounter his love and goodness. And we are mistaken if we think his promise to personally experience him is for some time other than right here and right now. God never intended for us to have just enough of him to get by. He has more than enough, and he longs to reveal his goodness to us every single day.

Revelation creates expectancy. As our understanding of God increases, our expectation of how he wants to encounter us expands. Excitement over what is possible is a natural result of learning more about God. It is perfectly normal that a new or increased revelation of God as the Great Physician, the compassionate Healer, and a really good Father leads to fresh hope. Each testimony in this book is an opportunity for our understanding of what's possible with God to grow. We can be encouraged by what he's doing around the world through people like you and me. And because he is unchanging, what he has done in one place through one person is a demonstration of who he is to all people everywhere. What he's done he will do again.

Our study about God is to lead us into an encounter with him—an encounter where he supplies the proof our heads require. The apostle Paul wrote, "My message and my preaching were not with wise and persuasive words, but with a *demonstration* of the Spirit's power, so that your faith might not rest on human wisdom, but on God's power" (1 Cor. 2:4–5, emphasis added). It's one thing to discuss healing—it's quite another thing to be healed. I pray that God's healing touch ministers to you as you read this book.

MINISTRY

I know from experience that it's possible to be a lifelong, devoted Christian and never quite encounter God's personal love for yourself. The good news is you don't have to wait another minute. Like the devoted dad who responds to a child's wish to be tucked in at night, our heavenly Father always comes when we call. An encounter with him may be powerful or subtle, but it will be personal, it will be good, and it will contain the love we were created to receive. There is nothing too small to bring before him, and he is real enough, close enough, powerful enough, and good enough to do something about it.

Papa God, you are better than I can imagine. Your goodness is limitless, and you are kinder, more real, more personal, and more loving than I ever thought possible. I will never find the end of your love for me. Thank you that you long to encounter me with your love even more than I want to be encountered. Please come and show me your love. Encounter me right here, right now. I must have more of you today. Amen.

3

THE QUESTION OF
WHO WE ARE

...

The sunny, late-spring day is quickly turning into a chilly night as my three friends and I traipse across San Francisco to our car. One day removed from the end of our first year of ministry school, we decided to celebrate with a day in the city.

"Does anybody remember where we parked?" I ask, shivering from the cold. Baseball, a city to explore, and some spicy Asian food made for a dream outing, but the day's length and the long walk back to the car are wearing on me.

"We know where we parked," Mark jauntily replies. "We just don't know how to get there."

His optimistic response doesn't help my rapidly declining mood. Pausing to pull my coat closer in an attempt to block the wind blowing off the bay, I look longingly at a brightly lit coffee shop.

"We can't be far now," Maria encourages me. "Come on!" She grabs my arm and drags me at a quick trot to catch a changing light.

Caught up in conversation, Maria and I are several blocks away before we realize the other two aren't with us. "They're not picking up," I tell her, ending the call on my cell phone. "I bet they stopped at that coffee shop."

My attitude steadily deteriorates as we backtrack to the café. Pictures of my friends warming themselves over steaming cups of chai lattes dance through my head. "Do you think we could send Mark to get the car while we warm up inside?" I say as we turn the corner. When Maria doesn't respond, I ask, "What is it?"

I follow her gaze down the street to our two companions, who are standing in the cold and talking to a man whose request for money I ignored only a few minutes earlier.

"Here are the other two." Mark introduces us and proceeds to fill us in on the man's hard life story, one that includes a long list of ailments and broken bones.

"Are you two like these two?" the man asks.

"In what way?" I reply.

"Angels in disguise." The wonder in his voice and the tears in his eyes tell me we walked right into a divine moment—God is encountering this man's heart with his love.

"No, we're not angels." I smile as my unwarranted irritation melts away. "But I would love to pray for you if that's okay."

Though the response comes easily from my mouth, my heart nearly beats through my chest. This is it. Here is my first opportunity away from the safe confines of church and ministry school to share and demonstrate the love of God in words and power—power I am confident will bring healing to the man's hurting and broken body. A deep, unwavering conviction that God is about to heal the man comes over me; I wish I always felt that certain when I pray for healing. I don't. I often pray out of obedience or conviction, but this particular time God gives me a gift of faith, a complete certainty of what is about to happen.

The man agrees, and we command the pain to leave and pray for his body to be healed. "Pain, you need to go now in Jesus' name. Every part of this body be made new right now. Holy Spirit, come and show him just how much the Father loves him." To our great joy, that's exactly what happens.

He starts testing his back, first by squatting and then by bending over to touch his toes. "It doesn't hurt!" the man says, smiling through his tears. "I go to the doctor every month for shots to handle all the pain, and it never makes me feel this good."

"Thank you, Father," I praise, tears welling in my own eyes.

"You," Mark says to the man, "are the beloved son of God. He loves you right now, exactly as you are."

We pray for the presence of God to encounter the man, for God's love to envelop him. And there on a dirty sidewalk on the wrong side of town, I watch as a man forgotten and overlooked by so many—myself included—falls to his knees under the overwhelming weight of God's love.

We smile and laugh the rest of the way to the car, the damp cold long forgotten. God graciously gave us an opportunity to witness one of his children encounter his all-consuming love for the very first time, a storybook ending to our first year of ministry school.

It's an unbelievable honor to be part of someone's encounter with the Father's love, an honor I do not take lightly. But that encounter in San Francisco was significant for us for another reason as well—it served as the crowning moment to our school year and the culmination of a recurring conversation in which we imagined what it would look like to walk in the love and power of the gospel in our daily lives.

For both Mark and me, it was the moment when we knew something shifted in our faith from "I think God can" to "I know he will." This shift directly related to our increased understanding of God's fatherly nature and our identity as his children.

Before digging into some of the deeper theological questions surrounding healing, we need to be secure in our identity as God's daughters and sons, or healing becomes just another way to work for love instead of a demonstration of the immense love we've already encountered. When we work from the security of our position in him, we are connected to an unending supply of love that never runs out or dries up.

THE FATHER'S CHILDREN

A remarkable thing happens to a husband and wife upon the addition of a child to their family: They become a father and mother. At any given moment, I'm a daughter, granddaughter, sister, aunt, niece, and cousin, but I'm not a mother because I don't have children. For God to be a Father, he must have children. The good news is that he does have kids—he has us. And if God is all that the Bible says he is, we are the unconditionally adored and beloved children of a ridiculously good Father.

At some point, many of us lost the simple truth that since God is our Father, we get to relate to him as his children. This relationship requires us to believe and behave like his children. In other words, as our revelation of the Father's nature grows, our revelation of our identity as his children needs to keep pace. If that doesn't happen, our increasing awareness of God's greatness will create an imbalance that restricts us from approaching him and receiving the love, affirmation, and security intended for his children. And he really likes his children.

Anything that restricts or limits our ability to receive the love of the Father is not of God. His love and affirmation are necessary for sustained spiritual and emotional health. His love drives away our fears, and his affirmation emboldens us to take risks (1 John 4:18). We can fearlessly put our faith into action, live the abundant life, and walk in the destiny we were created for because of his immense, unending, and unquestionable love. It's the Father's love that makes us brave.

A CHILD'S ACCESS

There are few things that I remember from my childhood with such fondness as visiting my grandfather downtown at his retail store. I was the apple of my grandpa's eye and loved playing hide-and-seek among the store's inventory. The drive was impossibly long as I thought about my grandpa and the inevitable treats that came with a visit. I felt I would burst as my dad parked in the side lot and helped us out of the car. I would run to the front entrance where I'd wait for my dad to open the heavy wooden door, and then like a horse released from the starting gate, I'd run unabashedly through a doorway into my grandpa's office and his waiting arms. It wasn't until many years later that I noticed the doorway was marked PRIVATE. Undoubtedly, the sign stopped customers from entering uninvited, but it never slowed me down from seeing my grandpa; our relationship trumped regulation. No one has access to a father like his child or grandchild.

Our heavenly Father is remarkably kind to his children, granting us access to all he is and has. Being a daughter gives me certain rights and privileges that only a child possesses. Jesus restored my access to the Father, but I didn't make full use of my privilege because of false piety, a culturally shaped works mentality, the lies of religion that told me I was unworthy, and—worst of all—ignorance of my access. Sadly, for much of my life I was like the customer outside the office instead of the unashamed girl who ran to her grandpa. God had already given me permission to approach him, but I didn't understand (see Eph. 3:12; Heb. 4:16).

Fortunately, God foresaw this problem and graciously provided a response to my question of identity and access long before I asked it. The second half of one of the Bible's most familiar parables, the parable of the Lost Son, addresses this topic:

> *Meanwhile, the older son was in the field. When he came near the house, he heard music and dancing. So he called one of the servants and asked him what was going on. "Your brother has come," he replied, "and your father has killed the fattened calf because he has him back safe and sound."*
>
> *The older brother became angry and refused to go in. So his father went out and pleaded with him. But he answered his father, "Look! All these years I've been slaving for you and never disobeyed your orders. Yet you never gave me even a young goat so I could celebrate with my friends. But when this son of yours who has squandered your property with prōstitutes comes home, you kill the fattened calf for him!"*
>
> *"My son," the father said, "**you are always with me, and everything I have is yours.**"*
>
> **LUKE 15:25-31 (EMPHASIS ADDED)**

Children need affirmation and recognition from their father. How painful it must have been for the elder son to watch as his heart's valid longing was given to another. After years of dutifully working for his father, he felt he deserved the recognition and reward lavished upon his unworthy brother. The first son didn't understand that his father's love was something to receive, not earn. His father lovingly clarified the access the son already and always possessed.

Perhaps the person with the greatest revelation of his identity as a child of God was the apostle John, a man forever known as the Beloved (John 19:26). Not surprisingly, our position as God's children was a recurring theme in John's writing. John opened his

Gospel by writing, "To all who did receive him, to those who believed in his name, he gave the right to become children of God" (1:12). Later he wrote with unbridled joy, "See what great love the Father has lavished on us, that we should be called children of God" (1 John 3:1). John understood what took me years to learn: We are nothing less than God's adored children. It is the most favored position in his kingdom and he lavishes it on us. Everything we need—affirmation, affection, encouragement, identity, and the truth of our great destiny in him—has already been made available to us. As God's daughters and sons, we needn't wait another minute to run into his loving, unconditional embrace.

FROM SERVANTS TO SONS AND DAUGHTERS

Before I took a position with the nonprofit in Southeast Asia, I desperately wanted to serve God on the mission field in some capacity—I just had no idea where I was supposed to go. It was a few years after my healing, and I was extremely frustrated by God's apparent silence on the subject.

"God!" I would cry out in my bedroom as I paced back and forth. "Where do you want me to go? What do you want me to do?"

Silence.

"God," I pleaded. "My life is yours! I'll go anywhere."

Again, no reply.

My frustration and volume increased with each turn through the room. "Just tell me where to go."

I wish I could say that I heard God's audible voice, had a vision of some far-off nation, or felt a strong impression, but nothing happened. I was like an obedient Christian soldier waiting for marching orders that weren't coming, completely unaware that God isn't looking for soldiers, slaves, or even servants—he is looking for sons, daughters, and family. It was some time before I realized that God's silence *was* his response. He trusted me to make a decision based on the things already in my heart to do.

God is much, much more like a dad teaching his child to ride a bicycle than a general issuing orders. Our heavenly Father walks beside us with both hands on the bike as we begin to pedal unsteadily. Then he jogs beside us with one hand on the handle bars and finally runs beside us as we ride alone. He's there to steady us if we falter, catch us when we lose our balance, and clean us up if we fall. Instead of orders and commands, he teaches and develops us, molding us into the mature sons and daughters he created us to be so we can walk in the full, amazing destinies he designed for us. So, too, the Bible teaches us far more frequently *how* to think than it does *what* to think. At times God tells us what to do, but as we mature, we are given greater freedom to make decisions for ourselves and on behalf of our families.

Jesus is the access point, and salvation is the doorway to a life of intimacy with God. All those who love God serve him but, for some of us, we can become so busy doing things *for* God that we forget our primary role as his children. For many years, I was comfortable and confident in my role as a servant, but my service to God prevented me from grasping my primary position—I was not merely a servant but his daughter.

To be clear, my access to God's presence never changed, but my *awareness* of my access changed drastically. Instead of waiting like the dutiful soldier on the outside for God to give an order, I am invited into his presence simply to enjoy his company. As my awareness of my true position grew, the motivation for my life changed—instead of living and working *for* love, I found I was living *from* love. And amazingly, as I rested in my identity as a daughter, I did more and saw greater fruit in my life than when my Christianity was defined by discipline and duty.

No discussion of sonship negates service and obedience. As God's children, we seek to be obedient and serve him. In fact, the children of a house can look like servants in many respects. Both children and servants obey and serve the master, but only children receive the father's name and inheritance. It's one thing to be obedient and quite another to willfully serve God without being asked or told what to do. As we mature, we have the freedom to willfully choose the things of God's kingdom, revealing what's in our hearts.

Family life includes chores, projects, and work, but it also includes playtime, laughter, celebrations, and vacations. Wrongly emphasizing one side of the equation throws our lives out of balance. Passion and love inspire, energize, and motivate us and will take us to places we never dreamed possible.

STEALING HIS JOY

When I was living on the West Coast, I would often visit my parents back in the Midwest, and every time I stepped through the front door, I experienced the same treatment. I would find my preferred kind of coffee conveniently set beside the coffeemaker and the refrigerator and pantry stocked with treats—and this was only the beginning. My favorite meals were cooked, the house heat was set a few degrees higher (to keep my California blood warm in Minnesota), and there was always a night or two when the family came together for a big dinner. If I visited and didn't use any of the special gifts intended for me, assuming my parents had given me enough in the past or that the gifts were for someone else, my well-intended abstention would actually hurt them. My pleasure in receiving their gifts remains a large part of their joy in giving.

Much like my parents, our heavenly Father is extremely biased toward his children. His favor is apparent in what he does for us, what he plans for us, and what he loves to give us. God gives to us out of an overflow of love and generosity. If we choose not to receive what he wants to give us because we believe his blessings are for someone else, for some other time, or we feel unworthy, we actually grieve him. God has made his heart vulnerable to us. It's beyond my understanding that my actions affect God's emotions, but that is exactly what happens.

As I said earlier, I used to think it was noble to refrain from receiving from the Lord, so there would be more to go around. I was afraid of becoming "that girl," the one who demands attention and asks for too much. But our Father delights over us, rejoices over us, and even sings over us (Zeph. 3:17). He "has blessed us in the heavenly realms with every spiritual blessing in Christ" (Eph. 1:3). He's the one "who did not spare his own Son, but gave him up for us all," and he will graciously give us everything else along with him (Rom. 8:32). I missed the truth that he already gave me everything; I have his Son and "every spiritual blessing." Failing to receive all that God has for us keeps us from the abundant, full life designed for us and robs our Father of his great joy in giving to his children.

We are called to make earth like heaven (Matt. 6:10), a place of unending communion with our loving heavenly Father. Only those who have personally experienced this communion can share it with a lost and hurting world. Likewise, we can give away only what we first receive. As God's children, we are positioned to personally experience his love, blessings, and grace. Everything he has is ours. It's time to grab hold of our divine inheritance—the gifts, promises, and blessings that Scripture states are ours—and allow God to lavish us with all he is and has.

BECAUSE OF OUR FATHER

Roger Federer is arguably the greatest male tennis player of all time. He's won a record number of major titles, which are the sport's pinnacle events. His name and "Wimbledon champion" are practically synonymous. Federer is also the father of four children, and upon the birth of each of his kids, talk in the tennis world would circle around the possibility that one of them would become a future champion. While the discussion was lighthearted, a slight undercurrent of possibility ran through the conversation: The children might be future champions based solely on their father's greatness.

While I may not be the daughter of a Wimbledon champion, I am the daughter of the King of kings and Creator of the universe. By nature of my relationship with my heavenly Father, expectation (hope), provision, and greatness surround my life. Just as the Federer children have done nothing apart from inherit their parents' genes to merit their possible inclusion amongst future champions, my potential is limitless, and I am nothing short of amazing because of who my Father is.

Pride is awful. It's corrosive and quickly destroys wherever it gains a foothold. But pride is not just expressed in arrogance. It is also found in its subtler, more acceptable form: false humility. We are nothing without Christ, but unfortunately for many believers, "I am nothing" is where our identity starts *and* stops, and we forget our call to change the world. For too many years, false humility robbed me of fully believing and therefore behaving like the incredible person I was created to be. I carefully downgraded and even denigrated my own value out of fear of pride. Thinking less of myself than God does dishonors my Creator and prevents me from becoming all I was created to be. It also keeps me from attempting, let alone accomplishing, the works he planned for me to do. The truth is, God is a master Creator, one who doesn't make mistakes, and he made me.

True humility is not thinking less of ourselves but thinking accurately of ourselves. The apostle Paul raised the subject of true humility: "The only accurate way to understand ourselves is by what God is and by what he does for us, not by what we are and what we do for him" (Rom. 12:3 MSG). God is the one with proper perspective of our identity. In the same way we love because he loves us and we step out in faith because we know he is faithful, we are nothing short of awesome because he is awesome. To avoid pride and false humility and to think accurately of ourselves, we need to know what God thinks of us—and the short answer is that he thinks so highly of us that he willingly died in our place. Our heavenly Father is beyond description or compare, which makes us absolutely amazing by default.

FROM SINNER TO SAINT

My mind begins to wander and I look at my watch. Forty-five minutes until the end of class. It isn't that I'm bored. Actually, it is quite the opposite. After several hours of revelation-packed, paradigm-shifting classes at ministry school, my brain feels like Jell-O. I am drinking from a fire hose and getting waterlogged. *Forty-five minutes,* I think and attempt to refocus my attention.

"The biggest lie in Christendom," I hear my teacher say, "is that you're a sinner saved by grace."

The saturated feeling in my brain quickly gives way to alarm. *What?* What does that mean?

"You are not a sinner saved by grace," he continues. "You were a sinner, Jesus' grace saved you, and you've been transformed into a saint. Anyone who is a believer in Jesus is a new creation."

A sinner working for salvation is not part of the gospel, but that day in class, I suddenly realized that that was exactly what I had been practicing. Memories of feeling like I didn't do enough flooded over me. I never seemed to read the Bible enough, pray long enough, share my faith enough, or be generally good enough to silence the accusations. Paul's words to the Galatians might as well have been written for me: "How foolish can you be? After starting your new lives in the Spirit, why are you now trying to become perfect by your own human effort?" (3:3 NLT). I lived like a sinner who was trying to prove herself worthy of what was already freely given. Clearly, there was a disconnect between what I knew to be true in my head and what I actually believed in my heart. A truth upgrade always means greater freedom (see John 8:32). In the time it took for my teacher to expound his statement from Romans 8, two things happened: The paradigm I used to interpret the Bible completely changed, and I felt unexpected and new freedom wash over me.

You may have heard all your life that you're a sinner, but it's simply not true. You *were* a sinner until God's grace saved you and transformed you into a saint and an entirely new creation (2 Cor. 5:17). Sinners do not walk in the freedom and confidence of a son or daughter; their attention is focused inward as they perpetually fight a battle against self that Christ already won. Instead, they could be looking upward in communion with the Father and outward toward the world they are called to transform. God sees us far above and beyond anything we dare dream. The more our minds are renewed to the reality of our identity as saintly sons and daughters, the more we become and behave like the royal priests we are (see 1 Pet. 2:9).

CHAPTER KEYS

Studying the theology of healing is relatively straightforward. But pursing a lifestyle of healing—one where we regularly pray for and see people healed—requires more of us. I want every person I pray for to be healed, but unfortunately, that's not the case yet. This means it's of paramount importance that I am entirely convinced (in an "I know that I know that I know" sort of way) of God's goodness and our Father-daughter relationship, so I am prepared to weather storms in advance, long before the clouds form. If this foundation isn't in place, I am likely to question God's goodness in the face of my own disappointment and pain, allowing my experiences to dictate God's character and nature instead of relying on Scripture. And if I'm not convinced of my position as a daughter right now, before I pray for even one person's healing, then each person healed will at some level be a performance-based attempt to earn the affection I already possess.

A.W. Tozer famously stated that what we think about God is the most important thing about us.[4] Who we believe we are is the second most important thing; our beliefs translate to actions and embolden us to take risks. We are the children of an amazing Father—a reality that bestows identity, calls us to greatness, and releases destiny. We have continual, unlimited access to all that God is, does, and has, and we bring our Father joy by receiving all he intends for us.

Finally, along with being daughters and sons, we are saints, the righteousness of Christ (2 Cor. 5:21). There is nothing to gain by starving when the pantry is full. God's storehouse of love, affection, and blessing is fully stocked; he is limitless and so are the good things he gives his children. Because we are his children, we are encouraged to come boldly before him to receive all he has for us today and then again tomorrow. And the next day. And the day after that.

As children secure in our identity, we think, believe, and act from a place of love. Our identity in no way minimizes a life of humility and service to God. Everyone who loves Jesus serves him. But we get to serve our family with perseverance and passion inspired by love; we serve in a way that a person bound by duty never could. Sonship does not negate our service requirement. It expands it.

When the clock is running out and the game is on the line, you want the ball in the hands of a confident player, one who knows she will make the shot. We were born for greatness, to clearly reflect God's image to the world and see his kingdom come. And we were born again into an incredible family with a call and destiny to see the world transformed. What Jesus started is now ours to complete (Matt. 28:18-20). God trusts us to take the shot. We were born for it.

---

4. A.W. Tozer, *The Knowledge of the Holy* (New York: HarperCollins, 1992), 1.

MINISTRY

For me, the transition from servant to daughter came in big, "ah-ha" moments, but it also came slowly as I spent time with God, asking him a simple, childlike question: "Father, how much do you love me?" This question is part of my daily routine. I ask him about his love for me before crawling out of bed in the morning and wait until he answers. Sometimes this means physically feeling a tingling sensation I've come to learn is God's presence. Sometimes it's him speaking words of his extreme love into my heart with that still, small voice. Still other times, I feel led to different passages of Scripture about his love for me; the words leap off the page and fill my heart in a fresh way. Abiding in his love for me protects, encourages, and empowers me to live as the daughter he created me to be.

You are the child of an incredible Father. You are already successful. You already delight him. You are a son or daughter of God with a full inheritance and all the blessings such a position entails. This is the perfect moment to ask God what he thinks about you, remembering that he sees you perfected through the lens of Christ. You are his beloved child. Let his love come touch your heart. Whether it's the first time or the thousandth time, his love changes everything.

Heavenly Father, thank you for your incredible, world-changing love. There is truly nothing like it anywhere else in existence. I want all that Jesus won for me. I want to know you and be known by you as your child. Please show me right now how much you love me. Father, show me your love in a way that I can receive it. Speak courage into my heart, replace fear with love, and shower me with all the love you've stored up for this very moment. Transform me by your love so I am more like your image and the child you created me to be than ever before. Thank you, my loving Father. Amen.

4

THE QUESTION OF
WILL: PART 1

...

I arrive a few minutes before the prayer meeting begins, eager for God to work a great miracle for a friend who is to undergo a complicated surgery later this week.

"Rebecca, you're here!" my friend exclaims as I walk into the kitchen. "Well, I guess that means we can pray now." His smile tries to wipe away the tension readily apparent on his face. I can see it on the faces of many others present as well.

I respond with a lighthearted comment and begin to pray silently. If hope is the confident expectation of coming good, I can feel my hope for something incredible colliding with a collective lack of hope. It seems to me that something other than heaven is setting the general expectation for the evening.

The gathering opens with a hymn, but the atmosphere is noticeably flat, as if many people agree with our friend's grim prognosis instead of expecting their prayers to powerfully effect a change. *Don't they know that you are the Great Physician, Father?* I ask silently. I begin worshiping quietly, refocusing my attention on the one who heals instead of the one in need of healing. Whatever we focus on grows in size; when we focus on an impossible situation, it feels impossible and our prayers become desperate pleas reflecting our despair. However, when we focus on Jesus, we are filled with awe for our God, who destroys impossibilities, and we pray expectantly from a place of victory.

The people present at the prayer meeting tonight vary from long-time believers and leaders in the local church to newer believers and even some non-Christians attending to lend moral support. I continue my inaudible worship as I wait for someone to stand up and pray boldly for our friend to be healed. But that doesn't happen. Instead, prayers for wisdom for the doctors and strength and peace for the family are accompanied by the phrase "if it's your will."

After the meeting, I sit in my car unmoving and slightly stunned. My fellow Christians' general lack of familiarity with God's healing grace grieves my heart. "They don't know they can ask for healing, Father. They don't know you *want* to heal."

We tend to fall into one of three categories:[5]

1. We believe God no longer heals today.
2. We believe God heals today but we have little or no personal experience that supports our belief (i.e., we have rarely or never seen someone healed).
3. We believe God heals today and regularly see people healed.

Until relatively recently, I belonged to the second category. I believed that God heals, but outside of my own healing, I had no experience of it, nor did I know where to go to gain experience or learn

---

5. I first heard these categories neatly laid out by Bill Johnson in his Healing Collection teaching series.

about it. This disconnect between what I believed to be true and what I experienced was extremely frustrating—so frustrating that I could no longer drown it out by spending more time volunteering at church, taking the next Bible study, or reading another book written by someone who also had no personal experience with healing. My ever-increasing discontentment and frustration led me to admit to the offensive idea that I was missing something and forced me to search until I found it.

It is easier to believe God no longer heals today than it is to believe that he heals and see someone we love sick. The pain caused by this tension can inadvertently lead to reinterpreting the Bible to justify our experience. We re-tailor our beliefs to explain our experience instead of asking why our experience doesn't match what we read in Scripture. This produces disempowering lies that many Christians believe are orthodox realities of the day. Instead of theology that appeases the dissonance we experience, we need to upgrade our beliefs about healing until they mirror what God believes about healing.

I had to set aside much of what I thought was true or was taught in favor of asking myself challenging, uncomfortable questions as to why my life *didn't* reflect many of Jesus' great promises regarding healing. In other words, why wasn't I producing the fruit the Bible says is natural for believers?[6] I could no longer live with the dissonance; the questions needed to be answered. Like Jacob, I wasn't going to give up wrestling until I received a blessing.

"IF IT'S YOUR WILL"

Praying for healing, even just a few years ago, was an extremely rare occurrence in my life. Most of the time, I prayed for strength to get through a situation or wisdom for the doctors instead of

---

6. For starters, check out Mark 16:15–18; Luke 10:9; Jas. 5:14–16.

praying for God to actually heal the person. Like any child, I copied the prayers, faith, and hope modeled for me. My prayers were full of caveats that allowed God a free pass in case the person wasn't healed. I attached "if it's your will" to everything because I wasn't convinced it was his will. Countless uncertain prayers later, I stopped to ask an important question, repeating the words I so often prayed: Is it God's will to heal?

Our questions are rarely centered around God's ability to heal but rather his desire to heal. We don't doubt that he's *able* but if he *wants* to. A prayer with faith—a prayer with expectation attached to it—even if it is as small as a mustard seed, will move mountains and please God (Matt. 17:20; Heb. 11:6). In fact, it's the prayer offered in faith that Scripture says "will make the sick person well" (Jas. 5:15).

To be clear, God is not dependent on our faith to heal. He can and routinely does heal in spite of a person's lack of faith, but faith attracts heaven and opens a door for God to move in our lives. If we are to pray in faith, we need to clarify our beliefs about healing and answer the questions that swirl around the subject: Is it always God's will to heal? Does he want to heal everyone? Does he send sickness? What about the person who isn't healed? If we're uncertain about the answer to any of these questions before we pray, we end up offering tentative prayers, second-guessing ourselves instead of approaching his throne of grace with confidence. We find ourselves praying faithless and powerless prayers riddled with doubt concerning God's ability or willingness to heal.

In the next two chapters, we will tackle head on the question of God's will. We will start by looking at what the Bible says about God regarding healing and then examine the three places where God's perfect will was or is always done: Eden, heaven, and in the life of Jesus. Our really good heavenly Father has a strong opinion about healing, and it's imperative we discover what that opinion is.

JEHOVAH-RAPHA

I soon realized that most of the teaching I'd received about healing was less about divine healing and more of an attempt to make sense of loss and pain.

Questions about loss and pain inevitably arise when we pursue healing, but I needed to know if God *wanted* to heal someone in the first place. I decided to set aside everything I thought I knew and begin with the Bible to find the answer to the question I so frequently asked.

The Bible is always our starting place when studying theology or God's will. Scripture frequently states God's desire for humankind. His heart is not for us to languish in uncertainty over his will for a given situation; he loves to tell us who he is, what he does, and how he wants to interact with us. In fact, a unique aspect of God's unchanging character and nature is revealed in every one of his names listed in the Bible.

Regardless of the subject, a helpful Bible study tool is to examine how God defines himself in Scripture, paying special attention to statements like "I am the LORD," followed by an action (e.g., "I am the LORD, who makes you holy" in Exod. 31:13). Also pay attention to names and titles given to him. God says a lot about himself throughout Scripture, and it's important to let his own words define how he thinks and feels.

Another great tool is to look at Jesus. Jesus is the image of the invisible God, and God's will is always done in Jesus' life (Col. 1:15; John 17:25–26). If we ever have a question about God's will in a situation, we can look at Jesus, who perfectly demonstrated the character, nature, and will of our Father, and find the answer.

Let's look at two familiar examples of how God's name reveals his character and nature and how Jesus models those aspects of the Father.

Jehovah-Raah

Our first example is *Jehovah-Raah:* "The Lord my Shepherd." This name speaks of special intimacy, friendship, and protection found within God.[7] It reveals his nature and desire for an intimate relationship with his people. King David personally encountered this tender side of God and wrote in his most famous Psalm, "The LORD is my shepherd, I shall not want" (Ps. 23:1 NASB).

Jesus perfectly demonstrated God's character, nature, and will, so it's no surprise that he fully embodied the nature of *Jehovah-Raah.* He walked in intimate friendship with His disciples and protected his sheep from the enemy (see John 17). In fact, Jesus said of himself, "I am the good shepherd; I know my sheep and my sheep know me— just as the Father knows me and I know the Father—and I lay down my life for the sheep" (John 10:14–15).

Even if we don't feel we've experienced this aspect of God, Scripture tells us he is the "Lord our Shepherd" for every single person. That is his character and nature.

Savior

Angelic hosts introduced the newborn Christ to the world and introduce us to our second example of how God's name reveals his character and nature. The angels proclaimed, "Today in the town of David a Savior has been born to you; He is the Messiah, the Lord" (Luke 2:11). Before Jesus uttered a word, we knew his will to save because of his title *Savior.* He later described his mission in life "to seek and to save the lost" (Luke 19:10). Jesus is called the Savior because his character and nature, and thereby his will, are to save.

---

7. Strong's 7462.

Most of us are familiar with the nature of God our Shepherd and God our Savior. He cannot be separated from his name and nature as our Shepherd and Savior, even if some people feel they have never experienced him as either. Our inexperience with certain aspects of God's character and nature does not change who he is or how he desires to interact with us. There is a very real tension that exists between what is ultimately true and the facts of our lives. We may feel the dissonance between biblical revelation and what we experience, but that does not diminish the reality of who God is and his will for the world.

Let's look at one name that directly impacts our study regarding God's will to heal.

Jehovah-Rapha

Wandering through the desert provides ample opportunity for testing. The sun's searing rays beat down relentlessly, while the night brings a cold that seeps into your bones and makes you forget the burning heat of noonday. It doesn't take long in this harsh climate to become irritated with others, especially your little brother.

Picture Miriam and Aaron traveling through this unforgiving climate. They are short on sleep; it's offensively hot; and they are probably experiencing an emotional letdown after their last few weeks of plagues, the pursuing Egyptian army, and a dramatic sea crossing. And they are taking orders from their little brother. I imagine that one day their patience simply ran out, and they began to grumble. Instead of confronting Moses directly (I'd be a little intimidated after recent events to say something to him, too), they take it out on his wife. Maybe that's not exactly what happened before the grumbling began, but Numbers 12:1 says, "Miriam and Aaron began to talk against Moses because of his Cushite wife, for he had married a Cushite."

Grumbling never worked for the Israelites in general, and Miriam and Aaron discovered this for themselves as God himself came to Moses' defense. The Bible says, "The anger of the LORD burned against them," and when the cloud of his presence lifted, Miriam was leprous like snow (Num. 12:9–10). This intense scene called for immediate action, and Aaron quickly confessed their foolishness and asked Moses to pray for Miriam. Being a good brother, Moses cried out, "O God, please *rapha* her! Heal her!" And God did (Num. 12:13–15).

We have a luxury Moses didn't: the rest of the Bible, complete with countless healing testimonies. In light of our modern understanding, it's easy to miss the significance of what transpired that day. Up to this point—aside from a brief demonstration at the burning bush where his hand turned leprous and back to normal as a sign for the Israelites (Exod. 4:6–7)—Moses had not seen God heal. Instead, he had regularly witnessed death and destruction from the plagues in Egypt. So why did he immediately turn to God for Miriam's healing?

Moses knew God would heal Miriam's leprosy because God had already revealed his name—and therefore his nature, character, and will—to him: "I am the LORD, who heals you" (Exod. 15:26). With this powerful introduction, God declared himself to be *Jehovah-Rapha,* the Lord Who Heals.[8] Moses called on God to do exactly what he said he would do when he revealed himself as *Jehovah-Rapha.*

Predictably, Jesus perfectly demonstrated the nature of God the Healer throughout the New Testament. He traveled throughout Galilee, "teaching in their synagogues, proclaiming the good news of the kingdom, *and healing every disease and sickness among the people* . . . People brought to him all who were ill with various

---

8. Strong's 7495.

diseases, those suffering severe pain, the demon-possessed, those having seizures, and the paralyzed; *and he healed them"* (Matt. 4:23–24, emphasis added). Jesus fully embodied the character, nature, and will of *Jehovah-Rapha* as he brought emotional, spiritual, and physical healing everywhere he went.

• • •

God is never separated from his nature. When I attached "if it's your will" to my prayers, I was effectively asking whether or not his nature changed instead of fully trusting that he is who he said he is. Regardless of our past experience and disappointments, we can have complete confidence that God will always act in alignment with biblical revelation and who he declared himself to be.

When we wonder if God *wants* to heal the person in front of us, be it from muscle spasms or multiple sclerosis, we can call to mind his revealed and unchanging nature as the Healer and know that his will is always to act in accordance with his nature. This doesn't mean we see every person healed (yet).

Unfortunately, not everything God wants for humanity occurs, nor is his will always accomplished on the earth—if it were, he wouldn't tell us to pray for his will to be done (Matt. 6:10). But it does mean that God is unquestionably *Jehovah-Rapha* in any and every situation.

Circumstances can change, but God's love and promises endure forever. The Bible must set our understanding and define who God wants to be to us even if the facts of our lives don't yet match the truth of Scripture. We cannot afford to reduce our beliefs to the lowest common denominator of our experience.

Instead, acknowledging the tension, we must continue to raise our expectation level until it matches the level Jesus lived by and Scripture sets for us.

A GARDEN AND A CITY

With my newfound revelation of God's character and nature as the Healer, I continued my pursuit to discover his will for healing by studying the two locations in the Bible where his will is perfectly actualized: the garden of Eden and heaven. Both places give a glimpse of God's will for humanity without the effects of sin muddying the water.

EDEN

Take a minute to picture a gorgeous tropical garden. The hibiscus are in bloom, the palm trees sway in the breeze, and birds of paradise sing happily in the canopy overhead. The leaves and palm fronds are a vibrant green. Everything feels so alive that you can almost hear the grass growing. The breeze carries that fresh, salty scent announcing the ocean's presence, and running water acts as the bass track for the birds and insects.

Imagine a path in front of you that leads into the forest. Walk down the path through jungle vines to where it opens beside a waterfall. Hear the water crashing into the dark pool below. See how the rays of light turn the rising mist into a rainbow. Feel your skin prickle as the breeze coats you in the cool spray. Now make your way down the path through brilliant pink and white bougainvillea as the roar of the waterfall grows quieter and quieter and is replaced by a new sound—the steady pulse of waves breaking on a nearby shore.

Suddenly the trees and vegetation stop, replaced by a beautiful white-sand beach. Walk down to the wet sand at the water's edge. Stand unmoving as the warm, frothy water rushes over your feet. Match your breathing to the rhythm of the waves; take a deep breath in and release it. In and out, in and out, filling your lungs with the fresh ocean air.

Take a look at yourself standing on that beautiful beach. What are you wearing? What do you look like? For me, I have a healthy tan and that bleached-blonde hair I get whenever I spend time at the beach. And I'm dripping from swimming in the breakers.

As fun as this little mental vacation is (especially if you're reading this midwinter), I want to highlight one point: Even if your hair is dry, or you prefer to look at the waterfall instead of jump off of it, or you find sitting on the beach more enjoyable than body surfing—I can guarantee that you didn't picture yourself with the kidney disease that's ailing you, the arthritis that cripples you, or the cast currently on your foot. Just as we picture a vacation with sunny skies and without the stress of work or everyday life, when we picture ourselves in paradise, we tend to see ourselves in perfect physical health.

Not surprisingly, when we look at the Bible's first paradise, the garden of Eden, the scene was in many ways the same as our mental vacation destination. There was no sin to corrupt and no pain to endure. Evil hadn't taken a toll on body, soul, or spirit. In fact, Eden means "pleasure."[9] God put man in the middle of his pleasure on earth. Unfortunately, contrary to God's desire, our story took a catastrophic turn. We lost perfection and life without pain and sorrow, yet even then, God's redemption plan was already in place. When we study life in Eden, we can clearly see God's original desire for us to live free from pain, disease, and illness.

HEAVEN

Anyone who has spent more than a day or two in a hospital will probably say the nights are the worst part. Loneliness and fear can quickly creep up on you when the distraction of visitors ceases and the lights go out. I remember one night when I felt particularly alone

---

9. Strong's 5731.

and afraid, my body wracked with pain. I repeated the words of my then-favorite verse over and over: "There will be no more death or mourning or crying or pain, for the old order of things has passed away" (Rev. 21:4). I consoled myself with deep longing for that day. "No more pain. One day, no more pain . . ."

The biblical promise of freedom from pain and sickness brought comfort but no change to my circumstances. Unwittingly, I allowed the verse to reinforce my belief that healing and the absence of pain were reserved for that glorious day when I'd meet the Lord face to face; my understanding of a healthy life was limited to heaven. I was unaware that instead of Scripture, my experience with sickness was dictating my expectations. We can daydream about the beauty of Eden past or heaven future without diminishing the truth that we have access here and now to all Jesus paid for at Calvary.

In summary, we have two settings where we can observe the perfect will of God without the consequences of sin disfiguring the picture. There's no pain, no illness, and no disease. The garden of Eden, God's original plan for humanity, is devoid of any trace of the devilish trio. Nor is there any sickness, illness, or disease to be found in our final, perfected state of life with God in heaven. God's desire is for man to live without these maladies. As we will see, health and healing were never intended only for Eden past and our heavenly future—but for right here and right now in our current lives.

CHAPTER KEYS

Our experiences ebb and flow, but God's Word stands firm. It is absolutely imperative that Scripture defines God's will for us, a will revealed in his name *Jehovah-Rapha,* the Lord our Healer, and demonstrated in two places free from all effects of sin: the garden of Eden and heaven. My investigation of Scripture regarding God's will for healing reinforced something I knew to be true in my head but had trouble believing with my heart—the Bible needs to define God's will for me. His perfect will is not always done here on earth. We live in the very real tension that exists between two kingdoms: the kingdom of this world, which is subject to physical laws, affected by human will, and under demonic influence; and the kingdom of God, the place where God's will is always done. His kingdom is here now *and* on its way. In the midst of this tension, we cannot afford to create a theology that rewrites God's will, desire, or nature in order to justify our experiences. God is unchanging. We can put all our hope and expectation in him and entrust our very lives to the reality that he is who he said he is, and he will be who he said he will be.

MINISTRY

Just like I did, it's possible you've unintentionally placed limits around how you expect God to move or interact with you based on your experience instead of the truths of Scripture. The good news is that we are blessed with the presence of the Holy Spirit, who leads us into all truth (John 16:13).

Take a moment to ask him to free you from beliefs that keep you from experiencing all he has for you and to break down any walls that are hindering you from the fullness of life in his kingdom and deeper relationship with him.

> *God, thank you so much for your Word and the truth it reinforces about who you are. You're consistent and consistently good. You're beautiful and more wonderful than I can imagine. Father, please forgive me for thinking less of you than you said you are, for allowing my experience to define you instead of relying on your Word. I ask for your Spirit to come now and upgrade my thinking about who you are and how you want to interact with me. Encounter me with the truth of how wonderful you are. Amen.*

5

THE QUESTION OF WILL: PART 2

...

One night when I was still living in Northern California, we invited a group of friends to come over to celebrate my roommate's birthday. We cleaned, decorated, cooked, and finished all the regular party preparations in anticipation of our guests' arrival. Taking advantage of the climate, we set a table on the patio underneath strings of bistro lights, and soon our kitchen and backyard were filled with the happy din of friends laughing and enjoying themselves.

One friend was slightly less than his normal, joyful self. After a few minutes of conversation, he shared that he'd hurt his back at the gym. It was causing him so much pain that he'd had to call in sick to work.

"Well, let's pray for it," I suggested, and without hesitation he agreed.

A minute later, he bent over and touched his toes with no ill effects, a maneuver that would have been extremely painful before the prayer. We high-fived, thanked God, and proceeded to have a fun evening.

That simple anecdote serves as an example of how far my beliefs have come regarding healing. Several years ago, I wasn't sure if God even *wanted* to heal us, nor did I have any confidence to pray for healing. Though seeing someone healed is now a rather common occurrence in my life, it has not diminished my joy and excitement in partnering with God to heal. It was a long, painful road for me to get to this place where I now see people healed regularly. Before any of that could happen, I needed to be convinced to my very core that God actually *wanted* to heal the person in front of me. Did I really believe it was God's will to heal this person? What if he actually wanted this person to be sick? And if it were God's will for the person to be sick, would praying for his healing be in direct contrast to my desire to live in agreement with God's will?

In the last chapter, we began to look at the cornerstone question concerning healing: Is it God's will to heal? If we want to see God's healing power at work in and through us, we must answer that question once and for all, or we will continually ask it in our prayers.

"I AM WILLING"

It started slowly. At first it was hardly noticeable, just a little rash. The man thought nothing of it the first day nor the second or third. It was only as the rash began to spread that he became concerned. The growing signs of leprosy on his body were matched only by his growing terror.[10]

Being a righteous man, he swallowed his fear and showed himself to the priest as commanded by the Law. His anxiety increased as the priest told him to separate from the community for the prescribed seven days. All week he worried about his wife and their four young children; what would they do without him? On the seventh

---

10. Leprosy in biblical times was not the same as modern-day leprosy or Hansen's disease, but it was a catchall for skin diseases that potentially disfigured and unquestionably ostracized the sufferer from the community.

day, a defeated man, he presented himself to the priest knowing full well the coming pronouncement—leprosy and a life of isolation.

Dehumanized and forced to beg for survival, the man made it from the beginning of each day to its end by replaying memories of his children laughing and holidays celebrated with his family. His past life felt like a distant dream. He was a forgotten man, robbed of the things that define the human existence.

Rumors of a miracle man eventually reached his deformed ears. Daily he heard new accounts of a man who walked from village to village healing the sick like the great prophets of old. As the rumors became reported fact, a new feeling began to blossom within the leper: hope.

And then it happened. While sitting in his usual place outside the town, he saw the miracle man approach. There could be no mistaking him. Running on mutilated feet, the leper fell facedown before the man. "Lord!" he cried. "If you're willing, you can make me clean!"

With tenderness and compassion, the miracle man looked at him and did something no one had done in years—Jesus touched him.

Jesus reached out his hand and touched the man. "I am willing,"
he said. "Be clean!" And immediately the leprosy left him.

LUKE 5:13

I love how Jesus answered a question we regularly ask of him with both an action and words. The word Jesus used for "willing" in this verse is the Greek word *thelō,* which carries the connotation of taking pleasure in and to like doing something.[11] Jesus was willing to heal the man, and he actually *enjoyed* healing him.

In this chapter, we will pick up two keys that unlock answers to common questions about God's will to heal. The first is found by

---

11. Strong's 2309.

examining Jesus' life, and the second is found by diving deeper into the Father's heart, which Jesus so perfectly displayed.

JESUS, GOD'S WILL DISPLAYED

This is one of my favorite questions to ask friends (particularly on long car rides): If you could witness one moment from the Old Testament, what would it be and why? My answer used to be either creation (for obvious reasons—wow) or Moses' encounter with the glory of God in Exodus 33.

But this summer, my answer changed. My Bible-in-a-year plan led me to Solomon's dedication of the temple in 2 Chronicles and reminded me of another astonishing event:

> *When Solomon finished praying, fire came down from heaven and consumed the burnt offering and the sacrifices, and the glory of the LORD filled the temple. The priests could not enter the temple of the LORD because the glory of the LORD filled it. When all the Israelites saw the fire coming down and the glory of the LORD above the temple, they knelt on the pavement with their faces to the ground, and they worshiped and gave thanks to the LORD, saying,*
>
> *"He is good; his love endures forever."*

2 CHRONICLES 7:1-3

Can you imagine this moment? It's absolutely incredible to me. The visible glory of God was so strong that the priests could not enter the temple. What was it like for the whole nation to witness such a magnificent event? Fire fell from heaven, God's glory descended, and spontaneous worship rose from every prostrate person. What I wouldn't give to see that!

This spectacular scene continually amazes me as I meditate on how Jesus physically embodies the glory that descended on Solomon's temple. Jesus is "the image of the invisible God," as well as "the radiance of God's glory and the *exact representation* of his being" (Col. 1:15; Heb. 1:3, emphasis added). Jesus is God's glory revealed. In other words, he perfectly displays the Father's nature, character, and will in every situation.

Whenever we want to know God's will or intent for a situation, we can look in the Gospels and see it in action in the life of Christ. Jesus said, "For I have come down from heaven not to do my will but to do the will of him who sent me" (John 6:38). So great was his desire to heal that he "went around doing good and healing all who were under the power of the devil, because God was with him" (Acts 10:38). He never told a sick person, "I won't heal you," "I choose not to," or "It's not your time." Never. Everyone who came to him for healing was healed without condition or exception.

Some parts of the Bible are difficult to read and not just because of hard-to-pronounce names. We can struggle reconciling what we read in the Old Testament with what we know about the loving, kind, and gracious God we see in the New Testament. God's seemingly dualistic nature can hinder us from trusting him completely and lead to questions regarding his will for us. But God does not change. Jesus is *exactly* what our Old Testament God looks like. It took a heaven- sized dose of revelation for me to understand that what Jesus declared is true: "Anyone who has seen me has seen the Father" (John 14:9). In other words, when we read about God in the Old Testament, we need to remember that same God is Jesus; Jesus is our "cheat sheet" for understanding the Old Testament and discovering God's will. Any conclusion we come to about God that is inconsistent with the life of Jesus is a wrong conclusion.

When we're confronted with someone who needs healing, we can look at Jesus—God the Healer incarnate, the one who healed everyone who came to him without exception—and pray bold, confident prayers absolutely certain of God's desire to heal.

THE FATHER HEART OF GOD

Just a few weeks ago, my friend and I had the opportunity to pray for a man suffering from hepatitis C and liver cancer. He came to church for prayer and was simultaneously hopeful and inhibited. It quickly dawned on my friend and me that the man thought he deserved to be sick. We told him about the goodness and kindness of our heavenly Father and how he is filled with compassion for his children. We shared about the truth of Jesus' victory on the cross and how God thinks we are worth the price he paid two thousand years ago for all our sins, guilt, and shame. And as we reintroduced the man to the God who loves him, something miraculous did indeed happen: He received God's free gift of salvation.

Jesus' life is God's will displayed for us in human terms. His life provides overwhelming evidence in favor of God's will to heal, but our journey to understanding God's will to heal would be incomplete without also examining the kind, loving nature of the Father's heart.

A good dad doesn't wait for a convenient time before taking his daughter with a broken arm to the hospital. Absolutely not. A good dad helps his child who is in pain regardless of whether that pain is from the normal bumps and bruises of life or something self-inflicted. By comparison, our heavenly Father makes a good dad look uninvolved, unconcerned, and careless. The Father heart of God doesn't say, "Better luck next time," or "I hope you learned your lesson." The Father heart of God leads him to do everything necessary to remove us from harm—even death on a cross.

Many of us actually think we deserve whatever is causing our pain, but poor choices and flawed decisions do not change God's nature.

He never stops being a good Father to all his children. His nature as the Healer and his desire to heal are not changed even if our pain or illness is the direct result of our sin. He is gentle and forgiving. He is moved by compassion toward his children. "A bruised reed he will not break, and a smoldering wick he will not snuff out" (Isa. 42:3).

I chronically underestimate God's goodness. I don't mean to, but it's just that I keep learning he's better than I last thought. I've yet to plumb the depths of his grace, compassion, or mercy, let alone his goodness. So, too, we routinely miscalculate his love and kindness, drawing the boundary at what we think we deserve instead of what he desires to give. God is a Father of indescribable goodness and will stop at nothing to bring love and life to his children. If we wonder if it's his will to heal, we just need to pause to look at our heavenly Father, who possesses greater mercy, more compassion, and a deeper love for the person in front of us than we ever could, and we'll see the answer.

RAISE YOUR EXPECTATIONS

I vividly remember my first hurricane. The whir of power drills was the only thing that marred the otherwise perfect beach day as hurricane shutters were installed and patio furniture carried indoors. "So if it gets really bad, do we go to the basement?" I asked.

Stifling a smile, my Florida-native friend told me there wasn't one. I suddenly realized that my expectation for the approaching storm was a category or two shy of reality. I felt like an AA minor league baseball player who suddenly found herself facing major league pitching—I was unprepared. After countless hours of brilliant lightning, roaring thunder, and deafening wind, we emerged from our bunker to find yard décor from homes miles away scattered throughout our yard and bizarre-looking palm trees devoid of fronds. The next time a hurricane barreled through the Caribbean, I was ready (at least mentally).

In the same way that my expectation for a hurricane was tremendously undersized due to my experience with significantly smaller midwestern thunderstorms, my experience set my small expectation for healing and dictated my understanding of God's will. Instead of encountering God as he revealed himself in the Bible, I encountered God in a size strikingly similar to the box of my theology. Instead of believing in the God who heals, I believed in the God who gives you enough strength to get through something. I was guilty of seeing the word *healed* and reading *emotionally or spiritually healed* because that was the range of my experience. God certainly heals us emotionally, mentally, and spiritually—but we can also *expect* him to heal our physical bodies. Where God writes *hurricane,* he doesn't mean *rain shower.*

Likewise, when the Bible says Jesus healed someone, it doesn't mean the person walked away with emotional peace while the physical problem persisted. The woman with the issue of blood left with more than peace and courage to continue her quest to find the right doctor; she touched the hem of his robe and the blood stopped (Mark 5:23–34). The deaf and mute man left with more than hope; his encounter with the God who heals gave him his hearing and speech (Mark 7:31–37). And Lazarus left the tomb alive, physically restored (John 11). There can be no mistake: Jesus healed the whole person—spiritually, emotionally, and physically.

We greatly limit our interaction with God the Healer when we replace our expectation for physical healing with an expectation to receive courage for the battle, hope for the process, and peace amidst uncertainty. These things are wonderful gifts, especially for the times when we must exercise enduring faith, but they are not the fullness of what God is able and desires to do. Inexperience or disappointment cannot limit our hope for what we will receive from our Father. It is imperative that the reality of who God is and the validity of his Word set our hope level.

It's time for Christ's body to raise our collective expectation for healing to match that of our exalted Head.

CHAPTER KEYS

Is it God's will to heal?

In the past two chapters, we examined what God said in the Bible about his will to heal. We started by studying his name *Jehovah-Rapha,* the Lord Who Heals. Then we took a refreshing stroll through paradise and realized that pain, sickness, and disease were noticeably absent; sickness, too, is nowhere to be found in heaven. We looked at Jesus' life, which is God's will perfectly demonstrated, and discovered that without condition or exception, he healed all who came to him. Finally, we examined the nature of our kind, loving, and compassionate heavenly Father who paid the ultimate price required to free us from the effects of sin. He looks forward to the day when his will is always done on earth as it is in heaven. The unmistakable conclusion from Scripture is that it is God's will to heal every person of every disease every time we pray.

The burning question that immediately rises is this: If it's God's will, why doesn't it always happen? We will address this more in later chapters, but the short answer is that God's will isn't the only will at work. First, we have an enemy actively undermining God's will and, second, God gave us free will, which means we can challenge and defy his will. Both the Christian and non-Christian feel the effects of sin. To say that "all things" are the will of God means that *all things* are within his heart for humanity—including murder, war, and other tragedies. Declaring it's God's will to heal every person of every disease every time we pray does not mean we currently see everyone healed. It means that our Healer-God's desire is for everyone to be healed. It means Jesus saw everyone healed when he prayed. It means that when we pray for healing, we are praying in alignment with God's will whether we see a miracle take place or not. It can sound offensive to say it's always God's will to heal because each of us can think of someone we loved who wasn't healed, but even more troubling is letting something other than Scripture determine our theology while withholding faith from our prayers and trust from our heavenly Father.

It's easier to conclude it wasn't God's timing or his plan when we're confronted with someone chronically ill or when someone we pray for isn't immediately healed, but those ideas aren't biblically sustainable. Instead, we need to continue pursuing healing in the midst of our disappointment, confusion, and pain. Calling chronic illness, disease, and even death "God's will" or placing them under the heading of his sovereignty saves us from the very real heartache and disappointment caused by living in the tension of his kingdom here and coming. Sweeping our heartache under the rug doesn't heal the pain, and calling disease "God's will" disempowers us from effecting change and divorces us from actual responsibility.

What if the opposite is true? What if we are authorized and empowered to see sickness bow the knee to the name Jesus? What if we, as Christ's body, carry the solution for the one suffering in front of us? Suddenly, we are empowered to live nothing short of the abundant, powerful life promised to us (John 10:10, 14:12). The Bible is clear even where our experiences are cloudy: God's will is for all to be healed—a fact that makes our prayers extremely powerful.

MINISTRY

Healing is not a safe subject. Declaring that it's always God's will to heal doesn't lessen the hurt of losing a loved one. And it certainly is not meant to bring condemnation. You don't know what you don't know. Any accusation, guilt, shame, or condemnation you may feel is not from God. Instead, there is grace available to receive his love that moves us past fear and through pain.

It's also entirely permissible to have questions. It's okay to disagree with me. It's even okay to assume that each of the stories I've shared about healing is my fling at fiction writing. I personally walked through all these stages. But ask yourself if your discomfort is caused by a desire for accuracy and a defense of God's honor, or if it arises from past disappointments or different teachings you've received. Take a moment and ask God to reveal to you his heart for healing.

Father, thank you that you're good. You're better than I can imagine. Thank you that your plan for me is always for my benefit. Forgive me for confusing my experience with your will. Please come and calm my fears and confusion, encounter me with your love in those places. Clarify your heart and desire regarding healing. And may your perfect will be done in my life, my family, my church, and throughout the world. Amen.

6

THE QUESTION OF COST
AND KINGDOM COME

...

It was my last night visiting a close friend in her hometown, a western European capital. Over the course of a week, we spent hours wandering streets older than America, took in the sites, shopped, and encouraged one another with conversations about what we saw God doing in each other's lives. And we ate—a lot.

No surprise, our final evening together finds us in a market with large plates of cheese and charcuterie in front of us. At the table next to us sits a girl in her early twenties wearing a cast on her wrist.

"Do you want to pray for her?" my friend asks, following my gaze.

I observe the girl in the midst of her family, all of them enjoying their meal. "No, she's eating; we're eating. It's fine."

"Are you sure?"

In America, people may be surprised by your offer to pray but almost always accept. I understand that the response is quite different in this country, where offers to pray are often met with a strong aversion for both the question and the questioner. Again,

I look at the girl. "Yeah, it's fine," I say in an attempt to convince us both.

This is the perfect end to my time here, I think, looking around at our very European surroundings. *Being coldly snubbed by that girl would be such a sour note to end on.* But as that thought drifts through my mind, I suddenly realize, *That's not my thought! That's not how I think, and it's definitely not how Jesus thinks.* As the family starts to gather their things to leave, I can't push away the feelings of compassion and anger bubbling inside of me: compassion because the girl is in pain, and anger because I know Jesus paid an exorbitant price for her complete healing. Turning to my friend, I ask if we can pray for the girl.

"Excuse me," my friend says in the vernacular and proceeds to explain that we want to pray for her.

I understand enough of the conversation to realize the girl is receptive to our offer. My friend lays her hand on the cast, and I join in, silently commanding the bone to be restored. The girl thanks us, kisses our cheeks in the European manner, and says goodbye.

"Wow!" my friend exclaims. "You don't know how rare it is to actually get to pray for someone around here." We celebrate that small victory as she quickly fills me in on the parts of the conversation I didn't understand.

As we discuss the encounter, our eyes are drawn to an approaching figure.

"Did she forget something?" my friend suggests.

"No, I think she's coming back for us," I reply.

Sure enough, the girl walks right up to us and asks to speak with us for a minute. "Why did you pray for me?" she asks.

As my friend translates, I tell her, "Honestly, I saw you in pain and felt compassion for you. Jesus already paid for your broken bone to be healed." We share a little more about God's specific love for her before we say goodbye again. This time, it really is the perfect ending to a great week.

A couple of weeks after my return to the States, I awake to an excited message from my friend in Europe: "Guess who texted me after re-visiting her doctor?" I rub my bleary eyes and read the rest of the message. The girl from the market had texted my friend a full update: At her next checkup, the doctor was confounded by the newest X-ray. The bone showed no sign of ever being broken. Her cast came off six weeks early.

WHY WE PRAY

I used to get stymied by questions of *how* to pray, but I've learned it's of far greater importance to know *why* I pray. Seeing others freed from pain and devastation is great motivation—I will never tire of watching the look on someone's face when she realizes Jesus healed her—but the healing a person experiences, incredible as it is, is not the only reason I pray. Along with the compassion I felt for the girl that night in the market, I felt a burning conviction for Jesus to receive everything he bled and died for at Calvary. The first and greatest reason I pray for healing is that Jesus deserves it. He deserves the full reward of his suffering, which includes our freedom from all torment, sickness, and disease. My prayers for healing are part of winning for Jesus his full reward—the champion's prize that cost him his life.

Our prayers are not mere triage stations in our fight against the enemy. Prayers for healing are a forward-operating base from which we launch attacks into enemy territory. Healing is a sign that the kingdom of God is present and that it possesses greater authority than the kingdom of this world (see Luke 10:1–12). Our prayers for healing are offensive weapons that aggressively expand God's kingdom territory. We don't pray just so people are healed—we pray so the earth looks like heaven.

In this chapter, we will unpack these two statements:

1. Jesus won the full healing of our bodies once and for all at Calvary.
2. Healing is a demonstration of the presence, rule, and reign of the kingdom of God and Jesus' messianic identity.

The more we learn about what Jesus won at Calvary, and the greater our understanding of the rule and reign of God's kingdom on earth, the bolder and more confident our prayers become. If Jesus paid for our full healing, this impacts how and why we pray. It changes *how* we pray because our authority increases when we understand God ruled in our favor two thousand years ago, and it changes *why* we pray because we passionately desire to see our Lord Jesus receive everything he won.

IT'S BOUGHT AND PAID FOR

If my mom sends me to the bakery to pick up her order, I need to know what she bought. Wheat or rye? Cake or cookies? If I don't know or am uncertain, it will be difficult to double check that I received the full purchase, answer any questions that arise, or—more likely—I'll forget something needed for dinner and toss in an extra sticky bun or two. But if I know what was bought, I can collect the order with confidence.

If Jesus' atonement paid for *all* pain, injury, and illness, then as his followers filled with his Spirit, we have the authority to collect on that payment. In other words, we can have complete confidence each and every time we pray for healing, knowing that God already won *this* healing.

When we know what Jesus bought at Calvary, we know what to collect, and we can do so with the authority of the one who paid for it. This poses the all-important question: What did Jesus win for us at the cross?

Fortunately, the prophet Isaiah answered that question long before we asked it:

> *Surely he took up our pain*
> *and bore our suffering,*
> *yet we considered him punished by God,*
> *stricken by him, and afflicted.*
> *But he was pierced for our transgressions,*
> *he was crushed for our iniquities;*
> *the punishment that brought us peace was on him,*
> *and by his wounds we are healed.*

ISAIAH 53:4-5[12]

Jesus was crushed, wounded, and pierced for our healing. The King of kings endured a terrible beating, one where "his face was so disfigured he seemed hardly human, and from his appearance, one would scarcely know he was a man" (Isa. 52:14 NLT). He did this because it meant our healing. Jesus was so swollen, bruised, bloody, and broken that he no longer looked like a man. And he suffered that excruciating violence because he knew Isaiah's prophecy; he knew that with each lash of the whip and every stroke of the soldier's rod, he bought our healing. With his eyes fixed on you and me, Jesus carried all our sickness and physical pain to the cross, where sin's curse was eternally defeated. By enduring an unimaginable beating and crucifixion, Jesus once and for all won our complete and total healing from every injury, illness, and disease.

---

12. How often I read this passage without grasping the full meaning! The word *pain* in verse 4 (sometimes translated as "griefs") literally means sickness (Strong's 2403), and the word *suffering* (also translated as "sorrows and pains") means physical and mental pain (Strong's 4341). Jesus defeated physical, emotional, *and* mental pain.

SIN AND SICKNESS, SPIRIT AND BODY

Maybe the people came to witness miracles. Maybe they came to hear someone make daring claims about God's kingdom. Or maybe simple curiosity drew the crowd. Regardless of the reason, people packed into the house to hear Jesus speak. Undeterred by their inability to gain entrance through the door, a group of men intent on bringing their paralyzed friend to the Healer made a hole in the roof and lowered the man on his mat until he lay at Jesus' feet.

"Son, your sins are forgiven," Jesus told him.

A collective gasp echoed through the room. Who dared forgive sins but God alone? Jesus might as well have passed out stones to the dissenters, so open was his blasphemy. Jesus responded to their unspoken thoughts:

> *"Which is easier: to say to this paralyzed man, 'Your sins are forgiven,' or to say, 'Get up, take your mat and walk'? But I want you to know that the Son of Man has authority on earth to forgive sins." So he said to the man, "I tell you, get up, take your mat and go home." He got up, took his mat and walked out in full view of them all. This amazed everyone and they praised God, saying, "We have never seen anything like this!"*

MARK 2:9–12

I'm routinely amazed by the faith and persistence demonstrated by the man's friends. They literally removed every obstacle that kept him from Jesus. However, it wasn't until recently that I saw the connection between the forgiveness of sins and the healing of the body woven into this story and that Jesus demonstrated his power and authority to do both. While I've known about the effects of sin on my spirit and my absolute need for a Savior, I never thought about the effects of sin on my body—or more precisely, that it corrupts, destroys, and ultimately kills my body the same way it does my spirit. Sin is to the spirit what sickness is to the body; one brings spiritual disease that leads to spiritual death, while the other brings physical disease that leads to physical death. This is actually good news because Jesus saved us from *all* the effects of sin.

It's one of life's oddities that after buying a new car, you start to notice that same kind of car on the road. This happened to me after getting my Jeep. Suddenly I saw Jeeps everywhere and learned there's even a special "Jeep wave" one driver gives another. Similarly, upon realizing the relationship between sin and sickness, I began seeing it on page after page of the Bible. Sin and sickness are what Peter spoke of when he quoted Isaiah's prophecy about Jesus: "'He himself bore our sins' in his body on the cross, so that we might die to sins and live for righteousness; 'by his wounds you have been healed'" (1 Pet. 2:24). It's the theme David sang of long before Jesus went to the cross. He penned, "Praise the LORD, my soul, and forget not all his benefits—who forgives all your sins and heals all your diseases" (Ps. 103:2–3). The atonement bought our spiritual *and* physical salvation. Jesus was brutally beaten, crushed beyond human recognition, and underwent extreme physical suffering so that we, his beloved, wouldn't have to.

Medical advances routinely benefit those who only a few years ago would have perished. In some cases, the blind see, the deaf hear, and the paralyzed walk. Yet even with continual breakthroughs in medicine and technology, there's still one realm that can't be touched: No one except God can forgive sins. When Jesus healed the paralytic, he demonstrated his authority to remove all the effects of sin, answering the charge routinely put to him: "If God gave you authority to do this, show us a miraculous sign to prove it" (John 2:18 NLT).

This brings us back to Jesus' question: Is it easier to say, "Your sins are forgiven," or "Get up and walk?" If, like me, you grew up in the church where the gospel of salvation was regularly preached, the idea of sins being forgiven is a no-brainer. I know Jesus alone can remove sins, so I take zero responsibility when leading someone to Jesus. In fact, even that phrase points out how little responsibility I take—all I do is *lead* the person. Connecting the person in front of me to Jesus is my only task, which removes the burden of responsibility and places it squarely on Jesus' shoulders. However, with the concept of healing, since it was new to me, I felt extremely responsible for the result, even though the process for healing is exactly the same as it is for salvation: Connect the person to Jesus.

One challenging thing for us about healing is that it's often immediately verifiable; in many cases, either the person gets out of the wheelchair or he doesn't.[13] The fear and what-if questions that surround healing make it feel harder to us, but in reality, both healing and forgiving sins are easy for God. The atonement bought our salvation and healing at the same time. Jesus emphasized that his ability to heal the man (a visible miracle) proved his authority to forgive sins (an invisible miracle). Likewise, when we pray for healing, we are demonstrating the authority of God's kingdom that has the power to heal our bodies and spirits.

A GREATER KINGDOM

You know the exact moment you cross California's southern border into Mexico. Only a few feet away from the United States, there are noticeable changes: A different flag flies, the officials speak Spanish instead of English, and the acceptable customs vary to match the culture. Contrast this with crossing California's northern border into Oregon, where the only perceptible change is the gas price. Differences do exist between states, but they pale in comparison to the

---

13. However, I've seen many healings manifest days or even weeks after the initial prayer.

differences between nations. The ruling authority determines much of what we experience. Consequently, when the authority changes, so does our experience.

Throughout the Gospels, the announcement of a new government was repeatedly declared: "The kingdom of heaven has come near" (Matt. 3:2). We know the kingdom of God has come the same way we know we've crossed the border into Mexico—the government, laws, and authority have changed. And just as the Mexican or American flag is a sign of the governmental authority, so, too, healing signals the arrival of the kingdom of God.

Our job description hasn't changed much since Adam and Eve received their assignment in the garden. God told them to "fill the earth and subdue it" (Gen. 1:28), and he still plans to use us to expand his kingdom—territory marked by the heavenly standards of righteousness, peace, and joy in the Holy Spirit (Rom. 14:17). This bench-clearing, everyone-gets-to-play reality is far different and more fun than I ever thought possible. Where once sin ruled, we bring the pronouncement of mercy and grace. Where fear tormented and stole, we bring freedom and peace. And where sickness reigned, we bring divine health and life.

Before I realized that the kingdom of God's ultimate authority means I am part of administering its laws, I was handcuffed to a theology that hindered any response other than sympathy and any action except prayer for peace. I could hold the door open for a person in a wheelchair but lacked the knowledge of my power and authority to help him out of it. Now when sickness crosses my path, I smile to myself in the same way a hunter does when her prey walks into view. It is *illegal* for sickness and disease to exist within the kingdom's jurisdiction, and *I* represent that kingdom. I am armed and authorized to bring healing everywhere I go.

The way God does things is a mystery often contrary to the worldly wisdom surrounding us. We needed saving, so God the all-powerful became a helpless baby. We needed a relationship with the God of all love, so he became one rejected and despised. We needed a way back to the God of all holiness, so he became our sin. It makes little sense that we, frail and corruptible humankind, play an intricate role in bringing his kingdom, but in his infinite wisdom, God decided the best plan for the world was to hand us the job. Remember, a very real tension exists between the established territory and the coming arrival of this kingdom. It's here and on the way; we live in the established kingdom *and* play an active role in its establishment. Yet in the midst of this now-and-not-yet tension, it bears pointing out that Jesus is already reigning. And wherever Jesus reigns, the laws of his kingdom are in effect.

MISTAKEN IDENTITY

I travel a fair amount. I'm five feet ten and blonde, and I frequently find myself in Asia, where blending in is rarely an option. Often, and for reasons I have yet to understand, people ask to take their photo with me. Consequently, it was with great anticipation that I boarded a flight to Norway, both because I was attending the wedding of a dear friend and because I was to travel in a country where I might *not* stand out.

Upon arrival, I deplaned, glanced around, and was soon addressed *in Norwegian.* No one seemed to take any notice of me—that is, until I went with my friend to the family farm on the tip of a breathtaking fjord. It was one of the most stunning places I've ever seen. It turned out that I wasn't alone in this opinion; cruise ships daily emptied their passengers into the little port to enjoy the exquisite beauty, and many of these tourists wanted nothing more than a picture with a Norwegian. Instead of the anonymity I expected, I was once again the subject of numerous photographs, albeit this time *because* I looked like a local.

"Tusen takk!" they'd say, attempting to express their thanks in Norwegian.

"Værsågod. You're welcome," I'd answer, good-naturedly playing along and using the only Norwegian phrase I knew.

In small-town Norway, a tourist mistaking a tall, fair-headed girl for a Norwegian is entirely reasonable. I am the embodiment of a tourist's Norwegian stereotype. What's far less understandable is how those who witnessed Jesus healing multitudes of people in fulfillment of Old Testament messianic prophecies still somehow missed his identity. Speaking of the Messiah's healing ministry, Malachi prophesied, "The sun of righteousness [the Messiah] will rise with healing in its wings" (4:2 NASB). Similarly, Isaiah—the prophet who spoke most frequently about the Messiah—foretold healing as evidence of his advent:

> *Then will the eyes of the blind be opened*
> *and the ears of the deaf unstopped.*
> *Then will the lame leap like a deer,*
> *and the mute tongue shout for joy.*

ISAIAH 35:5-6[14]

Does that description sound familiar? We regularly sing in church about the blind seeing, deaf hearing, and lame walking, and it's also the answer Jesus gave when asked to verify his messianic identity. "So he replied to the messengers, 'Go back and report to John what you have seen and heard: The blind receive sight, the lame walk, those who have leprosy are cleansed, the deaf hear, the dead are raised, and the good news is proclaimed to the poor'" (Luke 7:22). Matthew went one step further, drawing the connection between Isaiah's messianic prophecy and Jesus' actions for us:

---

14. See also Isa. 29:18, 42:7, 53:4.

When evening came, many who were demon-possessed were
brought to him, and he drove out the spirits with a word and
healed all the sick. This was to fulfill what was spoken through
the prophet Isaiah:

"He took up our infirmities and bore our diseases."

MATTHEW 8:16-17

Jesus' messianic identity was confirmed every time he reached out his hand to heal, a point the apostle Matthew made explicitly clear. So, too, we announce the message of Messiah every time we do the same. When we bring healing in place of sickness, we boldly proclaim and demonstrate Jesus' identity as the Son of God to the world. Our actions fully embody the apostle Paul's words: "My message and my preaching were not with wise and persuasive words, but with a demonstration of the Spirit's power, so that your faith might not rest on human wisdom, but on God's power" (1 Cor. 2:4-5). Our actions, particularly healing the sick, reinforce to the world the truth that the Messiah has come and his kingdom reigns. We don't merely present this truth—we get to demonstrate it.

God is abundantly gracious and kind to us. He knows how our brains work with our love of logical arguments and our need for empirical evidence—he made us to function that way. Jesus told his disciples, "Believe me when I say that I am in the Father and the Father is in me; *or at least believe on the evidence of the works themselves"* (John 14:11, emphasis added). In other words, sometimes we believe before the healing and sometimes it's the healing that gives us the grace to believe. We get to proclaim Jesus the Messiah and then, like he did, back up our claim by bringing healing to broken bodies, souls, and spirits. Jesus is the answer to every problem facing the world, and as those who have his Spirit dwelling within us, we carry that answer everywhere we go.

CHAPTER KEYS

Martin Luther reintroduced the world to the beautiful truth that it's faith alone by the grace of Christ that saves us, a truth that was subsequently taught by each generation following him. By the time I came on the scene, I was introduced at a young age to the idea that I could have complete assurance of salvation the very moment I confessed Jesus as Lord. I inherited a mindset and spiritual reality from countless others who prayed for, taught, and received salvation in the atonement as an undisputed fact. Though some of us may personally question whether or not we've received salvation, or haven't experienced the peace that comes with it, we can have that assurance and peace right this very minute. All that is required of us is to declare verbally, "Jesus is Lord," and believe in our hearts that God raised him from the dead, and we will be saved (Rom. 10:9).

In the same way salvation through the atonement has been taught, believed, and built upon to a level where we are completely certain of it, I can see where our beliefs about healing are headed. My excitement level rises when I daydream about what healing will look like when we embrace the truth that Jesus won our bodily healing at the same moment he paid for our salvation. What will it look like when we corporately apprehend, teach, and believe the truth that healing is as easy as praying with someone to receive salvation?

I didn't wake up with a burning conviction of the truth about healing. Frankly, I never spent much time considering how healing as part of the atonement could affect my prayer life. Nor in all my years of reading about the coming of God's kingdom did I ever stop to consider what it looked like when that kingdom actually came. When my heart realized what my head knew for so long—that Jesus won a total victory over sin and all its effects, including sickness—my confidence and boldness in praying for healing skyrocketed. Likewise, when I grabbed hold of the reality that I carry the fullness of God's kingdom within me, what I expected to happen when I entered a situation went from *peace to get through it* to *power to transform it.*

More than anything else, we need to understand we are lovers of God. Administering the kingdom of God's laws is always second to love. As I experience more of God's uniquely personal love for me, I am enabled to love him more, which overflows to those around me. It's this love that motivates me to act, but it's his act at Calvary that empowers me to do so.

The atonement, the coming of the kingdom, and Jesus' messianic identity are all tied together and perfectly demonstrate the Father's heart. Our God loves healing. In life, Jesus healed as a messianic sign—a bold statement of what was to come. In death, Jesus vanquished sin and sickness forever, thoroughly defeating evil and its stronghold over us. And in his resurrection and ascension, he handed the expansion of the kingdom to us, to those who possess it internally, that we might demonstrate it externally.

MINISTRY

This burning passion to see Jesus get his full reward and establish his kingdom's rule is transferable. It is simply more of his presence in our lives.

If you want this passion, all you need do is ask for it. He will say yes. It could come like a blazing bonfire or it could start as a few glowing embers, but it will come. I encourage you to pray the following prayer with me and then wait until you hear him speak to you—until you tangibly feel his love and presence. He may not come as you expect, but he will always come.

Jesus, thank you for the extravagant price you paid for me to live in complete freedom—body, soul, and spirit. I want to see you receive everything you paid for. I want to see your kingdom advance. Cause a burning passion rooted in your love to rise up in me right now. Pour out your Spirit on me. Empower me, embolden me, and fill me with passion to proclaim and demonstrate the coming of your kingdom with words and power. Jesus, receive your full reward. Amen.

7

THE QUESTION
OF ORIGIN

• • •

At the beginning of this book, I briefly told you of my encounter with Jesus in which I was healed after years of illness. I was purposely vague when describing that exchange.

First, what occurred was difficult for me to understand, and second, I needed the proof of my transformed health to fully believe what happened. What follows is a more detailed account of that life-changing encounter.

• • •

It's dark by the time I pull up to my friend's house and park my car. I spent the afternoon in a daze, questioning the morning's events. Does God really speak that clearly? Is it really that easy? Am I making it up? That morning, I had prayed with my friend's mom for well over two hours as she acted as counselor and confidante, encouraging me to persist until God replaced the root lie—

an underlying belief contrary to God's belief about a situation—with his truth. I feel like I am seeing the world right side up for the first time.

I enter the house, and we start our second prayer time the same way we began the first: by asking God to bring to my mind anything he wants to address. As I sit with my eyes closed, I "see" a picture in the same spot you can "see" the ocean right now, if I asked you to imagine it. I see thick, lacking-any-light, oily black darkness. I try to convince myself that the darkness is my imagination. I open my eyes, look around, and close them again. Immediately, I see the same picture, only this time when I peer into the darkness, I see a hideous, inhuman face that terrifies me.

"What are you seeing?" my friend's mom asks and listens as I describe the picture to her. "Oh, that's not a problem," she assures me. "But let's get my daughter to join us in prayer. She's dealt with demons before."

"Demons?" I exclaim. The word greatly disturbs me. *I'm a Christian. How can there be a demon?* The closest I've come to the demonic was reading *The Screwtape Letters* by C.S. Lewis.

Mother and daughter return and begin to silently intercede. "Why don't you ask Jesus what he wants to tell you about this?" my friend's mom suggests.

So I pray, "Jesus, what do you want me to know about this?"

Internally I hear his voice tell me, ever so gently, "This is a demon whose name is Pain. He's been afflicting you since you were a little girl." I break into frightened tears. The idea of this vile creature's nearness is nauseating.

"Jesus, what do you want to do about this?" I manage to ask.

And then something wonderful happens. It is more wonderful than anything I've ever experienced. Dressed in brilliant white, Jesus enters my vision of darkness. He is unbelievably bright, like flashes of lightning. He is so bright I can't look directly at him.

In the midst of my confusion, Jesus is entirely untroubled, serene in the storm. "Just look here," I hear him say, and in one motion he extends a sword toward the demon. The demon and darkness vanish. There is no fight. There isn't a struggle. Jesus points his sword and the demon is gone.

"You are healed," Jesus tells me.

As real as the exchange feels to me, I still have trouble believing it is truly happening. A small, lingering thought tells me I am imagining the scene, that Jesus isn't *really* there and I am not *really* healed. The thought grows in size as I listen to it. What if I am making this up? What if I still wake up sick tomorrow after telling people Jesus healed me?

"You mean, I *will be* healed or I'm going to be healed one day," I clarify, turning my focus back to Jesus. His tangible love envelops me. His eyes burn through me, quieting my fear. And then a second choking thought bombards me: I only know how to live with this illness—who will I be without it?

"Child," he says tenderly. "It's past tense. It's complete. You are healed."

This second battle, the one for my identity, lasts far longer than the first. After several minutes that feel like hours, I relay what I've seen and heard with my eagerly awaiting friends. Immediately, tears of joy mixed with laughter overcome us. We hug each other and thank God, and then, with a new lightheartedness, go out for ice cream to celebrate.

DOES GOD SEND SICKNESS?

The idea that a demon could somehow "attach" itself to my life and cause me physical pain was the stuff of nightmares and beyond my comprehension. I found myself in completely new territory with none of the familiar markings or signposts I had learned on Sunday mornings or from the Christian lives modeled around me. As with anything new, there was an element of fear to overcome, but I was ready to run into this new land that looked more like the Gospels than anything I'd ever witnessed. Each day that I woke up without pain was an astounding gift. It was full steam ahead into this land where God's love is tangible and his power readily demonstrates itself.

At least, that was what I wanted to happen. I'd love to say that I ran into this Promised Land without any hesitation, but at times I doubted the validity of my encounter. I even called my friend the morning after my healing to double check that I hadn't imagined it, a phone call I repeated a few months later, the first time I felt less than my best. If healthy boundaries took time to find (it turns out that no one feels good on a couple of hours of sleep or on a diet consisting mainly of banana milkshakes and coffee), it took me far longer to make sense of my theology.

Until Jesus healed me, I firmly believed that God sent my illness either to teach me a lesson or to somehow glorify himself. But Jesus spoke about the impossibility of being both a cause and a cure, declaring that a house divided against itself cannot stand (see Mark 3:23–26). If God made me sick in the first place, why would Jesus remove something his Father sent?

In many ways, my belief that God was the source of my illness kept me in bondage to my illness. I was entirely ignorant of God's passion for healing and was unwilling to pray for my own healing, believing it would be contrary to his will. Interestingly, this didn't stop me from going to doctors—which, if similar logic were applied, should have been out of the question. If any part of us believes that God causes illness or that he receives glory from our physical suffering, we will abstain from seeking him for healing and we will second-guess our prayers, as well as ourselves. We need to determine the source of sickness and pain in our lives. If God is the source of sickness, illness, and disease, we can respect his decision and live the best life possible in light of our circumstances. But if he is *not* the source of these things, we don't have to wait any longer—we get to stand up and fight against them with every ounce of our strength.

THE GOODNESS OF GOD

Take a moment and imagine yourself in heaven's throne room. Wipe away any trace of harp playing on fluffy clouds that may be running through your mind—heaven is vibrant and full of activity. Creatures and elders throw crowns and sing praises, incense and prayers arise, and it's very, very loud (see Rev. 4). In the center of all of this is the brilliant one, Jehovah God himself. I love the apostle John's attempt to describe God's appearance. He stumbles over the most exquisite things he can think of and still falls short. He describes God's appearance like "jasper" and "ruby" with a "rainbow that shone like an emerald" (Rev. 4:3). The very brightness of heaven, illuminated by God's glory, is too wonderful for human language to express (Rev. 21:23).

Stop and really engage your God-given imagination. Picture the elders and the living creatures bowing. Hear the shouts of "Holy, holy, holy!" Smell the incense. Now take a minute and look—can you find any evil? Or anything like famine, war, or pain? In the same way that there is no dark corner in a brightly lit room, the presence of God negates the presence of evil. There is no poverty within him, no strife or pain. In fact, there are no colds, no arthritis, no cancer, and no death found within him. There is no evil in God. None.

Not surprisingly, Jesus' life sheds light on the question of origin. He came to "destroy the devil's works" (1 John 3:8) and actively healed great multitudes. Every person who came to Jesus for healing or merely touched the edge of his cloak was healed (see Acts 10:38; Mark 6:56). If God sent or caused the sickness of even one person Jesus healed, Jesus actually destroyed the work of God instead of the devil. Though most within the church would readily agree to God's goodness, we expose our confusion on the subject when we attribute pain, illness, and disease to him. Good things, not bad, come from him. The apostle Paul wrote, "Everything God created is good" (1 Tim. 4:4). This refrain began at creation and continues today.

God's goodness is the message he's aching for us to grasp. He longs for everyone to personally encounter his goodness. He is so incredibly good that he takes the hurt and broken areas of our lives and transforms them into something wonderful. This does not make him the *origin* of our pain, but he is wonderfully sovereign in the midst of it. When I assumed God sent my illness, I operated from a mindset contrary to Scripture and confused good with evil and God with the devil.

I cannot give you something I don't have. Likewise, for God to be the origin of pain and disease, it means he must possess these things in the first place. God's goodness is so complete that it's impossible for evil to exist within him and, therefore, impossible for evil to come from him.

EVERY GOOD AND PERFECT GIFT

It was Christmas Eve and the presents were piled several deep under the tree. I can't remember how old I was, but I can recall sitting within arm's reach of the gifts, obediently looking "only with my eyes." The memory jumps forward to the next morning, only now I'm smiling widely as I hold the unwrapped package containing brand new inline skates. (Why I asked for inline skates instead of ice skates in the middle of a Minnesota winter is beyond me.) Undeterred by my inability to skate outside, I happily skated circles around the basement until the snow melted some months later.

Though I may not remember every gift I've received over the years, I can confidently write that never once did my parents give me something harmful or something that brought me pain, loss, or illness. Everything they gave me—whether it was a much-desired Christmas gift, a practical stocking stuffer, or the things I failed to notice like dinner every evening and a bed to sleep in every night—was given out of love and for my benefit.

I'm blessed to have grown up in a loving, secure home with parents who modeled generosity. But compared to our heavenly Father, my parents come off worse than the Grinch. Jesus asked in Matthew 7:9–11, "Which of you, if your son asks for bread, will give him a stone? Or if he asks for a fish, will give him a snake? If you, then, though you are evil, know how to give good gifts to your children, how much more will your Father in heaven give good gifts to those who ask him?" This is the nature of our heavenly Father in action. He does not give us cancer when we ask for health or an accident when we ask for safety, yet that was what I unwittingly assumed when I believed my illness came from him. God's good and loving nature goes even further than not giving us bad things—he actively gives us good things. If he has something good to give us, he does (see Ps. 84:11). There's no earning, no working, no striving involved. He gives good things because he likes to, and he likes us.

His goodness even goes beyond giving us good things—his goodness is the origin of every good thing. James wrote, "Every good and perfect gift is from above, coming down from the Father of the heavenly lights, who does not change like shifting shadows" (1:17). Whatever God gives is wonderful, *and* everything wonderful comes from him. I have no fear that today he will bestow his love, but tomorrow he might give multiple sclerosis. None. I know his nature is good; he is a good Father, which means he's got a treasure trove of wonderful things he can't wait to give me. According to Jesus, all we need to do is ask.

WHAT MAKES US SICK?

As I began to piece together the realization that God was not the source of my illness, it occurred to me that without my semi-fatalistic "God caused this" approach to illness, I didn't actually have an answer when asked its origin. Of course, I could point to the fall of man as the root of evil in our lives, but that felt like a cop-out, a generic generalization that only swept the matter under the rug without truly answering it. I actually needed to ask and answer the question of origin. If God isn't the source of illness, who or what is?

A Fallen World

Many people have trouble accepting the reality of God due to the presence of pain and suffering in the world. We question the goodness of a God whose creation is subject to catastrophes like earthquakes, tsunamis, and hurricanes. We attribute to him the suffering we witness, assuming his sovereignty is synonymous with culpability. In reality, humankind's sin subjected the whole earth to an existence outside of God's original intent. Creation itself does not operate according to God's design. Paul wrote:

> *For the creation waits in eager expectation for the children of God to be revealed. For the creation was subject to frustration, not by its own choice, but by the will of the one who subjected it, in hope that the creation itself will be liberated from its bondage to decay and brought into the freedom and glory of the children of God.*

ROMANS 8:19-21

It's not within God's heart to see the sun burn our skin or give us cancer, nor is it his desire to see his children suffer from natural disasters. Sin changed man's relationship with God *and* the earth we walk upon (see Gen. 3). The effects of our fallen world can cause illness, disease, and pain through the degradation of cells and the deterioration of life—both within our own bodies and the earth itself. We often point our finger at God when calamity strikes, but we need to take the responsibility for our actions and how they've negatively affected creation, as well as the natural order we were entrusted to steward. Creation, too, awaits full redemption. Until that time, creation itself, broken and behaving outside of the Creator's intent, is a source of sickness, illness, disease, and even death.

Humankind

Sometimes we get sick because creation isn't behaving as God intended, but creation isn't the only thing operating outside of God's initial design. Humanity at large is directly responsible for much of the sickness and disease that exist on the earth. War kills and maims on the battlefield, leaving famine and disease in its wake. Corruption keeps electricity, clean water, medication, and food from the people who need it most. When we ask how God could allow such terrible things, we demonstrate our memory loss: God gave us free will to choose good or evil, and our choices ripple outward, all too often affecting the most vulnerable.[15] It's a strong symbiotic relationship: The greater my influence or the closer our relationship, the greater my decisions will impact you and your health—regardless if you like, approve, or acknowledge my decisions.

Likewise, the person typically most impacted by my decisions is me. God gave me free will, which means I can actively choose harmful things with negative consequences that could include pain and

---

15. Perhaps this is part of the reason that God concerns himself with the poor, the widow, the orphan, the refugee, and the immigrant in the land (see Exod. 22:21-22; Deut. 10:18, 27:19; Ps. 146:9).

disease. If I forgo several nights of quality sleep in order to meet a deadline or hang out with friends, I leave myself susceptible to infection. If I eat only delicious European cheeses and pastries while neglecting other elements of my diet, I open the door to things like high cholesterol and other lifestyle-attributed ailments. Too often we blame God for causing or allowing a disease or injury when we are simply reaping the consequences of our decision-making. We accuse God instead of recognizing the extremely costly gift of free will, which allows us to make decisions—for good or ill—in the first place.

This is not to say that if we are sick due to poor decisions or reckless behavior that God withholds healing. I recently had a headache I knew came from dehydration. I asked God to remove it and he graciously did—and then I drank some water. God routinely, willfully, and lovingly frees us from the consequences of our actions the same way a dad dives into a pool to grab his small child. It doesn't matter to a father if his child accidentally fell in or foolishly jumped in; God mercifully saves us from ourselves and blesses us with a greater understanding of the connection between our decisions and our health.

The Enemy

Finally, the spiritual realm can also dramatically impact our health. The Bible says, "Your enemy the devil prowls around like a roaring lion looking for someone to devour" (1 Pet. 5:8). It is the devil's goal to destroy us in an attempt to hurt our Father, and this goal can affect every aspect of our lives: spiritual, emotional, mental, and physical. Often in the West we disregard the demonic as a possible source of pain, but having little understanding or conscious interaction with spiritual beings does not negate their presence. Paul reminded us of the battle waging in the unseen realm when he wrote,

"For our struggle is not against flesh and blood, but against the rulers, against the authorities, against the powers of this dark world and against the spiritual forces of evil in the heavenly realms" (Eph. 6:12).

Demonic influence is a concept commonly understood in the developing world where the interplay between the natural and spiritual is taken for granted. In these areas, exorcising demons or demonic influences is a normal part of healthcare. Witch doctors live in most villages and charge substantial sums to bring a cure or perform a curse. When I've asked to pray for someone for healing in the developing world, instead of needing to explain how prayer can change a physical situation, I've been asked how much I charge. While living in Southeast Asia, I regularly heard stories of illness and pain caused by demons or of strange diseases that no doctor could diagnose, no medicine could treat, and which were cured only through prayer. An acquaintance of mine began struggling with migraines around the same time she was given an ornate doll. After a couple of days of headaches, she made the connection between the doll and the headaches. She commanded the demonic spirit to leave and was never troubled by the mysterious headaches again. Whether we're cognizant of it or not, the spiritual world impacts the physical one.

Our Western minds can struggle mightily with these kinds of stories. Often we write them off as fiction or the result of an uneducated, overly spiritual population trying to make sense of life. For months, I struggled with doubts concerning my healing mainly because it was so contrary to my understanding of the interplay between the spiritual and physical worlds. The proof of my radically changed health finally convinced me of the encounter's validity. I grew up in the church, but I'd never heard a similar testimony or received biblical teaching on the subject, even though the Bible is full of stories of Jesus healing those who were demonically oppressed.

Healing is a demonstration of God's victory over Satan and part of Jesus' mission to destroy the devil's work. Not surprisingly, many of the healings in Scripture are actually deliverances or the removal of the demonic influence in the individual's life. A worthwhile study is to go through the Gospels noting every place Jesus heals and casts out demons at the same time.

One great example of this is found in Matthew, Mark, and Luke's parallel accounts of the man who brought his demonized son to the disciples for healing and deliverance. Notice first how the Gospel writers record the father's request (emphases added):

*"Lord, have mercy on my son," he said. "He has **seizures** and is suffering greatly. He often falls into the fire or into the water. I brought him to your disciples, but they could not **heal** him."*

MATTHEW 17:15-16

*A man in the crowd answered, "Teacher, I brought you my son, who is **possessed by a spirit** that has robbed him of speech. Whenever it seizes him, it throws him to the ground. He foams at the mouth, gnashes his teeth and becomes rigid. I asked your disciples to **drive out the spirit,** but they could not."*

MARK 9:17-18

*A man in the crowd called out, "Teacher, I beg you to look at my son, for he is my only child. **A spirit seizes him** and he suddenly screams; it throws him into convulsions so that he foams at the mouth. It scarcely ever leaves him and is destroying him. I begged your disciples to **drive it out,** but they could not."*

LUKE 9:38-40

The accounts of Mark and Luke focus on the child's need for deliverance while Matthew doesn't even mention it. Now read the different accounts of Jesus' interaction with the boy (emphases added):

> Jesus **rebuked the demon,** and it came out of the boy, and he was **healed** at that moment.
>
> MATTHEW 17:18

> When Jesus saw that a crowd was running to the scene, he **rebuked the impure spirit.** "You deaf and mute spirit," he said, "I command you, come out of him and never enter him again." *The* **spirit shrieked, convulsed him violently and came out.** *The boy looked so much like a corpse that many said, "He's dead." But Jesus took him by the hand and lifted him to his feet, and he stood up.*
>
> MARK 9:25-27

> Even while the boy was coming, **the demon** threw him to the ground in a convulsion. But Jesus **rebuked the impure spirit, healed the boy** and gave him back to his father.
>
> LUKE 9:42

The three accounts focus on different details, but each records the boy's deliverance and Jesus rebuking the demon. Matthew emphasized the boy's healing while Mark focused on the deliverance, and detail-oriented Luke, who was a doctor, recorded the deliverance and healing. Taking all three accounts together, we see that Jesus delivered the boy from the demon and healed his physical issues, demonstrating the direct correlation between deliverance and healing and his authority to do both.

Dark things are attracted to dark places. Pain, illness, and disease can create an environment attractive to a spirit of illness or affliction that acts upon the believer and non-believer alike, sometimes in addition to the physical ailment itself. The idea of possible demonic influence or involvement in my life used to terrify me as I imagined shadowy figures bent on my harm. In my fear, I'd temporarily forget the reality of Jesus' complete and total victory over the entire demonic realm. We are in a battle and the enemy is present, but Jesus is far superior to any demon or the devil—a created being himself, the opposite of an angel, not God. While the word *deliverance* may invoke thoughts of horror movies, it is not frightening. Instead, deliverance is a normal occurrence when truth unseats lies and God's superior kingdom is made manifest; it's what naturally happens as our minds are renewed. Deliverance is the defeat of evil and the binding of Satan's power and authority. And we, as members of Christ's body endowed with his Spirit, are equipped to heal and bring freedom from demonic affliction.

The enemy comes only to steal, kill, and destroy (John 10:10). Contrarily, Jesus brings healing and life (Matt. 9:35). In fact, Jesus *is* life (John 14:6). Satan and his demons intend to bring pain and destruction in whatever way possible, and their presence can impact our physical well-being. Wherever there is pain, destruction, disease, or death, the enemy is at work. Where God is moving, there is redemption, restoration, healing, and life. Whether through direct demonic attack or simply through hindering the establishing of God's kingdom, the third source of illness, death, sickness, and pain on the planet is Satan himself.

CHAPTER KEYS

My unquestioned belief that God made me sick reflected a teaching prevalent in much of American Christian culture, a teaching so commonly reinforced in conversations and sermons that its familiarity makes it sound true, but a lie never becomes orthodox, no matter how frequently it's repeated. The common belief that God sends disease, or allows an accident or illness to teach us a lesson or for a mysterious purpose known only to him, confuses the work of God with the work of the devil. My beliefs surrounding the origin of my illness led to a strange disconnect; I sought medical answers while simultaneously believing God wanted me to be sick. For too long, we have given Satan authority to work among us by confusing good and evil, God and the devil. God cannot send something he does not possess. God is not the origin of disease. He is the author of life, not its destroyer. A fallen world, our own choices, and an enemy working overtime to undermine God's kingdom cause the sorrows around us.

God is the source of healing. Regardless of what we encounter along the way—the highs of victory or the very real agony that accompanies sickness and disease—we cannot afford to accuse God of causing anything evil in our lives. Nor can we identify Jesus as the source of something he died to remove. No matter what happens, we know with all assurance that God is good and his attitude, will, and heart toward us are also good. Scripture is clear: God's plan for us is better than we could ever think possible.

MINISTRY

God is a benevolent and kind Father. He's thoroughly good and is the origin of all good things. He's at work right now to redeem the effects of sin and remove all demonic influence in your life. Let him breathe fresh understanding into you. Let his Holy Spirit bring glorious freedom to your mind, heart, and body.

Papa God, thank you that you are entirely good. Thank you that you are my hope for healing. Please come and realign my thinking about sickness and disease to match yours. And right now, I ask your Holy Spirit to come and remove any demonic attachment and influence from my life. In Jesus' name, I command every spirit of pain, infirmity, and affliction to leave me and never return. Jesus, come fill me up with more of you and more of your presence. Amen.

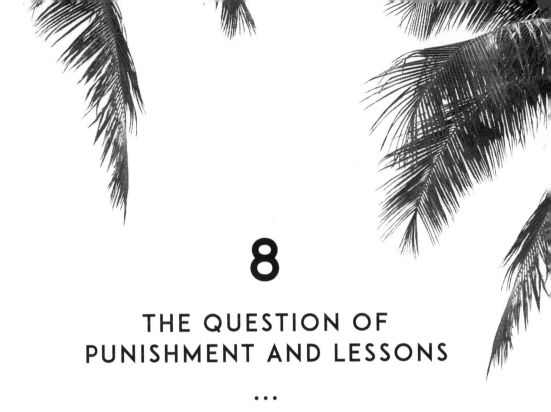

8

THE QUESTION OF PUNISHMENT AND LESSONS

• • •

It's my third flight of the day, and my early morning is beginning to catch up with me. Sighing, I glance at my boarding pass and continue down the aisle to my seat near the rear of the plane. I'm not supposed to be on this flight; I was supposed to have flown a more direct route a few days earlier, but a bad cold grounded me and forced a change in my plans.

Soon a slightly crotchety octogenarian and a middle-aged woman join me. The woman's bright blonde hair matches her outgoing and bubbly personality. Before the flight takes off, she introduces herself. "Are you traveling for business or pleasure?" she asks, genuinely interested.

"A little bit of both," I respond, explaining that I am on a ministry trip with a friend who is speaking at a church that weekend. "We'll get to explore the city a little, but I'm here as part of his ministry team." I talk about how I will teach breakout sessions, help run the services, and pray for people.

I tend to be a little wary of telling people about my work in ministry. It's not a neutral profession like accounting. It evokes a response, be it a quick end to the conversation or a discussion of different beliefs. As is often the case, my answer starts a religious conversation. The elderly gentleman between us quickly joins in, sharing his strong opinions about sin, and he tells the woman that she is guilty of multiple sins.

To clarify, I don't take sin lightly, but you and I both have the ministry of reconciliation (2 Cor. 5:18). It's the kindness of God that brings people to repentance. We get to share the great news of how Jesus made a way for us to come into relationship with a loving Father. The Holy Spirit is really good at convicting hearts and leading us into righteousness. I'd rather leave that work to him—especially when I just met the person.

Our conversation is halted by the safety announcement and take-off. The woman turns awkwardly with her hand on her neck. "Sorry," she apologizes. "It's difficult for me to talk when my seatbelt is on because of the fused disks in my neck. I can't turn my head without turning my body."

People often tell me about their pain, usually adding that they don't know why they're talking to me about it. Whenever this happens, I believe they're unknowingly asking for prayer. The woman's statement was like a flashing neon sign to me. "Is your neck hurting you right now?" I ask.

"Yes, I'm actually going to have surgery on it in a couple of weeks."

"I've learned that God likes to heal people, and I've actually seen him heal all sorts of problems. Would it be okay if I prayed for you?"

In all honesty, I would prefer praying for her right before we land instead of right after we take off. There is a thread of doubt running through my mind. If this doesn't work, it's going to be a really long flight. But I ignore the thought, and before the wheels are in the body of the plane, I reach across the man and gently place my hand on the woman's neck.

"All pain leave, in Jesus' name. Neck, be healed. Amen."

The woman bursts into tears. "It doesn't hurt anymore. It doesn't hurt!" she exclaims, turning her head left and right.

We exchange high fives as she realizes she has full range of motion and no pain. "God really loves you, and he cares about your neck," I tell her.

She thanks God as the man between us watches open-mouthed.

A little while later, while the woman is in the lavatory, the man turns to me still in shock. "Okay, I've been a Christian longer than you've been alive. How did you do that?"

"I didn't do it," I assure him. "I have no idea how to heal a neck, but I know the one who can, and I know what he likes to do."

"But God was punishing her for her sin," he argues.

"All I know is that she's the daughter of God, whether she knows it or not—and whether she's actively living that way or not. God doesn't want to see any of his children in pain. I don't want to condemn someone or simply talk about God's love. I want to demonstrate the gospel and the power of God's love."

As I pursued a greater understanding of health and healing, I began to see the murky picture of God I had painted for the world, one where I said he is both perfectly good *and* might give you cancer. I firmly believed that God sent or allowed my illness for my benefit and, at the same time, I did everything I could to get rid of it. I never thought to ask why, if Christ died to defeat something, would he later use it as a tool to make me more like him?

EXPECTING ILLNESS

Most teenagers can remember their very first paycheck. I don't mean one for babysitting or mowing lawns (or in Minnesota, shoveling snow) but their first *real* paycheck from a *real* job. It's a fundamental rite-of-passage moment that instills pride and a strong sense of accomplishment—until the envelope is opened and the new work-force member sees that some guy named Fed took a healthy chunk for himself.

"Who is Fed and what's he doing taking so much money from me?" I asked my parents. They exchanged a knowing glance before explaining the premise of a federal income tax. "How can you stand it?" I asked. It was a poignant adult moment when I learned to accept and expect paying taxes.

Whatever we accept as a normal part of life we tolerate when it inevitably occurs, even if, like taxes, it's not the most pleasant experience. If I accept illness as a normal part of life or as God's punishment or teaching tool, I tolerate its presence when I get sick.

In many cases, our familiarity with certain diseases, such as the "common" cold, allergies, or the seasonal flu, validates their presence and effectively concedes ground to the enemy that's rightfully ours to possess. Merely changing our mindsets doesn't keep us healthy, but it is the first step to claiming biblical promises and seeing the kingdom of heaven made manifest on earth. In other words, positive thinking alone doesn't change the situation, but believing what Jesus believes is paramount to transformation (see Rom. 12:2).

If Jesus' death meant the destruction of illness' power, I need to take a hard look at any thinking that permits, creates expectation for, or generally tolerates the presence of illness in my life. In this chapter, we will examine a few mindsets that lead us to expect illness in our lives as God's discipline, punishment, or promised suffering. We'll also examine the radical truth of God's sovereignty and goodness that transforms even the most broken places in our lives into something beautiful.

FEARING PUNISHMENT, ENDURING DISCIPLINE

Countless sermons, Christian books, and my own biblical interpretation reinforced my belief that God sends or allows sickness to teach us valuable lessons. Likewise, my conversation with the gentleman on the plane revealed a belief held by many in the church: God uses illness as a form of correction or punishment. I didn't consider my illness to be God's punishment, even though more than one well-meaning believer suggested I examine my life for sin, but I did believe that God sent or allowed my illness for a "greater purpose" he alone knew and I might never fully understand.

Punishment looks backward. It is "the infliction or imposition of a penalty as retribution for an offense."[16] Discipline, on the other hand, looks forward, shaping an individual for future success. Punishment says, "You acted wrongly and deserve a negative consequence." But discipline says, "For where you're heading (someplace unique and wonderful, an amazing God-designed destiny), you can't afford to have that behavior in your life." God disciplines us, his beloved children, because he deeply cares about us. Sin is always harmful to us and our destinies. When God sees sinful behavior in our lives, he corrects us, knowing that we cannot afford to think or behave that way if we are to become the people he created us to be. This is the polar opposite of a wrath-filled deity lashing out with maladies and accidents whenever we make a mistake. God is "compassionate and gracious" and "slow to anger, abounding in love and faithfulness" (Ps. 86:15). In fact, God's discipline brings freedom and life (see 2 Cor. 3:17). We know when God is at work because we are freer and feel more alive than we did a moment ago. His discipline is how he reshapes the clay until it becomes what he, the potter, intended: a display of his glory.

---

16. *Oxford Dictionaries*, s.v. "punishment," accessed April 10, 2017, https://en.oxforddictionaries.com/definition/punishment.

One of the clearest examples in the Bible of God's discipline is found in Deuteronomy 8. Moses wrote:

Remember how the Lord your God led you all the way in the wilderness these forty years . . . He humbled you, causing you to hunger and then feeding you with manna, which neither you nor your ancestors had known, to teach you that man does not live on bread alone but on every word that comes from the mouth of the Lord. Your clothes did not wear out and your feet did not swell during these forty years.[17]

DEUTERONOMY 8:2-4

The Israelites wandered in the wilderness as a direct result of their own decision and unbelief. When given the opportunity to enter the Promised Land, the people feared their situation more than they trusted God. God humbled the Israelites by allowing them to reap the consequences of their decision and then disciplined them by meeting their needs. There was manna to collect six days a week with a double portion the day before the Sabbath, which was a *daily* testimony of God's faithfulness. For forty years, their clothes didn't need patching, which was a *visible* reminder of God's provision. Day in and day out, the children of Israel encountered God's provision and learned to rely on his faithfulness until they were equipped with the faith they needed to possess the Promised Land.

Even though eating the same thing for forty years sounds rather trying and I'd miss my jeans I intentionally bought with holes already in them, I can't help but think of how ingrained God's faithfulness would be in me, as well as the culture around me, after forty years of daily miracles. God's discipline prepared the Israelites to trust him fully, so they would be ready the next time to believe God's Word

---

17. I first heard pastor and author Nathanael White point out this example.

instead of their situation. Similarly, when God disciplines me, he prepares me to inhabit his promises. His discipline doesn't look like suffering from a kidney infection, a broken arm, or an autoimmune disease; it looks like teaching us about his faithfulness by meeting our needs.

Jesus is another incredible picture of God's discipline. Any conclusion I come to about God that I can't verify in the life of Christ is a wrong conclusion. Jesus perfectly displayed the Father's heart, will, and intention in his actions. I fully believed my sickness was God's disciplining tool to make me more like him, even though that idea was never validated by Jesus' life. Jesus never looked at a person in need of healing and said, "You deserve this," "I'm using it for a greater purpose in your life," or "This issue is here for your benefit." Never. Jesus freely forgave, lovingly restored, and unconditionally healed all who came to him. The idea of God disciplining me with a disease—an enemy he died to destroy—is contrary to Scripture and our heavenly Father's tremendous goodness.

To be clear, the Bible indisputably tells us that God disciplines those he loves (Prov. 3:12), but his discipline looks like our loving Father pruning the barren branches, so we are more fruitful (John 15:1–8). Typically when God disciplines me, it takes me a moment to realize that's what's happening. He's kind and gentle. His goal is relational connection. He does not use sickness to make me more like him, the Healer. Instead, his discipline calls me into who I truly am. It doesn't crush, scourge, or harm me for being something I'm not.

When we're tempted to think God uses illness to discipline us, it's good to remember that this idea is inconsistent with the life of Christ. Instead of punishing, Jesus forgave. Instead of imparting illness, Jesus healed. And instead of disciplining us with sickness, Jesus "was pierced for our transgressions, he was crushed for our iniquities; the punishment that brought us peace was on him, and by his wounds we are healed" (Isa. 53:5).

When parents see their child in pain, they desperately wish they could trade places with that child, enduring the pain for her. Our heavenly Father saw us in great pain and joyfully took our place. Our understanding of God needs to reflect this truth. It's essential that the God we describe to the world looks like Jesus. If he doesn't, we've misunderstood or misinterpreted something along the way. John the Beloved wrote, "There is no fear in love. But perfect love drives out fear, because fear has to do with punishment. The one who fears is not made perfect in love" (1 John 4:18). There is no need to fear God sending cancer when he already sent his Son.

We cannot afford to have a theology that teaches God heals *and* sends illness or tolerates its presence. It's time to re-present our God to the world as the perfect Father who mourns when we mourn and weeps when we weep. His hand is one extended in love, not drawn back in anger.

BEAUTY FOR ASHES

And a sword will pierce your own soul, too.

Abruptly, Mary awoke from a fitful sleep. More than thirty years later, the words old Simeon prophesied at the temple over her and her newborn son still caused a cold chill to run down her spine.

Looking outside, Mary saw the first gray fingers of dawn inching across the sky and got up to stoke the embers of the small kitchen fire. She stared into the growing flame and remembered all the extraordinary events surrounding the birth of her firstborn.

A faint smile curled the corners of her mouth as she recalled the angel, the precious time with her cousin Elizabeth, and the look of sheer wonder on the weather-beaten faces of the shepherds that first night in the stable. Yet the warmth of her memories could not erase the cold she felt when she thought of the years of torment that followed as she was routinely ridiculed regarding her son's questionable paternity. She protected him as best she could from the untoward remarks when he was young, but with a glimmer of tears in her weary eyes, she thought of her inability to protect him from the recent threats.

Destined to cause the falling and rising of many in Israel, and to be a sign that will be spoken against, so that the thoughts of many hearts will be revealed. She remembered the old prophet's words.

"And a sword will pierce your own soul, too." The sound of her own voice startled her back to the present. Sighing heavily, she tried to shake off the feeling of foreboding, but it remained. "Mighty one," she prayed. "Has not my heart been pierced enough?"

Her prayer was interrupted by a frantic shout. "Mary! Mary!" Her son's youngest disciple, John, burst through the door. "They've taken Jesus. The soldiers have him. Come quickly!" His words came as a confirmation rather than a surprise.

Wrapping her cloak around her, Mary followed John into the pre-dawn darkness.

What followed was horrifying. From a distance, Mary watched as her son was dragged from one authority to another, brutally whipped, scourged, and beaten, and finally condemned to death by crucifixion.

For Mary, minutes passed like hours, hours like days. Finally, too fatigued to summon any more tears, she stood silently by her son's cross, willing her presence to comfort him.

Jesus, hideously disfigured and gasping for breath, turned toward Mary and the others with her. "Woman, here is your son," he said to her. And then to John, "Here is your mother."

Nodding in acknowledgment, John put his arm under Mary, supporting her exhausted frame. Together they watched as her son drew his final breath.

• • •

Tears filled my eyes as I wrote this account of what those last hours might have been like for Mary. Even a fictional taste of the soul-piercing sword was almost too much for me. If the story ended here, it would be the most un-gospel-like story in existence. But this is not the end. Long before Mary and John stood at the foot of the cross, the prophet Isaiah proclaimed our God gives "a crown of beauty instead of ashes, the oil of joy instead of mourning, and a garment of praise instead of a spirit of despair" (Isa. 61:3). Time will not run out nor the clock strike midnight before every place that looks and feels like a pile of ashes is radically transformed into a crown of beauty. It is impossible for a story to end without God's beauty shining through. Easter Sunday always follows Good Friday.

In my years of illness, I never dreamed God would use my experience to see others healed and set free. That is only the beginning of God's sovereign work in my life. Likewise, Mary and the disciples couldn't imagine in the dark hour of Jesus' crucifixion that God would turn it into the greatest good the world has ever known. Even the devil did not understand the significance of the moment. The apostle Paul wrote, "None of the rulers of this age understood it, for if they had, they would not have crucified the Lord of glory" (1 Cor. 2:8).[18] With the benefit of hindsight, we can see what they couldn't: Jesus' death meant salvation, restored relationship with the Father, and the indwelling presence of his Spirit. God was faithful to turn the death of Christ into history's glorious turning point; he will be faithful to make something beautiful out of every situation we face. God does not cause sickness, illness, and disease, but he will work a mighty miracle and use a point of pain for our benefit. This truth bears repeating: If it's *not* too good to be true, it's not the end of the story.

---

18. Steve Backlund says, "If the devil had a biography, it'd be titled *It Backfired Again.*"

ALL THINGS FROM GOD VS. ALL THINGS FOR GOOD

Often we hear stories of how Dad's broken leg meant the priceless revelation he needed about his relationship with his son or how a battle with cancer brought a much needed re-prioritizing to the survivor's life. We are so grateful for the good resulting from our sickness and pain that we are thankful for all of it—even the part that didn't originate in God. God is a master at turning terrible situations into beautiful ones, but there's a very great difference between God *using* a broken leg and God *causing* it.

The devil is shortsighted. He does not believe that God will follow through in making beauty from ashes in every situation, even though this is God's declared intent (see Isa. 61:1–3; Luke 4:16–21). Some situations in life are so terrible that we cannot begin to imagine how good could ever emerge. These are moments when we can see only the cross and not the empty tomb. It's here that we must apply the promise of Romans 8:28 (emphasis added): "And we know that in *all things* God works for the good of those who love him." If it were readily apparent how all things were used for our good, we wouldn't need this promise in Scripture.[19]

It wasn't hard for me to accept that God will use everything for my benefit—but I did struggle with another idea, one that suggested God might not have initiated something, but he did allow it, which made him ultimately responsible. For some, that idea may seem like semantics, but for me, it was a tough issue to wrestle with. I thought that since God is able to destroy cancer cells before they multiply, their very existence makes him at least partially culpable. As I worked through this, I saw more and more how much of the responsibility is actually on our shoulders. God greatly respects our free will. Instead

---

19. Bill Johnson was responsible for initially unpacking this promise for me. He has much more to say on the subject, and it's well worth checking out.

of forcing his way into a situation, our prayers open the door for God to intervene without violating our will. Our intercession, proclamation, and demonstrations of the kingdom actually allow him to stop pandemics before they start and dissolve tumors before they form by giving him legal access to do what's in his heart to do. Instead of asking God how *he* could allow disease to exist, I realized that at some level, the question was actually this: How could *I* have allowed it? The concept grieved me to no end. As I repented to the Lord for my inaction, my thinking was renewed and my emotions lifted. The revelation of my responsibility wasn't sorrowful or condemning—it was good news. God is reigniting power within his church to see his will done on earth as it is in heaven. The truth James penned so many years ago still holds true: "The prayer of a righteous person is powerful and effective" (5:16).

Beautiful endings are evidence of God's unfathomable sovereignty, faithfulness, and goodness, not his responsibility for the initial devastating illness or tragedy. God is not the origin of everything that happens, but he will take everything that happens and make something wonderful out of it. He will use illness to our benefit, but he does not cause it. He flawlessly weaves together the things outside of his will to make good out of evil. Whether we live to see the good conclusion or not, the conclusion will be good. Whether we celebrate now or later, we will celebrate. Until that day, we can stand confidently on God's promises, knowing that all things will be used for good. He is big enough, powerful enough, good enough, and creative enough to teach us a lesson without breaking our leg, but rest assured that if we break a leg, he will use it to our advantage.

THEOLOGY OF SUFFERING

A few years ago, due to an increased travel schedule, I earned an elite status on an airline. Airline status was something I never thought much about apart from wondering what was behind those club doors at the airport, but it took only a few months of free checked luggage, upgrades, and priority boarding before I was caught up in the program hook, line, and sinker. Upon realizing I didn't fly enough with that airline to maintain my status this year, I began calculating how I could earn enough miles before January 1 to keep it. The prospect of waiting in lines at check-in and security nearly motivated me to book a transcontinental flight with the sole purpose of earning miles. Status and the perks that go with a recognized identity are a huge draw to the frequent flyer. Reward programs work.

Every one of us has a basic need to be known. We desire recognition. Not necessarily in-front-of-the-adoring-public, movie-star-style recognition, but recognition for our faithfulness, character, or commitment. It's why we hope our boss or professor notices when we work hard on a project. Being recognized for what we accomplish or endure adds to the overall picture of who we are; it is part of our face to the world, our identity. Sometimes that recognition is a positive thing, like a reputation for excellence forged by years of consistently high achievement. Brands like Rolex, Harvard, and the New York Yankees are great examples of this. Other times that recognition is neutral, neither good nor bad, and tells us nothing about someone's character, such as my (sadly former) airline status. But from time to time, recognition can actually be harmful, lauding something that shouldn't be praised.

As followers of Jesus, we will inevitably face persecution and suffer for Christ; Jesus guaranteed it. We expect to be ridiculed for our faith, face hardships and discrimination for our beliefs, and encounter painful situations where we have the privilege of choosing Jesus over safety and comfort. Unfortunately, many of us have taken the promise of persecution and created a theology of suffering that gives permission to the sustained presence of illness and disease. This theology of suffering wrongly commends all suffering as fulfillment of Jesus' words and generates a strange faith hierarchy for long-term and chronic sufferers (i.e., their faith is greater because of what they have suffered). It is of paramount importance to recognize that Jesus promised persecution for our faith, not suffering caused by illness. He stated, "Remember what I told you: 'A servant is not greater than his master.' If they persecuted me, they will persecute you also. If they obeyed my teaching, they will obey yours also" (John 15:20). Jesus was not referring to illness here; his suffering was not from sickness but persecution. The promise of hardship means there is a cost to pursuing a life like his; it doesn't mean we have to patiently suffer long years of crippling diseases like muscular dystrophy or Parkinson's. It means that we will inevitably face persecution for choosing to live a righteous life in an unrighteous world. It means we choose to believe, think, and act according to a higher standard. And it means we have the opportunity to faithfully live in the tension that exists between God's promises given and God's promises actualized.

Not until after I was healed did I discover I had a misplaced sense of accomplishment and identity that kept me from pursuing healing. I wrongly assumed that Jesus received additional glory for each page in my medical file, every trip to the doctor, and my general suffering borne without complaint. My growing list of ailments became a source of identity and pride. My willingness to endure what I assumed was God's plan for my life "proved" my love for him. I've since come to understand that I wasn't alone in this misplaced sense of accomplishment and identity. Many Christians believe their sickness is a cross to bear instead of an enemy to fight.

Praising those who endure chronic illness without fervently seeking healing feeds an unorthodox doctrine that unintentionally upholds suffering as a higher value than the finished work of the cross. Obviously, my aim here is not to minimize the courage displayed by individuals who face tremendous physical challenges and chronic illness—but to draw attention to this disempowering theology that has permitted the continued presence of something Christ died to destroy. It takes great bravery to get up each morning and say, "Now is the time of God's favor, now is the day of salvation" (2 Cor. 6:2), especially when yesterday, last week, and the months before felt like anything but the day of salvation. Keeping one's heart tender toward God while in need of healing requires both incredible character and divine grace. It is our privilege as a body of believers to encourage one another with the reality that the kingdom of God is at hand. Today *is* the day. And if it doesn't happen today, we get up tomorrow with fresh expectation for our new day to be the day of breakthrough, the day heaven comes to earth.

VALIDATING DISEASE

Whether through my misplaced identity in suffering from sickness or from my misinterpretation and misapplication of Scripture, two passages in particular kept me from pursuing healing: Jesus' encounter with the man born blind (John 9) and the description of the apostle Paul's thorn in the flesh (2 Cor. 12:1–10).

John 9: The Man Born Blind

In John 9, Jesus and his disciples happened upon a man born blind. The story of his healing and subsequent confession of faith is, for me, quite possibly the most poignant coming-to-faith moment described in Scripture. It's also the source of much confusion surrounding God's work in our lives. John the Beloved wrote:

> As he went along, he saw a man blind from birth. His disciples asked him, "Rabbi, who sinned, this man or his parents, that he was born blind?"

135

"Neither this man nor his parents sinned," said Jesus, "but this happened so that the work of God might be displayed in him. As long as it is day, we must do the works of him who sent me. Night is coming, when no one can work. While I am in the world, I am the light of the world."

After saying this, he spit on the ground, made some mud with the saliva, and put it on the man's eyes. "Go," he told him, "wash in the Pool of Siloam" (this word means "Sent"). So the man went and washed, and came home seeing.

JOHN 9:1-7

The confusing part of this passage isn't the healing. The healing is direct and to the point; the man couldn't see, Jesus intervened, and a miracle occurred. Instead, just as it did for the disciples, our trouble starts as we attempt to determine the cause of the blindness. When Jesus stated, "This happened so that the work of God might be displayed in his life," I understood him to mean that God caused the blindness so he could heal it later. This conclusion led me to two wrong beliefs about illness: that illness glorifies God through patient suffering and continued faith in the midst of trying circumstances, and that God is both the cause and the cure of the illness.

When we don't understand and have a limited perspective, faith is beautiful and pleasing to the Lord—but illness never is. God's great distaste for anything that steals life from his precious children is evident throughout Scripture. Jesus said he came that we may "have life, and have it to the full" (John 10:10). Not a life of survival between migraines or treatments to keep symptoms in check, but a life consisting of everything we were created to partake of, experience, and enjoy. So, too, we know that God being the cause and the cure for something is the definition of a house divided, a concept Jesus rebuked (see Matt. 12:25–28). In addition, God won't *use* his children.

Causing a condition or illness and then healing it to gain a testimony or to demonstrate his power is entirely contrary to God's fatherly nature.

God will certainly use your testimony, but he's not dependent on you or your testimony to advance his kingdom; he doesn't need to create an opportunity to demonstrate his power and bring himself glory. In John 9, Jesus demonstrated the truth of Romans 8:28—he can use all things for good—when he took what was painful and used it to bring good to the man and glory to God. The disciples saw a desperate physical condition and questioned its origin, whereas Jesus encountered the same condition and saw an opportunity.

The work of God in John 9 was not the man's blindness. The work of God in John 9 was Jesus restoring sight.

2 Corinthians 12: Paul's Thorn in the Flesh

One of my best friends and regular travel companions is well over half a foot shorter than I am. On every transcontinental flight we've taken together, there's usually a moment sometime after the meal service and before the start of the second movie when I notice her sleeping soundly, curled in a position physically impossible for me to copy. Green-eyed jealousy attacks me as her gentle, rhythmic breathing fills my ears. Around this point, I typically begin to question the decisions that put me in this cramped, uncomfortable space, so I purposefully remind myself of all the good things awaiting me at my destination. As I start daydreaming about the people I will see and the fun to be had, my mounting discomfort and frustration melt away in favor of anticipation. My vision for what will happen in a few hours gives purpose to the pain of my current situation. Vision gives pain a purpose.

For many years, I believed that my illness was similar to the apostle Paul's thorn in the flesh—something from God to make me more like him. This helped give purpose to my pain as I assumed God was working through my illness. I even felt guilty for not fully appreciating "my thorn" whenever I longed to join the healthy kids playing outside. My guilt only grew with age as I became more aware of the normal childhood and teenage experiences I missed like sleepovers with friends, church retreats, and the prom. Calling my illness "my thorn" helped me endure countless doctors' visits, pain-filled days, and sleepless nights. It validated the chronic pain I endured with a promise of something greater than health, but it did not make me better or teach me to pursue divine healing. In fact, calling my illness "my thorn" derailed hope and chained me to a false belief that life with my sickness was better than life without it.

I've heard the apostle Paul's thorn in his flesh used more frequently than any other passage to justify the presence of illness in a believer's life. We label the painful things that don't yield the first, second, or even third time we pray "our thorn" and grow accustomed to their presence. But anything that creates space for illness in our lives is well worth reexamining. If our interpretation of 2 Corinthians 12 validates illness, we've missed something. It's time we tackle Paul's thorn, a stumbling block for many well-meaning believers, head on.

Concerning this thorn, Paul wrote:

Even if I should choose to boast, I would not be a fool, because I would be speaking the truth. But I refrain, so no one will think more of me than is warranted by what I do or say, or because of these surpassingly great revelations. Therefore, in order to keep me from becoming conceited, I was given a thorn in my flesh, a messenger of Satan, to torment me. Three times I pleaded with the Lord to take it away from me. But he said to me, "My grace is sufficient for you, for my power is made perfect in weakness." Therefore I will boast all the more gladly about my weaknesses, so that Christ's power may rest on me.

2 CORINTHIANS 12:6–9

Many brilliant scholars with countless years of biblical interpretation under their belts have debated this passage. It's possible that the interpretation I was originally taught—that Paul suffered from an eye disease that caused him great physical pain—is correct. It's also possible that it isn't. Maybe Paul's thorn wasn't physical at all. Maybe it was persecution. I don't know. And frankly, it doesn't matter.

I am very clearly not the apostle Paul. Though I hunger for more encounters with God and experiences like Paul's, I've never witnessed anything like what he described earlier in the chapter. And though I've worked hard on this book, it's *nothing* like authoring part of the New Testament—let alone over half of it. I haven't been entrusted with the incredible revelation of God's grace for all people like Paul was. In fact, I'm mining his revelation of God's grace and will continue to do so the rest of my life. I am not the apostle Paul, and though perhaps a thorn in the flesh was something this master builder of our faith required, it isn't necessary for me.

Frankly, not one of us needs a thorn, and if we think we do, we've missed the point. God skillfully took a terrible hardship in Paul's life and revealed another aspect of his incredible lovingkindness and goodness toward us: His grace powerfully works through our weaknesses. His grace doesn't empower us to remain in a lowly, broken state, but it lifts us up, calls us out, and transforms us "into his image with ever-increasing glory, which comes from the Lord" (2 Cor. 3:18). If our understanding of Paul's thorn in the flesh keeps us from pursuing healing or leads us away from hope about our current life situations, we've misinterpreted the passage. If we're ever tempted to validate the presence of sickness, illness, or disease as a God-given thorn to keep us humble, we can turn to Jesus, the one who bore a crown of thorns, and remember he died to destroy any trace of disease in our lives. Our theology cannot permit something to exist that Jesus died to destroy.

CHAPTER KEYS

We do not see the full picture or understand everything that occurs, but we must not reason away our disappointment when someone isn't healed by suggesting it wasn't God's will, wasn't in his timing, or that he's working a greater purpose than we currently see or understand. Instead, we can remember that Jesus revealed the heart of the Father, and he healed all who came to him without exception. Assuming God sends or allows illness as punishment or to teach us a lesson is a serious assertion. Likewise, a theology of suffering that includes sickness, illness, and disease wrongly praises suffering through illness instead of empowering us to fight the very thing Jesus died to remove. God *uses* all things, but he does not *cause* all things. He does not make us sick to transform us into his likeness—the Healer, the author of life, and the perfect picture of love.

This was a difficult chapter to write. I spent my childhood suffering from an awful illness I embraced as being from God. Now it is my dream to see this kind of thinking uprooted from the church. We cannot maintain a theology about something that shouldn't exist. Jesus suffered to rid us of sickness—we cannot justify its presence. If our study of the Bible leads us to hopelessness, we have misunderstood or misinterpreted the Scriptures.

Jesus is not hopeless about any situation in your life. He promises there will be a good ending. And if it isn't too good to be true, it's not the end.

MINISTRY

God's declared intent for your life is to turn your ashes into beauty, to anoint you with the oil of joy in place of your mourning, and to exchange a spirit of heaviness for a garment of praise. You will be called an oak of righteousness that displays his splendor (Isa.

61:3). Jesus died to remove illness, sickness, and disease from your life. Even if you've prayed hundreds of times for its removal, even if you've learned to live with it, *even* if you can see the numerous lessons God has taught you through it, go to the throne of grace. It's time to receive beauty for your ashes.

If it's your knee, put your hand on your knee. If it's your chronic migraines, put your hand on your head. If it's something else, like a place of emotional pain, disillusionment, or disappointment, bring it to him expecting something beautiful in exchange. Jesus died to remove this pain. It's time for it to go.

Father God, thank you that you are better than I thought possible. Thank you that your kindness toward me is without limit, without end, and beyond all description. I come to you again, like it's the first time, knowing that your will for me is good, knowing that your will for me is to be healed. Holy Spirit, come. Come with your life-giving presence. Come exchange my pain with your presence. Fill me afresh. Fill me to overflowing. Thank you, Jesus. Amen.

9

THE QUESTION
OF GIFTING

...

I'm in a divine moment—of that I am certain.

As we walk through the heat permeating the small South American city, every person I pray for is healed and every person I speak to about Jesus receives salvation. I witness God's Spirit radically heal and profoundly change lives all around me. It feels like I am in perfect alignment with heaven. There is literally no place on earth I'd rather be. When it comes time to leave, I plead with my team to go without me.

"Go!" I shout. "I'll find you later."

"Becca," my friend says, grabbing my arm. "What's the name of our hotel?"

I wince and admit, "No idea."

Her grip tightens. "That's what I thought."

I turn to meet her gaze. I can feel God's love for the people around me, and I think I'll burst if I don't share his love with another person. "Just one more. I have to . . ." I trail off, ignoring the tug on my arm, and address the woman next to me in broken Spanish.

"*¿Tienes dolor en su cuerpo?* Do you have pain in your body?" I ask.

"*Sí.*" She points to her neck, and I can see pain in her eyes.

"*En el nombre de Jesús,*" I pray, placing my hand on her neck. Tears fill my eyes as I feel the immensity of God's love for her.

Her face relaxes as the pain leaves, and she looks at me with a bewildered smile.

"Rebecca, we need to leave *now.*" My friend pulls me away as I look longingly at the crowd, wondering how Jesus ever made it from one town to the next.

The next day, giddy with anticipation, I join the group heading back to the plaza to pray for people we meet on the street. The crowd grows as we pray for more and more people and see scores healed.

"God loves you and wants to heal your bodies and your spirits," a Spanish-speaking friend tells the captivated audience.

"Jesus is the one who heals," we say, emphasizing the power is his and not ours. To demonstrate this, we ask if anyone wants to perform a miracle. A man whose back was healed only moments ago raises his hand.

"You have what we have," I tell him via an interpreter as I pair him with a man deaf in one ear. "It's God who heals through us. Tell his ear to open."

Copying our prayers, the man prays for the other man's deaf ear to open—and it does. Shocked, the formerly deaf man pulls out his cellphone and plays music, holding it up first to his left ear and then to his previously unhearing right. The man who prayed for him is overjoyed. In under ten minutes, he went from an interested observer to a miracle-working participant.

If I heard a story like this in the past, I was simultaneously awed by the goodness of God and the faith of the people involved while acutely aware of the reasons I thought something similar couldn't happen through me. I rationalized that the mission team possessed some special gifting or that it happened because it was an international trip, a unique place where this sort of thing still happens. For many years, I believed that miracles as a part of the typical Christian life were unfathomable.

There are two reasons I absolutely love this story:

1. I can think of nothing more fun than seeing healing and salvation break out—especially in ever-passionate Latin America.

2. It obliterates the notion that we must do something or be something other than saved by grace to bring healing. If God can use a random passerby to open a deaf ear, he can and will use you and me.

WORKING FOR A GIFT

I used to read Scripture with a disqualifying "it happened back then" or "it happened through them" mentality. While I believed there were people operating in the gift of healing today, I assumed you either had a gift of healing or you didn't, and since I'd never seen anyone healed, nor had I prayed for anyone to be healed, I thought I fell into the second category. Scripture said healing was a gift of the Holy Spirit, but I never considered asking him for a gift to heal. It somehow felt sacrilegious to ask for a spiritual gift the same way I'd ask for a new pair of boots for Christmas. Instead of piety, my ignorance to the approachability of my heavenly Father and the freedom to make requests of him revealed a religious mindset that promoted form without power and rules over relationship.[20]

I believed for a very long time that healing either came through individuals who spent years studying Scripture, fasting, and crying out to God or those whose divine insight and experiences set them

---

20. I first heard Bill Johnson define religion this way.

apart—they were unique, ultra-gifted Christians who had something I didn't have or knew something I didn't know. To make up for the touch of God I assumed I had missed, I attempted to find a "Christian formula." If I prayed for X hours, I would see Y people healed. If I fasted for X days, I would see a breakthrough in disease Z. Praying and fasting are wonderful disciplines that strengthen us to bear the weight that accompanies a greater measure of God's glory and gifting, but I quickly discovered they did not qualify me to be used by God. Contrary to what I had assumed, seeing people healed through prayer isn't reserved for just a select few.

Jesus didn't say, "Those who find the right formula and work really hard will see the sick healed." Instead, he promised, "These signs will accompany those who believe: in my name they will drive out demons . . . they will place their hands on sick people, and they will get well" (Mark 16:17–18).

I have some good news for you if you've longed to see people healed and set free when you pray: All of us who have received Jesus as our Savior fall into the "those who believe" category.

NORMAL CHRISTIANITY

"It's not better." My words echo in the empty kitchen.

I shut my Bible and take in my surroundings. A lizard clinging to the pale-yellow walls returns my stare. The evening call to prayer drifts through the open door, swelling like a wave moving from east to west as other mosques pick up the cry. I position the fan to blow the sticky air in my direction and reopen my leather-bound Bible purchased the last time I visited an English-speaking country. After spending the last week reading and rereading John 14–16, I keep hoping for a different conclusion to my question.

Here, far from the safety of my air-conditioned home church, I have seen too many things I can't explain or reason away. I've witnessed witch doctors demonstrate their power while I sat spiritually handcuffed, uncertain of what to do or how to respond. So once again, I find myself staring at the red letters, Jesus' own words, that boldly declare, "But I tell you the truth, it is to your advantage that I go away; for if I do not go away, the Helper will not come to you; but if I go, I will send Him to you" (John 16:7 NASB).

"It's really not better," I mutter. I write in my journal, "I don't see how it's to my advantage (or anyone's around me) that the person of Jesus isn't sitting right here at this table." Processing the verse and my thoughts, I look up and return the lizard's stare. "What am I missing?"

The lizard doesn't reply.

• • •

What would it look like if Jesus were physically present with you throughout a typical day? What would happen if he walked you to class, sat in your meeting, or waited with you for your flight?

He *is* with you just like that. He is doing all those things with you. What I was missing in my hot, Asian-sized kitchen as I read and re-read those passages in John was not a *what* but a *who.* I was missing who Jesus sent in his place—his Spirit. Jesus sent the Holy Spirit to us knowing that with the Spirit's help, we would become everything he dreamed for us to become and able to accomplish everything he planned for us to do. Suddenly, through the indwelling power of his very presence on earth, Jesus' life becomes more than just one life we study. With the enabling power of his Spirit, Jesus' life becomes one we imitate. He is not only our Savior—he is our model for ministry.

At first, the idea of Jesus as a ministry model felt heretical. How could I ever do what Jesus did or even dare think it was possible? He's the very Son of God. But as I studied this concept in the Bible,

I made a few startling discoveries, things I had always known to be true in my heart but hadn't quite put together in my head:

1. Jesus, though fully God, set aside his deity and became like us in every respect. The apostle Paul wrote that Jesus, "who, being in very nature God, did not consider equality with God something to be used to his own advantage; rather, he made himself nothing by taking the very nature of a servant, being made in human likeness" (Phil. 2:6–7).[21] It's a mind-blowing concept—God the Son, through whom all things were created, emptied himself of that which made him equal to the other parts of his triune self to become just like us. This doesn't make Jesus less God; it means he decided to set aside his divine nature for a time to fully identify with us. The author of Hebrews helped explain this concept, writing that Jesus was "fully human in every way, in order that he might become a merciful and faithful high priest in service to God, and that he might make atonement for the sins of the people" (Heb. 2:17). Jesus became like us and lived with all the limitations that come with being human. Jesus was just like you and me.

2. Given his self-imposed human limitations, Jesus did everything through the power of God's Spirit living in him. Isaiah foretold of the Spirit's power on Jesus, prophesying, "The Spirit of the LORD will rest on him—the Spirit of wisdom and of understanding, the Spirit of counsel and of might, the Spirit of the knowledge and fear of the LORD" (Isa. 11:2). This prophetic word was fulfilled at Jesus' baptism when "the Holy Spirit descended on him in bodily form like a dove" (Luke 3:21–22). In other words, Jesus

---

21. The Greek word translated as "nothing" is *kenoō,* which means to empty or make empty. It is specifically used to describe Christ, who "laid aside equality with or the form of God" (Strong's 2758).

didn't heal the sick, raise the dead, cast out demons, or even walk on water by his own power but by the power of the Holy Spirit in him.

3. Finally, with human limitations and the Holy Spirit's immense power working through him, Jesus was fully obedient to his Father's wishes. He said, "Very truly I tell you, the Son can do nothing by himself; he can do only what he sees his Father doing, because whatever the Father does the Son also does" (John 5:19). The Father's agenda was Jesus' agenda. The Father's will was perfectly demonstrated in Jesus' actions.

We can go down the list and see that our lives aren't that different. We are fully human. We possess no power of our own but are empowered by the Holy Spirit, and we long to do the work of our Father. Furthermore, as our minds are renewed to a greater understanding of what the Father desires to do through us on earth—like healing the sick—we become better at partnering with him. Jesus perfectly modeled what our lives can look like.

Obviously, we don't need to die Christ's death, but we can live a life like the one he modeled for us. It starts by redefining "normal" Christian life until it matches what Jesus' life looked like. We continually raise our expectations of what God wants to do in and through us until our expectations also match Scripture, which includes healing the sick. Jesus' life is the starting point for normal Christianity. He said, "I tell you the truth, anyone who believes in me will do the same works I have done, *and even greater works,* because I am going to be with the Father" (John 14:12 NLT, emphasis added). As Christians, we are empowered to do the things Jesus did—and even greater things. He is our reference and guide to the normal Christian life. He is our inspiration to do the Father's work so the blind see, the deaf hear, the lame walk, and the good news is preached.

Living the way Jesus did requires more of the Holy Spirit in our lives—and there's no limit to how much of him we can have. Even though we all receive heaven's greatest gift upon believing in Jesus, there's more. The same disciples Jesus breathed on and said over, "Receive the Holy Spirit" (John 20:22), were told to wait in Jerusalem until the Holy Spirit came on them again in power (see Acts 2). These same disciples cried out for more of the Holy Spirit and received yet another Holy Spirit filling later (Acts 4:23–31). I'm not saying there are second-class citizens in the kingdom of God or two categories of believers: those who don't have the Holy Spirit and those who do. But I am saying there is much, much more available than I ever dreamed possible. How much more? I don't know, but I'm not going to quit asking for more until I find out. As we pursue the working of the Holy Spirit in our lives, we are first and foremost chasing after greater relationship, deeper fellowship, and increased intimacy with our triune God.

As we further realize our identity as daughters and sons of God empowered by his Spirit to do his work, we get to discover the incredible things we can do. Or better yet, what *can't* we do? Jesus, our ministry example, healed all who came to him and then promised we would do greater things. There are no limits to what's possible in Christ.

HEAVEN TO EARTH

I wrote part of this chapter while sitting in a cozy bakery just outside Stockholm. As I sat watching steady streams of people come and go, ordering cinnamon rolls and drinking endless cups of coffee, I couldn't shake the sense that I'd been here before. And then it struck me: I felt like I had been here because, in a way, I had—I was in an authentic version of the many old-world, Scandinavian-style cafés found in Minnesota.

Just like an American café can recreate the experience of visiting a café in the ancestral homeland, our mission on earth is to reproduce the same feeling and experience of our true celestial home. Jesus taught his followers a daring, world-changing prayer: "Your kingdom come, your will be done, *on earth as it is in heaven*" (Matt. 6:10, emphasis added). This powerfully packed bombshell of a prayer empowers every believer to live a kingdom-advancing supernatural lifestyle until earth looks like heaven. It is our God-given mandate to bring heaven to earth.[22]

Our mission to bring the kingdom of God to earth is profoundly simple: If something is in heaven—like love, joy, and peace—we get to bring it to earth. For example, worship is found in heaven, so we fill the earth with worship and praise. Conversely, there is no hunger or famine in heaven, so we feed the hungry we encounter, work with governmental and charitable institutions to see hunger eradicated, and pray expectantly for God to intervene in times of famine. Likewise, illness, sickness, and disease are nonexistent in heaven, where health, wholeness, and love reign supreme. This means it's part of every believer's assignment to see the sick healed and illness removed from the earth. It's a job far too great for only a few individuals to accomplish; it requires every one of us to live like Jesus, believing what he believes and doing what he's asked us to do.

Jesus is faithful and true. His promises will come to pass. Earth will look like heaven, and illness one day will be eradicated. "For the earth will be filled with the knowledge of the glory of the LORD as the waters cover the sea" (Hab. 2:14). And the great news is that each one of us plays an important role. We are God's first choice in bringing heaven to earth.

---

22. For more on the subject of bringing heaven to earth, I highly recommend the book *When Heaven Invades Earth* by Bill Johnson (Destiny Image, 2005).

PERMISSION TO PURSUE

Semi-frequent power outages at my home in Southeast Asia meant the electricity that powered lights and the all-important air conditioner was an uncertain amenity instead of a foregone conclusion. One moment I'd be reading a book in a well-lit, comfortably cool room and the next I'd be sitting in darkness, beads of sweat forming on my forehead. I quickly adapted to my setting, learning to arm myself with a headlamp and iced beverage before sitting down to read.

My adaptability stayed with me when I moved back stateside, but what passed for contentment in one season deteriorated into apathy in the next. When the light bulb in my bedside reading lamp burned out, I "adapted" by pulling out my headlamp like I did in Asia. After (embarrassingly) a couple of weeks of this, my roommate asked why I didn't replace the bulb.

"I did this all the time in Asia when the power went out," I replied.

There was zero hesitation in her response: "Becca, you're not in Asia. Get off your butt and go buy a light bulb!"

Sheepishly admitting the complacency that had kept me in the dark (pardon the pun), I drove to the hardware store.

Living in contentment "whatever the circumstances" (Phil. 4:11) is an essential part of our Christian life, but any strength overemphasized is a weakness. Contentment overemphasized becomes apathy. An attitude that says, "I will remain thankful," can unwittingly become, "Things will never change." My thinking that said I would be happy with whatever God gave me was really a misplaced application of Philippians 4:11. Paul directed the church to "eagerly desire" the spiritual gifts, including the gift of healing (see 1 Cor. 12:31, 14:1). His word choice reveals more than a passing wish for the church to walk in power; the Greek word translated "desire" or "pursue" is a strong action word that is actually a command. *Zeloo* means to "burn with zeal," "desire earnestly," and "exert one's self for."[23] Sitting back and waiting for something to happen is contrary to Paul's directive. It is our right, privilege, and responsibility to go after the gift of healing and not stop until we receive the blessing.

There are times when we make do with what's available to us (headlamps in Asia) and times when we must leave the comfort of our homes to chase after more (driving to the hardware store). It takes spiritual maturity to distinguish between these two seasons—children are brought food to eat, while adults must get it for themselves. Contentment despite our circumstances, "whether well fed or hungry, whether living in plenty or in want" (Phil. 4:12), is essential to a life of abiding in Christ, but I cannot afford to become "content" with the measure of God's love I've personally experienced. Neither can I be content with my experience of his kindness, goodness, grace, and mercy, nor the level of his working through me.

In the past, this kind of false-contentment thinking led to prayers along the lines of, "God, I'll receive whatever gift you want to give me." Because my prayers were broad and without any expectation of where or how they could be answered, I didn't see them answered. I've since learned to make bold requests that require faith on my end and to have a specific goal in sight so I can recognize when that prayer is answered. For example, I now pray things like this: "God, please work through me to heal every person with a headache who crosses my path." This gives me confidence to pray for people suffering from headaches and encourages my heart as I see the direct result of my prayers. Specific prayer requests are part of earnestly pursuing the gift of healing.

By God's great grace I will be content whatever my outward circumstances, whether it's minus 15 degrees Fahrenheit and I'm hungry, or it's 80 degrees Fahrenheit and I'm on the beach with a

---

23. Strong's 2206.

smoothie in my hand. I will be content whether the world accepts me or not. But I will not stay content, sitting back and letting whatever happens happen, when something Jesus died to destroy exists around me. We have biblical permission to pursue more, and as grateful as we are for all we have and have experienced, we can't stop there; we must have more.

PRACTICE MAKES PERFECT BUT COMPARISON KILLS

I have friends who possess a much greater healing gift than I do. Invariably, they return from a trip to the grocery store with a testimony about someone leaving a wheelchair, whereas I typically come home from the grocery store with groceries. I love hanging out with these friends because they help raise my expectations of what's possible and recalibrate my definition of "normal" in a way that encourages me to step out and pray for others. Likewise, the Bible tells us that how we steward and value someone else's treasure exposes what we're capable of handling on our own (see Matt. 25:14–30). When I value someone else's testimony, gifting, and experience, thereby celebrating and honoring the gifting in her life, my gifting actually grows.

Most of the time, I'm ecstatic at the testimonies of God working through my friends, but there are times when I've fallen into comparison. Watching others move in their giftings, particularly when I long to operate similarly, can stir up feelings of inferiority and inadequacy, which leads to insecurity, performance, and praying for people to see a result instead of from the compassion and love of Christ. Few things discourage us faster than when we stop focusing on what God is doing and instead concentrate on what we can't do.

It's no coincidence that the apostle Paul addressed comparison and teamwork in the middle of his primary instruction about spiritual gifts:

Even so the body is not made up of one part but of many.

Now if the foot should say, "Because I am not a hand, I do not belong to the body," it would not for that reason stop being part of the body. And if the ear should say, "Because I am not an eye, I do not belong to the body," it would not for that reason stop being part of the body. If the whole body were an eye, where would the sense of hearing be? If the whole body were an ear, where would the sense of smell be? But in fact God has placed the parts in the body, every one of them, just as he wanted them to be. If they were all one part, where would the body be? As it is, there are many parts, but one body.

1 CORINTHIANS 12:14-20

I lose whenever I compare myself with someone else. Either I walk away feeling inferior or I find value in what I do instead of in who God says I am. It's a simple but important truth: I am the best person in the world at being me. If I try to be someone else, one of us will be redundant. Furthermore, I need to be fully myself if I'm to complete the works God has for me to do.

Developing spiritual gifts is like going to the gym—everyone who works out will get stronger, but some of us will find we naturally possess stronger arms, legs, or muscles built for endurance. We are a team working together. All of us get to heal the sick, but some of us will have a natural knack for and interest in it. (Good news: If you're reading this book, you probably fall into the latter category.) Paul wrote, "We have different gifts, according to the grace given to each of us. If your gift is prophesying, then prophesy in accordance with your faith" (Rom. 12:6). The same can be said of healing. Not all gifting looks the same, but that does not discourage us from growing in and stewarding whatever measure we currently possess. Just as in the natural world, where we practice to develop a talent or run to increase our stamina, when we use the measure we have, our giftings grow.

DAYDREAMING LIKE JESUS

A few months ago at the gym, I glanced at the television to see something that completely captivated me. A commercial for cancer research dramatized the day cancer is cured. It showed a man on his front porch picking up the paper that shouted in a huge headline, "Cancer Cured." A woman reading the report on her computer at work ecstatically informs her coworkers. There's a crowd frozen in place in Times Square as the screens above Forty-Second and Broadway proclaim the news. A daughter rushes home to tearfully embrace her cancer-fighting mother. With wet eyes, I returned to my push-ups with a new thought: What will it look like when there's no diagnosis of cancer to give? How will the world respond to the news that malaria and cholera have been eradicated? And what will it look like when the kingdom of God comes in fullness?

The increase of the reign of God's kingdom will be full of joyful celebrations like the ones dramatized in the commercial—celebrations that will make a Super Bowl victory look like a tame Columbus Day parade. We live in a remarkable time when ministry is expanding from the select few up front on a Sunday into the hands of the entire church body. As we imagine God healing others through us, we begin to believe he wants to use us, and we receive an impartation of boldness to step past our fears.

In the same way that smelling a delicious meal whets one's appetite, witnessing a miracle makes us hungry to see more. Each miracle I witness only increases my passion to see others healed. For years, I dreamed of seeing one miracle. Just one. I imagined what it would look like to see a frozen shoulder move or stiff knees bend freely. I am delighted that I've seen both of those miracles more than once, but they only made me hungry to see them again. Even more, observing those healings encourages me to dream about seeing more and different healings. But if I'm going to continue to take new risks, my dreams of what's possible need to outpace what I've experienced. Our dreams must surpass us. Currently I dream about seeing children with Down syndrome healed and the regeneration of missing limbs right in front of me. Allowing my heart to daydream with God prepares me to take greater risks. It helps me dream of living a life more and more like that of Jesus, one without limits.

Remember, eating natural food fills you up, but eating in the kingdom of God makes you hungrier.[24] We get to steward the tension that exists between gratitude and pursuit. I am extremely grateful for each miracle I witness, but I must see more. I will not let gratitude turn into false humility that slows my pursuit for more. I will not slow down until my life looks like Jesus! To that end, I regularly pray, "Father, thank you so much for all you've done, but I must have more."

CHAPTER KEYS

We've all heard it before: People don't care how much you know until they know how much you care. In other words, "if I have the gift of prophecy and can fathom all mysteries and all knowledge, and if I have a faith that can move mountains"—if I empty wheelchairs and clear hospitals of their patients—"but do not have love, I am nothing" (1 Cor. 13:2). Loving God and the people around us is our primary call. We have permission to passionately pursue more of God and his gifts until earth looks like heaven—but this is never, never, *never* at the cost of love.

Too often our pursuit of healing begins when we are in dire need of a miracle. While pursuing the gift of healing is a road

---

24. Again, thanks to Bill Johnson for this kingdom truism.

better walked late than never, starting with such intense pressure and emotional investment can be extremely painful. Concern for someone's physical well-being is a heavy one, and disappointment is a deep and dangerous pitfall. There is great wisdom in pursuing a lifestyle of miracles *before* you need one. Whatever your reason, now is an excellent time to begin.

There is no amount of study or righteous living that can qualify us to receive what Jesus freely gives. Jesus already made up his mind: Healing is the birthright of every believer. We get to live lives like Jesus modeled for us, doing what the Father is doing empowered by his Spirit, and bringing heaven to earth every place we go. Like us, Jesus was fully human, and he performed miracles, signs, and wonders by the power and presence of the Holy Spirit. He simply did whatever the Father desired done. Like Jesus, our love must move us to action. His love moved him to heal, and his love flowing through us empowers us to do likewise.

MINISTRY

Now is the time to begin pursuing a radical "normal" Christian life. I promise it is the most fun, fulfilling, and adventurous life you could ever imagine. If you've never asked for a gift of healing or you just want more, I encourage you to ask and keep reading this book, and the next time you see a man limping down the grocery aisle or a woman leaning on her crutches in the mall, pray for that person.

God, you love to give good gifts to your children, and you said you would give us whatever we ask in your name, so right now I ask for a gift of healing. Let the blind see, the deaf hear, the lame walk, and the sick be made well through the power of your Holy Spirit working through me. May I continue the work Jesus started and bring great honor and glory to his name. Amen.

10

THE QUESTION
OF FAILURE

...

I drop my backpack and grab my running shoes, eager to stretch my legs and get a little exercise after another long day of classes. Changing shoes and mental gears, I run out the door and relish the change of pace and scenery.

As I near the end of my regular route, I notice a group of preteens hanging out on bikes and skateboards. My stomach does a little nervous flip as the Holy Spirit draws my attention to them.

"Pray for them," I hear internally.

The swirling in my stomach increases as I jog closer to them. *What if I made that up? If that's me and not God, it's probably better if I don't talk to them.*

My internal justification seems logical, and they don't have any obvious prayer needs—no casts, crutches, or splints. I continue my internal monologue as I jog past the kids: *What if they laugh at me? Great, now it's even more awkward because I'd have to stop and go back.*

I keep my pace and begin bargaining with God. *Okay, Lord, how about a deal? I'll run around the block, and if they're still here when I come back, I'll pray for them.*

I groan as I turn the corner. It's an extra-long block, a sizeable distance tacked on to the end of my run. *Wow, Papa,* I tell him. *I was really afraid right there and that's not me. In you I'm not afraid or timid but powerful and full of love.* I continue to encourage myself and ask for boldness as I jog down a parallel street.

My route back to the kids momentarily takes me alongside a park where, to my surprise and delight, I look up to see a friend emerging from a trail along the river. "James!" I shout and run to meet him. "You are the answer to my prayers."

James laughs as I fill him in about my temporary fear of preteens. "Will you come with me?" He agrees, and we start down the street where I first spotted the kids.

They're still there. In fact, now there are *more* kids. Slowing to a walk, James and I approach them.

"Hey, guys. What's up?" James asks. He casually talks to them for a minute, garnering one-word answers and blank stares, as I stand by quietly, grateful for his company.

"Do you have anything?" he asks me under his breath.

I freeze. I have nothing. No word of encouragement, nothing I feel led to pray for or ask about, not even a casual icebreaker. Nothing. We awkwardly talk to the kids for another minute or two before making an uncomfortable exit.

"Well, that was awkward," I admit. "I've never felt so abandoned when I thought God led me to do something. Whenever I feel him prompt me to talk to someone, he always gives me something to share." That remains true, but in most cases, the "something to share" usually comes after I initiate the conversation.

"You were obedient and that counts for something," James consoles me before we part ways, heading for our respective homes.

While James' consolation is valid, I don't feel satisfied. "God, what was that?" I pray when I'm alone. "I *know* you said to pray for them, and when I hesitated, you sent a friend to encourage me."

"That," God says, his still, small voice interrupting my thoughts, "was failure."

"Failure?" I'm shocked.

"Yes, failure. You failed. Epically."

I can hardly believe what I'm hearing. God just told me I epically failed at something *he* led me to do? "Umm, can you please explain?" I ask.

He answers my question with a question. "How do you feel right now?"

"A little confused," I reply, trying to wrap my head around the bizarre interaction. "But I guess I'm okay." I think about it for a few seconds, noticing the awkwardness and embarrassment have worn off. "Actually, I'm really okay."

"Child," he replies, "that's as bad as it gets. You tried and fell flat on your face and you're okay. You don't need to be afraid of failing."

With God's gentle words, I feel a weight fall from my shoulders. Without realizing it, I've been carrying fear of failure and fear of rejection into every conversation and opportunity to pray. God purposefully led me into an encounter not to see people healed—but to free me from my fears.

FREEDOM FROM FEAR

Numerous things seek to derail our prayers for healing before we utter a word, the largest of which are doubt and fear. We doubt our motives, our ability to hear God correctly, and whether the person will be healed. We fear what people will think of us or what will happen to their faith if they are not healed. And we're afraid that we will misrepresent God or somehow dishonor his name.

There are plenty of times I am turned down when I approach people to pray. These dismissals are sometimes polite and sometimes not so polite, and there are also times when I've prayed for someone without seeing immediate breakthrough. But in the midst of these rejections and apparent failures, I've discovered that rejection and failure are little more than small shadows distorted to frightening sizes by smoke and mirrors. Even more important, I've learned that the healing is secondary to the revelation of faith, worth, and love people experience when we stop to pray.

The world is desperate to encounter the authenticity and faith required to take a risk based solely on our belief in God and his goodness rather than an assured outcome. Not everyone I pray for is healed, but everyone I pray for can be loved, experience value, and witness a demonstration of faith that says, "My God is real, he is good, and he is able." It's time to encounter God's perfect love and let him drive out our fear (1 John 4:18). It's time to face our fears of rejection and failure head on. It's time to turn on the lights and see that what once made us afraid in the dark is powerless to frighten us in the light.

IT'S A WIN-WIN

I love tennis. I dream of going to Paris in the spring—not to walk beneath the budding chestnut trees along the Seine or eat *pain au chocolat* while sipping coffee in a café but to attend the French Open, one of tennis' four major tournaments. (Okay, maybe 60 percent tennis to 40 percent pastries, but still mostly for the tennis.) During any of the four major tournaments, I spend a lot of time on my phone checking scores or texting my aunt about the latest upset. I even sound like a tennis commentator as I say things like, "Last time they played, she was up a break in the second before double faulting twice and losing in three."

Given my long limbs and obvious love of the sport, it's no surprise that many people assume I'm a halfway decent player. The only problem with this notion is that, well, I'm not.

So last week when a cute guy asked me to play tennis with him, I nonchalantly made an attempt at a witty tennis pun, and we set a time and place for our sporting date. I hung up the phone, cringed at my pun, and promptly freaked out. "Guys!" I shouted to my friends. "We're going to play tennis. What am I going to do? He probably thinks I'm good at tennis!"

"Oh, no! I'd be so nervous if I were you. Are you *so* nervous?" asked one friend.

Thankfully, a second friend cut her off. "Don't worry about how good you are. I doubt he's looking for a competitive match. He just wants to spend time with you."

Her reasoning helped calm my butterflies.

"Besides," she added, "if it's really bad, you can turn it into a lesson. No one said it had to be a competition."

I felt the light return to my eyes as her suggestion dawned on me. "I don't need to be good at tennis. It can be a lesson!"

"And you get to go hang out with him, so either way it's a win," she encouraged.

"Either way it's a win!" I enthusiastically agreed.

• • •

There's no such thing as a draw in tennis. One player always wins and one player always loses, so the idea of playing tennis with two winners and no loser took a minute for me to comprehend.

But as I realized that day, just because you're hitting balls on a tennis court doesn't mean you need to keep score. Redefining "winning" removed nearly all the pressure and apprehension I felt.

Likewise, when my "win" in praying for healing is about the person's post-prayer symptoms, I am nearly suffocated by pressure, self-doubt, and fear of failure. Not surprisingly, this results-focused approach means I pray for fewer and fewer people while carrying an ever-growing guilt over succumbing to fear. But in the same way that redefining the concept of winning can make playing tennis a win for both players, praying for healing can be a win-win for both the person praying and the person receiving prayer every time we pray.

Win #1: The Pray-er

Faith is not demonstrated by an outcome but by an action. The Bible describes faith as "confidence in what we hope for and assurance about what we do not see" (Heb. 11:1). The way we walk out that confidence is through our thoughts, words, and actions. This means that the proof of faith truly transforming our lives is in what we do.

For example, I have faith that exercise is good for my heart, even though I cannot physically see what happens to my heart when I exercise. I demonstrate my faith every time I hit the gym or attend a boxing class. If my thoughts about exercise had yet to mature into faith, I would regularly give in to the temptation to sit on my couch after work. That is why James wrote, "Faith by itself, if it is not accompanied by action, is dead" (2:17). Faith motivates us to act. It is the framework on which God breathes and we move. As John Wimber once said, "Faith is spelled R-I-S-K."

My win in praying for healing is not determined by the outcome of my prayer but by the moment I get out of my chair and take the first step toward the person in need of healing. In other words, I win the split second I act, regardless of how nervous I am or if the person is healed. God starts smiling as soon as we take a risk.

Win #2: The Prayee

The second win in our win-win scenario is centered on the person receiving prayer. It actually has nothing to do with the *results* of our prayers but whether the person we're praying for feels valued, honored, and loved. Instead of basing our success on the outcome, something we can't control, success is based on something we can control—treating the woman or man in front of us like a daughter or son of the High King of heaven. We have an opportunity for a win-win every time we pray for healing as we actively demonstrate our faith, and the person we are praying for is loved.

REDEFINING SUCCESS

I am meeting a couple of friends at a new coffee shop featuring locally roasted coffee and killer cold brew. We grab a vacant table while waiting for our drinks and start chatting. At the same time the barista calls my name, a girl in her early twenties leaning on a crutch finishes placing her order and moves to the other end of the counter.

"Hey, girl, what's up with the crutch?" I ask, taking advantage of the easy conversation starter.

"Oh," she says, turning toward me. I can see the emotional pain in her response. "I was in a car accident a couple of years ago and have lasting nerve damage."

"That's a serious bummer. I'm sorry." In the past, sympathy and a kind remark were all I had to offer, but now I'm aware of the compassion that moves me to action and the resurrection power inside of me. "This may sound crazy, but I've seen God heal all sorts of people. Would it be okay if I pray for you?"

Her eyes fill with tears as she responds, "Yeah, that'd be okay."

I proceed to pray for her. Twice. She doesn't notice a decrease in pain or an increase in range of motion, but that doesn't seem to matter. "This is one of the kindest things anyone has ever done for me," she tells me, wiping away a couple of tears.

"Jesus loves *you*. I'm sorry we didn't see any change, but that doesn't change how special and valuable you are—nor his desire and ability to see your leg 100 percent healed."

She nods and wipes away a stray tear. "Would it be okay—?" she stammers. "I mean, could I just have a hug?"

"Of course!" I hold her in a tight embrace and tell her that she is worth the price Jesus paid for her. Returning to my friends with our coffees, I fill them in on my most recent "failure." "We didn't see any physical breakthrough, but she felt loved."

• • •

A friend of mine recently recounted what happened to him on a flight. He noticed a woman in need of healing and asked to pray for her while in the air. He prayed several times, but they did not see any immediate change in her physical circumstances. My friend told her that he knew God's heart was for her to be healed and that he was still learning how to see that happen. He thought that was the end of the story, but unbeknownst to him, a man a couple of rows in front of him was intently listening to their interaction. This man was so moved by the faith and love he saw my friend express that he waited in the jet bridge after deplaning to ask my friend how he could have similar faith and love. My friend gladly introduced him to Jesus.

Time and again, I'm blown away by individuals' responses when they aren't healed. The faith demonstrated when praying for healing and the love the person experiences awaken a holy hunger for our loving God. And as my friend experienced firsthand on that flight, this isn't limited to those receiving prayer. In fact, I'm routinely approached by individuals who want to understand the hope and love they witnessed when my friends and I pray for healing.

I will never get tired of partnering with God and seeing miracles. Never. But even if there's no change in someone's physical symptoms, when we pray we have an opportunity to demonstrate the highest law of God's kingdom: love. There is no wall high enough or defense formidable enough to keep love out. It never fails. When my heart is set to love the person in front of me, whether or not she is healed, I am always successful.

TAKING ONE STEP AT A TIME

There's an old riddle that asks how one eats an elephant. The correct answer is one bite at a time. I'm not sure why we're eating elephants in the first place, but the tactic is useful when faced with a seemingly insurmountable task: Do what's in front of you to do, and worry about the next step later.

It's easy when talking about healing to recount the testimonies of bold, fearless people who see dozens healed on airplanes or in checkout lines and disqualify ourselves with thoughts like, *I could never do that.* The truth is that at one point they couldn't either. In the realm of faith, baby steps count just as much as giant leaps. The achievement isn't in the size of the step but in forward movement. By concerning ourselves only with the opportunity in front of us, our comfort zones grow at an astounding pace, and we soon realize the things we "could never do" have become a regular part of our lives.

One day a few years ago, I was on a cardio machine at the gym when I felt like God said he wanted to heal the woman next to me of a certain kidney condition. The idea scared me. What if I was wrong and she wasn't suffering from that disease, or what if she turned down my offer for prayer and I was embarrassed every time I saw her at the gym? So I turned up my music and tried to ignore the thought and the nervous feeling in my stomach. When that didn't work, I hopped off the machine and walked straight out the door. I was more than a little disappointed with myself on the drive home. "God, I'm so sorry that I let fear dictate my actions. Please forgive me and increase my faith. Empower me to act with love and boldness." After praying, I let go of what occurred and trusted that the next time I encountered a similar situation, I'd be ready.

I wish I could say this is the only time I backed down when I felt the telltale signs of an opportunity to step out in faith (dry mouth, quickened pulse, churning stomach), but that's not true. There have been many such moments and probably will be some in the future. Instead of beating myself up, I regroup, repent, and know I'm ready the next time a similar situation presents itself. Sometimes it takes several occasions of missing and regrouping before I get it.

That initial fear we feel is Satan throwing everything he's got at us to get us to stop. Every time we step past our fear, it loses its influence and we're less afraid the next time. As we focus on taking just the little step in front of us, we find that what once terrified us no longer holds the power to keep us from action. In other words, be encouraged—it gets easier.

PERMISSION TO FAIL

Now is a great time to be a basketball fan in Northern California. Stephen Curry and the Golden State Warriors put on a near-nightly hoops clinic in fun-loving team play and jaw-dropping three-point shooting. But even with their unbelievable skill in shooting the long-distance three-pointer, they still make less than 50 percent of the shots they take.[25] In other words, the NBA team captivating America and inspiring players of all ages to practice their long-range shooting still

---

25. The NBA team regular season three-point field goal percentage record is .4276 (just under 43 percent) set by the 1996–97 Charlotte Hornets. The all-time best shooting team still shot well below 50 percent (http://www.basketball-reference.com/leaders/team_fg3_pct.html).

misses more than half of its shots. Fortunately, missing a shot does not disqualify someone from shooting the next one. Whether it's basketball or praying for healing, everyone shoots and misses at times.

The more I learned about those who preceded me in praying for healing, the clearer it became that everyone not named Jesus sometimes fails to see immediate breakthrough—this includes the writers of the New Testament. The apostle Paul did "extraordinary miracles" (Acts 19:11) but still had to leave his friend and fellow missionary Trophimus sick in Turkey (2 Tim. 4:20). Only a few chapters earlier, the disciples "drove out many demons and anointed many sick people with oil and healed them" (Mark 6:13), but they didn't see healing when they prayed for a demon-possessed boy. Mark wrote:

A man in the crowd answered, "Teacher, I brought you my son, who is possessed by a spirit that has robbed him of speech. Whenever it seizes him, it throws him to the ground. He foams at the mouth, gnashes his teeth and becomes rigid. I asked your disciples to drive out the spirit, but they could not . . ."

When Jesus saw that a crowd was running to the scene, he rebuked the impure spirit. "You deaf and mute spirit," he said, "I command you, come out of him and never enter him again."

The spirit shrieked, convulsed him violently and came out. The boy looked so much like a corpse that many said, "He's dead." But Jesus took him by the hand and lifted him to his feet, and he stood up.

After Jesus had gone indoors, his disciples asked him privately, "Why couldn't we drive it out?"

He replied, "This kind can come out only by prayer."

MARK 9:17–29

On behalf of the people for whom they prayed, I wish Paul and the disciples saw everyone healed; however, I'm personally thankful they didn't, because this frees me from the fear of failure and offers a number of valuable lessons:

1. **We have permission to fail.** It's extremely liberating to realize that even Paul and the disciples had times when they didn't see the miracle occur. If it was okay for them not to bat 1.000, it's definitely okay for you and me to swing and miss.

2. **We can expect a miracle.** Instead of being surprised when their prayers "worked," the disciples were surprised when they didn't. Likewise, by trusting in God's faithfulness and love, Jesus' atoning work, the Holy Spirit's power in us, and the promises found in Scripture, we can expect healing when we pray for others.

3. **We pray for the next person even if we didn't see a miracle last time.** Paul and the disciples weren't disqualified from praying for healing because someone wasn't healed. Likewise, just because we don't see healing yet does not disqualify us from praying and pursuing healing.

4. **Our response when someone isn't healed is to turn to Jesus.** Introspection and self-doubt are never appropriate when someone isn't healed. As the disciples demonstrated, the only viable option when healing doesn't occur is to go to Jesus with our disappointment and questions.

5. **Healing is a lifestyle.** Jesus said the particular demon in Mark 9 came out only by prayer, but he didn't pray in the moment; he commanded the demon to leave and it did. Jesus received the anointing and authority to perform miracles before he needed it.

Our personal prayer lives—times of worship, thanksgiving, Bible reading, and encountering God's uniquely personal love for us—are an essential step to seeing healing. A lifestyle of intimacy with God equips us to believe like Jesus and perform miracles in his name.

6. **Pray for healing.** The disciples and early church regularly prayed for healing. This was a normal part of their lives, as it is to be in ours.

Doing things to the best of our ability is the kingdom principle of excellence. The counterfeit of excellence is perfectionism: a disempowering and impossible standard that wears us out and prevents us from trying. We are not defined by the number of times we pray for healing without seeing an immediate response but by our belief in God's character, nature, and will, and the love we demonstrate. Missing shots isn't a problem. Not playing the game is.

PERMISSION TO LEARN

One Christmas while I was still living in California, I flew home to the cold, white North to be with my family over the holidays. My niece's birthday is perfectly placed between Christmas and New Year's, giving us another reason to celebrate. At her birthday party, we watched her tentative first bite of birthday cake and her unbridled pleasure in the boxes her gifts came in, but the evening's highlight was watching her struggle to her feet and take several unsteady steps. Every effort ended in a little tumble that deterred neither the soon-to-be walker nor her audience. Instead, each fall was met with cheers and an ever-increasing number of iPhones capturing the moment.

Tumbles and mistakes are a natural part of learning any skill. Learning how *not* to do something is as important as learning how to do it. This is the reason companies have research and development departments and not just manufacturing and sales. Yet when it comes to the gifts of the Spirit, we often don't allow ourselves the privilege of a learning curve. In the beginning, I expected to see my healing gift dramatically reveal itself at wheelchair-emptying, hospital-clearing levels. I nearly disqualified myself with false assumptions when I asked for a gift of healing and there was no thunder, lightning, or writing on the wall. I was ignorant of the countless examples of great men and women of God who prayed for hundreds and thousands of people before they saw someone healed.

It's important to clarify that by "failing" I do not mean moral failure or abuse of the Holy Spirit's gifts. Unfortunately, error and abuse have produced fear within much of the church. The Holy Spirit's gifts are the power tools of kingdom building. Like any power tools, those wielding the tools can cause both untold good or harm—a power saw is a great tool, but if used incorrectly it can cut off an arm. The devil doesn't waste his time creating confusion around something of little importance. Flatly rejecting the gifts of the Spirit because of another's error is also error. Our response cannot be to shut down the gifts but, instead, we can develop healthy thinking and teaching about the gifts that encourage a powerful and safe learning environment and kingdom culture.

God graciously encourages us not to "despise these small beginnings, for the LORD rejoices to see the work begin" (Zech. 4:10 NLT). Starting small and making mistakes are part of the learning process. We learn through experience. Begin by asking for the grace to heal, and believe you have received it. Then start praying for people. And in all things, make the love of God and love for the person in front of you your chief aim. We probably won't start out sprinting, but our adoring heavenly Father is eagerly awaiting those first tottering steps.

CHAPTER KEYS

We are citizens of a kingdom where we live by faith and not by sight (see 2 Cor. 5:7). Assurance of an outcome does not motivate us to pray for healing. Instead, we are led to pray because of our relationship with our really good heavenly Father, who loves without limits and delights in healing. We are both permitted and encouraged to learn, crawling and walking before running, failing and falling as we try. As we pray for healing, success is redefined, moving from an end result to a win-win interaction based on love. With this in mind, we cannot lose because even if we "fail," love is demonstrated and the kingdom of God advances.

MINISTRY

It's extremely liberating to find yourself in your worst-case scenario and realize you're going to survive. Whatever your worst-case scenario for healing is, it's really not that bad. Love is our green light to act in faith and take new ground for the kingdom. And when we do try and "fail," the ever-present reward of stepping outside our comfort zones is an encounter with the Comforter.

God, thank you that I am successful every time I'm motivated by love to act in faith. Thank you that every situation you are invited into is irrevocably changed. You are the Healer, the Creator, and my Comforter. Please come and encounter me with your love in every place that's been touched by fear and rejection. Encourage me with the knowledge that in you I am already victorious and cannot fail. And fill me with a spirit of love and boldness that empowers me to act. Amen.

11

THE QUESTION
WITHOUT AN ANSWER

...

It's the start of my second month of ministry school. The first month was one of the best and most challenging months of my life. Daily, and somewhat painfully, my paradigm for understanding God's goodness, kindness, and love changes as I step into new freedom. Every morning I awake excited for class, and every afternoon I leave school with a numb feeling in my overstimulated brain.

Sitting in Bible class, I force myself to pay attention for the last twenty minutes. The previous night's assignment was to look for the overarching story told in Mark 5. The teacher reiterates the points our textbook makes: Life is hard, bad things happen, and Jesus gets you through tough times. Here our teacher stops to point out one thing he believes the textbook misses—Jesus' presence radically transforms each situation. The demonized man is delivered, the sick woman is healed, and the dead girl is raised to life. We are challenged to fully trust Jesus to transform a situation without reserving any of our heart or expectation (hope), knowing that if the worst comes, if the situation isn't radically reversed, then the one called the Comforter will be present to pick up the pieces.

My first opportunity to put this teaching into practice comes minutes later.

My best friends from university are eagerly awaiting the arrival of their first child. Checking my phone as I leave class, I see multiple missed calls and text messages. My heart sinks. Something feels wrong. Absent from the messages are the time, length, and weight customarily supplied with a birth announcement, and the urgency doesn't imply good news. I call to find my fears confirmed. The baby, a little girl, was born brain dead and is on life support.

A sharp ringing blocks out all sound, and my vision narrows until I am looking down a dark tunnel. Friends lead me to a chair while my world spins dizzily. This little girl would have known me as Aunt Becca, but instead she is likely to die before I have the chance to meet her. In the moment, I decide the only option is to fully trust Jesus to radically transform the situation. I'm not going to withhold any of my hope to protect my heart from disappointment and pain. He who brings the dead to life can surely bring life to my niece's brain. A couple of days later, with no change in prognosis, I cash in frequent flyer miles and drive through the night to the airport where I catch a cross-country flight.

Garbed in a hospital gown, hairnet, and shoe coverings, with vigorously washed hands and a lump in my throat, I meet my niece. Even with tubes running in and out of her body, I can see the strong family resemblance. She is an infant-sized version of her parents. I place my hands on her tiny frame and pray. I worship. I command and declare. And then I repeat the cycle again and again over the next several days, waiting for the great exchange to occur—life for death. I do everything I know to do and leave without seeing the miracle happen. Nor does it occur. Two days after I return to California, this precious baby girl dies.

I stumble down the stairs, overcome by grief. "She died," I manage to say before bursting into tears and collapsing into my roommate's hug. Quite suddenly, the emotional exhaustion hovering in the background since I first learned of my niece's prognosis descends on me. The full weight of the loss—which happened in spite of my cross-country trip, prayer vigil, and unwavering faith for a miracle—bears down on me. I catch myself staring down the precipice of a very dark line of thinking. I'm tempted to accuse God for failing to act, and part of me wants to vow to never again believe for a miracle without reservation.

After the initial shock wears off a little while later, I go out to the garage, knowing I won't be heard in my car. When I can't cry anymore and there is nothing left to shout, a calm comes over me from that quiet place that exists on the other side of the very last tear. "God," I whisper, "this really hurts. I need your peace that goes beyond my understanding, so I give up my right to understand."

• • •

To receive God's peace that goes beyond understanding, we need to surrender our right to understand.[26] It may seem like God failed or didn't care enough to heal, but questioning his ability or heart is both wrong and foolish. He never fails and his love never ends.

The false comforts of accusation and reservation, though very real temptations in the face of pain, are utterly disastrous. It's dangerous to accuse God of inaction when the truth is, he already acted; Christ's death and resurrection already defeated sickness, disease, and death. Likewise, relationships require trust. Accusation and withholding part of our hearts absolutely destroy that trust. Vowing

---

26. I heard Bill Johnson teach about grief multiple times while walking through my own. Bill's teaching brought much healing to my heart when I needed it. Check out "How to Overcome Disappointment," available at shop.bethel.com.

to withhold our emotions and expectations actually partners with a demonic false comforter that steadily eats away at our faith and destroys our intimacy with God and our ability to believe for anything, healing or otherwise, in the future.

The temptation to accuse God of not preventing a death or otherwise altering a situation surfaces when our experiences don't align with his revealed truth in Scripture. The injustice we suffered accurately triggers something within us that screams, "This is not how it's supposed to be!" Giving up our need to understand also means relinquishing any right we feel we have to accuse God or hold him responsible for our pain. When we accuse God, we actually assume that we care more for that individual than he does or that our compassion is greater than his. It is of the utmost importance that we protect our hearts from the hardening and bitterness that come from accusation. We do this by deciding against accusing him *before* we find ourselves in a situation where we are tempted to hold him responsible for our pain.

It's in these worst-of-times moments when we can powerfully confess, "God, you don't seem all good or all powerful, but I know that's not true. It's not you or your promises that are broken. It's my situation that's broken." It is here, in the midst of our very real pain and confusion, that God the Comforter meets us, wrapping us in an embrace that may not bring an answer but does bring his peace and calms our fears. And then, contrary to our feelings, we have the opportunity to give a very costly offering of praise, one we can offer only on this side of heaven.[27]

EMBRACING HUMILITY: WE SIMPLY DON'T KNOW

Even several years after the death of my niece, writing about her still stirs up pain. I put my whole heart and all my hope into

---

27. Again, thank you, Bill Johnson.

believing that God would radically restore her. When that didn't happen, when the miracle didn't come, I was crushed both by grief and disappointment. I tried to pray but struggled to find the words. After several dark, lonely days, I heard God speak. Not audibly, but with the still, small voice of his Spirit within me.

"Child," I heard him tenderly whisper to my heart, "this loss hurts me, too."

It wasn't the words but the tone that stopped me in my tracks. His voice was full of pain. It began to dawn on me that he cared far more for her than I ever could. I'd imagined her growing up, but he'd already seen it. I wanted to take her on trips and teach her all the fun things aunts teach nieces, while he'd already instilled giftings and talents within her. God created her with a distinct purpose, and he grieved the loss of the life he so lovingly and expertly knit together.

In the past, painful losses meant times of strained relationship and decreased intimacy with God as I sifted through my understanding of his goodness and sovereignty. This time was different. This time, in the face of painful facts that seemed to prove the opposite, I confessed my lack of understanding and proclaimed my enduring conviction of his goodness, faithfulness, and unfailing love. And then something happened that I'd never before experienced: God moved closer. He shared a measure of his grief with me the way you share your pain with a close friend. Humility, in the midst of our pain and often in spite of what we think we know, is essential to a continued lifestyle of intimacy with God. Admitting we don't understand is the door to places beyond human reason and our limited perspective. As difficult as it is in the moment, we need to agree with the apostle Paul's conclusion of life lived between two kingdoms: "Now I know in part; then I shall know fully, even as I am fully known" (1 Cor. 13:12). One day we will have full understanding, but until that day, we humbly admit our lack and lift our hands to worship the one still worthy of all praise.

Even though we know God's will is to heal, even though we recognize that Jesus died to destroy all the effects of sin, the world is not as it will be, and we are in a fierce battle, a battle with casualties. When the worst happens, when our hearts are broken, the pain is raw, and our minds cannot comprehend the loss, there is only one answer we can honestly give in response to our questions: We simply don't know.

DISAPPOINTMENT: THE SILENT KILLER

I hear the same story far too frequently. Someone who fully believed in God's desire to heal—even someone who moved mightily in healing and saw numerous people healed—experienced one tragedy too many or lost a close friend or family member and stopped praying for people altogether. Or worse, the person walked away from the faith. Rarely was one painful situation in and of itself destructive enough to evoke such a dramatic response; instead, it was the tipping point after years of mounting disappointment. If humility is what empowers us to worship God and continue to pursue healing in the midst of loss, disappointment is its antithesis. When ignored or invalidated, unprocessed disappointment exposes even seasoned spiritual warriors to direct demonic attack.

Sometimes there's no way around pain. It hurts when we don't see answers to our prayers. King Solomon wrote, "Hope deferred makes the heart sick, but a longing fulfilled is a tree of life" (Prov. 13:12). If not addressed, disappointment, and even the fear of disappointment, embitters and poisons our hearts. It eventually paralyzes us from action and makes our hearts sick. Disappointment keeps us from living with the constant, confident expectation of coming good intended for us (hope). Learning how to walk through disappointment while wholeheartedly trusting in God's goodness and faithfulness is an essential part of the Christian life. We humbly trust in his goodness while admitting our lack of understanding. Paul touched on deferred hope, perseverance, and disappointment in his letter to the church at Rome:

> *And not only this, but we also exult in our tribulations, knowing that tribulation brings about perseverance; and perseverance, proven character; and proven character, hope;* **and hope does not disappoint,** *because the love of God has been poured out within our hearts through the Holy Spirit who was given to us.*

ROMANS 5:3-5, NASB (EMPHASIS ADDED)

Hope does not disappoint. This means that in the places where hope feels like it's wavering and disappointment is circling, God has more intended for me than what I am currently experiencing. Instead of fearing disappointment, I can walk in supernatural empowerment (grace) and proclaim his faithfulness. I can fully rest, not spending one more minute of mental or emotional energy, in the knowledge that God will turn even the most painful of situations into a place where his glory is revealed and his goodness declared—even if I am not the one who witnesses the fullness of the promise. If it's not too good to be true, then God is still at work and it's not the end of the story.[28]

We cannot allow past disappointments to determine our future actions and current hope level. And we cannot afford to create a theology based on experience instead of Scripture. We have to tie ourselves firmly to the mast of God's revealed nature to weather any

---

28. Even death is not the end; God is faithful far beyond what we can begin to imagine. Though Abraham didn't live to see his descendants as numerous as the stars in the sky (Gen. 15:5), I don't think he died disappointed. I have a strong suspicion he will be one of the first and happiest people we meet in heaven as he welcomes yet another one of his children, each of us a testimony of God's unwavering faithfulness.

storms of doubt and disappointment that come when we decide to walk by faith instead of sight (2 Cor. 5:7).

Here in the midst of our disappointments, it's worth emphasizing the second half of Proverbs 13:12: Longings fulfilled are trees of life. If I'm struggling with disappointment and disillusionment, often it's because my focus shifted from what God has done to what hasn't yet happened. As I celebrate the answered prayers and areas of break-through, these things become the "trees of life" whose fruit sustain me through barren times and desert places. God *is* perfectly good, and his desire is for healing to be manifest on the earth. I don't know why some aren't healed, but I do know that in Christ I can take heart and find the courage to continue my pursuit of healing, for he has overcome the world (see John 16:33).

BEARING THE CROSS

I'm an avid sports fan. While living in California, I considered it a West Coast advantage that I could go to bed knowing the majority of the day's sporting outcomes. As exclusive as my support of Minnesota teams once was, living in different states meant I started cheering for the local team in addition to hometown favorites. I admit that I've had to internally justify my change in allegiance, but the combination of access and the recent success of Northern California sports teams has made my new appreciation easier to swallow.

I know that to any diehard sports fan, what I just admitted is tantamount to sacrilege. Ultimate fan-hood is defined by undivided support of one team instead of my broader (nobler) perspective of supporting the sport as a whole. While cheering for both the Florida Panthers and Minnesota Wild doesn't create too much internal tension, one area where we cannot afford to be fair-weather fans is in our devotion to God. There's no middle ground (see Rev. 3:15). The

Christian life requires an investment of our whole being. It's all or nothing (see Matt. 22:37).

We tend to hedge our bets when our hearts are involved, fearing to invest fully in anything we don't deem a sure thing. But we cannot separate our hearts from the prayer of faith. Its very nature necessitates emotional involvement. And emotional involvement always means risk. This makes praying for healing dangerous. We know what the outcome is supposed to be, but that outcome does not always occur—yet. This all-in, kingdom-bringing faith demands our full belief, full expectation, and our full hearts. It may feel foolish to hold on to hope and stand in faith in the face of a doctor's negative report, our past experiences, or our pain, but continuing to trust God without all the answers is the definition of boldly living for an unseen kingdom. Fully trusting God is extraordinarily brave, not foolish.

Praying for healing is costly. Every time we pray, we put our hope and faith on the line for a miracle that far too often doesn't manifest. It costs us emotionally, and it can cost us our reputations. Consider what trusting God initially did to the reputations of people like Noah, Jeremiah, and Mary. Though we celebrate their great faith now, their contemporaries likely thought they were insane, liars, or some combination of the two. Personally, I believe the emotional cost, disappointment, and nearly unbearable agony of loss when we don't see healing are part of what Jesus described when he said, "Whoever wants to be my disciple must deny themselves and take up their cross daily and follow me" (Luke 9:23). In the moments when I haven't seen the breakthrough, when the condition worsens or the friend passes away, I resolve to worship God and fix my eyes on Jesus, who "for the joy set before him he endured the cross, scorning its shame" (Heb. 12:2). The cost is high but is nothing compared to what Jesus paid. What a privilege it is to walk in the footsteps of our Exalted Head, who willingly bore the weight of all our sin, sickness, and disease.

SURRENDERING OUR RIGHT TO OFFENSE

Pulling the chain as far from the wall as possible, John tried to find a position that relieved the searing pain in his shoulder. Led by large guards, a steady stream of curious observers from the palace had come to see the prized prisoner, but slowly their numbers dwindled and he was left in this dank, dark hole with only cockroaches and rats for company.

"Who's there?" John called into the darkness. His ears told him the cell was empty, but a nearly overwhelming feeling of dread accompanied by a cold chill suggested otherwise. "I know you're here. Show yourself, you vile creature."

A cold face appeared in the shadows, and a slithering voice said, "Still in chains, I see." Satan stooped to lift one of John's shackles. "Didn't he say he would free prisoners? Yet here you are. What a shame."

"Even still, he is the Messiah."

"A Savior who leaves his greatest supporter to die in this hole?" the devil questioned.

"Leave, you disgusting speaker of lies," John growled, adding defiantly, "He will crush your head."

Satan backed away with a cruel laugh. "Just you wait and see. He will not come for you. He will never come for you."

John watched as the devil disappeared into the darkness, and then slowly, methodically, he began reciting the prophecies of the Messiah to himself.

Day after day this exchange occurred. At first, Satan's challenges were met with John's thunderous rebuttals, but hunger, exhaustion, and life in a cell too short to stand in began to take their toll. The seed of doubt planted in these encounters began to grow in John's mind. Maybe Jesus wasn't the Messiah after all. Maybe John was mistaken.

Finally, with his last spark of hope nearly extinguished, John managed to get a message to several of his disciples: "Go to Jesus and ask him if he is the one or if it is someone else."

John the Baptist was chosen before his birth to prepare the way for the Messiah. His parents knew it. He knew it. His followers knew it. Every aspect of John's life was centered on preparing for and recognizing the Lamb of God. Clearly, he knew Jesus' messianic identity. Scripture shows us the exact moment John recognized Jesus:

> *The next day John saw Jesus coming toward him and said, "Look, the Lamb of God, who takes away the sin of the world! This is the one I meant when I said, 'A man who comes after me has surpassed me because he was before me.' I myself did not know him, but the reason I came baptizing with water was that he might be revealed to Israel."*
>
> *Then John gave this testimony: "I saw the Spirit come down from heaven as a dove and remain on him. And I myself did not know him, but the one who sent me to baptize with water told me, 'The man on whom you see the Spirit come down and remain is the one who will baptize with the Holy Spirit.' I have seen and I testify that this is God's Chosen One."*

JOHN 1:29-34

If John was confident of Jesus' messianic identity, how could he go from complete certainty to sending his disciples to double check? Of all people, he knew that Jesus was the promised Messiah—the Messiah who would "proclaim freedom for the captives and release from darkness for the prisoners" (Isa. 61:1). Yet day after day, John sat in prison. Doubt began to seep into a place of certainty, and his conviction began to crumble in the very spot where all of us are vulnerable: the tension between what's promised and what we are experiencing. If the Messiah was supposed to free prisoners but John was behind bars, then maybe, just *maybe,* Jesus wasn't the Messiah.

In response to John's direct question of his messianic identity, Jesus gave a very interesting answer:

> *At that very time Jesus cured many who had diseases, sickness-*
> *es and evil spirits, and gave sight to many who were blind. So*
> *he replied to the messengers, "Go back and report to John what*
> *you have seen and heard: The blind receive sight, the lame*
> *walk, those who have leprosy are cleansed, the deaf hear, the*
> *dead are raised, and the good news is proclaimed to the poor.*
> *Blessed is anyone who does not stumble on account of me."*

LUKE 7:21-23

The New American Standard translates verse 23 this way: "Blessed is he who does not take offense at Me."[29] Instead of a yes or no, Jesus told John not to be offended by what *wasn't* happening. He essentially said, "Don't be discouraged or dissuaded by the prison, but focus on what God is doing."

The implication of this verse is huge. Often our response *is* offense when we see God do one thing and not another; our hearts can harden when what we hope for doesn't occur. Like John focusing on his chains, when we focus on what hasn't happened, we set ourselves up to trip and fall over our own offense. Focusing on un-answered prayers and unfulfilled expectations can actually lead us away from God. Instead of putting our attention on the areas where we've yet to see breakthrough, we can receive the divine grace that protects us from offense and empowers us to continue pressing in

---

29. The word translated in the NIV as "stumble" is *skandalizō* and includes "to put a stumbling block or impediment in the way, upon which another may trip and fall" and "to entice to sin; to cause a person to begin to distrust and desert one whom he ought to trust and obey." It is also a metaphor for "to offend" (Strong's 4624).

for the breakthrough. We actively choose to fix our attention on what God is doing. We do not accuse him or allow pain to change our understanding of who he is. His nature doesn't change. His promises never fail. Our situation may be broken and not fully reflect his truth, but the brokenness is not on God's end of the equation. If it's not too good to be true, it's not the end of the story.

"YOU GRIEVE"

Praying for healing is still relatively new for me. There were many years I didn't pray for it, nor did I even know I could. When I first started praying, nearly everyone was healed or received some measure of breakthrough. It was incredible. But then it happened—I put my whole heart on the line, prayed with all my might, did everything I knew to do, and didn't see the miracle. I was emotionally and spiritually devastated. Soon after, I asked a pastor whose ministry is renowned for miracles how to regain the unreserved hope and faith I'd experienced before my loss. The pastor recognized my question was not theoretical but personal, born of pain. "You grieve," she replied gently.

Grieving is the last stop in our journey through this question without an answer. It is an essential part of the healing process. We absolutely need to grieve both the loss and the disappointment of one more day without seeing the breakthrough. The Bible promises comfort to those who mourn (Matt. 5:4). The only requirement to this divine comfort is to mourn, to grieve our loss. We need to be honest with ourselves, acknowledge the hurt, and allow ourselves time and space to go through the process. And frankly, some losses take longer to grieve than others.

If you've suffered loss, take time from your regular activities, even from praying for healing, to allow God to comfort and restore you. Don't pretend it doesn't hurt, and don't skip the valley of the shadow of death (Ps. 23:4). If we don't grieve, we unintentionally set up camp there.

CHAPTER KEYS

In the book *The Lion, the Witch and the Wardrobe* by C.S. Lewis, one of the children asked Mr. Beaver if Aslan, the great lion and true ruler of Narnia, was safe. Mr. Beaver's response beautifully depicts the tension of our Christian faith:

> *"Safe?" said Mr. Beaver; "don't you hear what Mrs. Beaver tells you? Who said anything about safe? 'Course he isn't safe. But he's good. He's the King, I tell you."*[30]

Safety was never promised. Our hearts are not "safe" when we act in faith, but we can stand on his goodness. At the end of the day, whether we saw miracles or suffered great loss, his goodness and kingship are what we know for certain. We're not alone as we stand on the truth of who he is in the face of contrary evidence. Our biblical heroes "were still living by faith when they died. They did not receive the things promised; they only saw them and welcomed them from a distance, admitting that they were foreigners and strangers on earth" (Heb. 11:13). We put our hearts on the line every time we step out in faith. Our emotions and reputation are at risk. Every right we feel we possess to accuse, to demand answers, and to scream injustice is laid down in order to receive peace beyond our understanding and protect ourselves from bitterness and disappointment. We embrace humility and the reality that sometimes we just don't know the answer. We grieve and experience very real pain over our losses and continue our march onward. We bear the cross and the

---

30. Lewis, C.S., *The Lion, the Witch and the Wardrobe* (New York: HarperTrophy, 1994), 86.

painful tension lived between the facts of our situation and the truth of Scripture. And above all we cry out for more of God's kingdom to be made manifest on earth.

He is good. And he is the King.

MINISTRY

When we admit that we don't know why something that's supposed to happen hasn't, we create space for the Holy Spirit to minister to us, to breathe fresh hope and life into places that seem long dead. The prophet Ezekiel wrote, "I will give you a new heart and put a new spirit in you; I will remove from you your heart of stone and give you a heart of flesh" (36:26). God longs to remove the pain and disappointment that turn our soft hearts hard. The Holy Spirit longs to comfort those who mourn, to give beauty for ashes, joy for mourning, and praise instead of a spirit of despair. He calls you his oak of righteousness, a display of his splendor. Don't wait another moment for his healing balm and divine comfort.

Father, I don't understand why things happen the way they do, but I know you're good and you're faithful. I need you. I need your healing touch. I need hope where I've long been disappointed. Please come. Take my hurt and my pain, my accusations and frustration, and make me new. Give me a soft heart again. Send your Holy Spirit to empower me to trust in your goodness and rest in your love. Amen.

If this chapter touched a specific hurt or memory, please do one thing more: Invite God to show you his perspective of that memory. It's time for old wounds to be cleaned, for hope to be restored, and for you to experience his love anew in areas of past disappointment.

12

THE QUESTIONS
THAT LIMIT US

• • •

"We should fire our trainer and hire this girl!" one of the players suggests as he watches a second teammate healed in front of him.

"It's not me. I can't heal you. Jesus healed you," I respond. I look around slightly dazed, trying to process what is happening. One minute my brother and I are walking on the pier talking about sharks, and the next we are surrounded by a group of vacationing lacrosse players and praying for their healing. "Do you know who Jesus is?"

"We go to Catholic school."

"That's awesome, but do you know who Jesus is?"

"Isn't he God or something?"

"Isn't he God or something?" I repeat. And then, heart pounding, I speak for several minutes about Jesus' life, death, and resurrection to an attentive audience. "Do any of you want to know Jesus as your Savior?" I ask, looking around the circle before leading the group in prayer. Only later when we're recounting the story to our family does the enormity of what occurred start to settle in. We got to be part of something I had longed to see—a group of people saved and healed.

. . .

Even if we've seen healing in and through our lives, it's still possible to be hindered by mindsets that limit our expectations for healing in places where God hasn't limited himself. We usually don't even realize a limitation is there until we come up against it. For example, if I believe that healing is only a tool for evangelism, I may step out and pray for a limping lacrosse player, but I will walk by a brother or sister limping up the stairs at church.

Thankfully, God is not restricted to act only according to my understanding or expectation—but I want to be more like Jesus. I want to think like him, believe like he does, and have the same expectation for healing he has. Any belief we have that limits God deserves our attention.

This chapter will examine some of the remaining areas of confusion and misunderstanding that often surround healing and can hinder us from believing like Jesus. Fortunately for us (and the chapter's length), calling out wrong beliefs that influence our thinking is often sufficient in breaking their power. Most of a lie's strength is found in our ignorance of its presence.

It's time to "demolish arguments and every pretension that sets itself up against the knowledge of God" and "take captive every thought to make it obedient to Christ" (2 Cor. 10:5). So let's get to it. Let's displace darkness with the light of truth and clean out any remaining cobwebs regarding healing.

QUESTION #1:
Is Healing Only an Evangelistic Tool?

Our encounter with the lacrosse team in the opening story was incredible. What started as a simple step of faith in praying for one guy turned into sharing with half the team about Jesus. But what if the story had ended differently? What if I shared about Jesus and no one responded? Or what if I prayed for a few ankles and that was it? In other words, would I be satisfied with healing simply for healing's sake, or is it always meant to be a step toward salvation?

There is a prominent teaching in parts of the church that healing and the gifts of the Spirit are at work only in places where people have yet to hear the gospel. From this teaching, I believed that healing was only an evangelistic tool. I have since learned that healing is far more about God's love for us than it is about winning souls, though the two often go hand in hand. Healing demonstrates God's immense love and an individual's inherent worth; God loves to heal because he loves to see us whole and healthy. When we pray with someone for healing, there are times when it's natural and appropriate to share the message of salvation. And there are times when it's not. As we partner with the Holy Spirit, we seek to say and do what he's saying and doing and, conversely, not to say or do something he isn't saying or doing.

There's one other problem with the idea that healing is only for evangelism: It's contrary to Scripture. The Bible encourages us to pray for fellow believers. James directed us to "pray for each other so that you may be healed" (5:16). Furthermore, as believers we are distinguished from the rest of the world by the presence of God, the great Healer himself. God is in the midst of believers, and in his presence are health and healing (see Matt. 18:20). This means that the church has the potential to be the healthiest place on earth. Healing demonstrates God's love and kindness to those in need—whoever they are, wherever we find them, and whatever their beliefs.

QUESTION #2:
Don't Healings Only Happen "Over There"?

As anyone who's traveled in the developing world knows, prayers for divine intervention come easily when in traffic. There's something about weaving around motorbikes, pedestrians, and the occasional oxcart that naturally solicits our prayers. Be it the overcrowded boat with a crew member whose job is to bail water or the airplane that makes you think, *Huh, that's a lot of duct tape,* developing world transportation inspires intercession in a way its developed-world counterpart does not. In general, life in the developing world provides ample motivation to pray prayers normally left un-offered when at home.

It's more than increased opportunities for prayer that I noticed when away from home—my prayers actually felt different. I *expected* my prayers to impact my surroundings and change situations in a way I never had in America. What was behind this faith boost? Why did I suddenly believe my prayers were powerful and effective in Mumbai in a way I didn't in Minneapolis? There are several contributing factors, but at the root of it is something I call an "over there" mindset. An over-there mindset expects God to heal, perform miracles, and generally interact with us *over there* in a way he doesn't here. This mindset is based on two typically unaddressed ideas:

1. Miraculous healings simply don't occur in the United States or developed world.
2. We don't need miraculous healing in the United States or developed world.

Testimonies are fuel and accelerant to our faith. They are the cords of dry wood that keep us burning as we recount God's faithfulness, *and* they are the gasoline that ignites our imaginations, inspiring us to pray in ways we never have before. While I ate up every miraculous testimony and healing story I heard from missionaries—stories that always occurred outside of America—I was unaware of any healing testimonies that took place within the U.S. I assumed miracles didn't occur in America simply because I had never heard of any. The fruit of my ignorance revealed itself in my prayer life. I believed God would intervene outside of the normal patterns, laws, and structures of life only when I was away from home.

Of course, we need God wherever we find ourselves, but we're often less aware of that need when in a familiar environment. When I hop into my car in the United States, I don't think about my need for divine protection like I do when driving in India. Clearly, things that are a threat-level two in America can easily jump to a threat-level five in places where emergency first responders, medical care, and general infrastructure aren't in place.

Fortunately for us, it's not our proximity to medical care that moves God's hand. Nor does the presence of doctors prevent miracles—one of the main recorders of miracles in the New Testament, and the author of the books of Luke and Acts, was a doctor. Though God is certainly aware of my need (see Matt. 6:8), he's not motivated by it. Instead, he is motivated by compassion.

Our heavenly Father's character, nature, and will for healing are unchanging, regardless of where we find ourselves. What changes are our expectations for healing. God isn't limited by location, but there is a direct correlation between our expectation (hope), our action (faith), and the result (healing). He doesn't choose to heal based on available medical options. He already chose to heal and demonstrated that decision at the cross.

God does not draw a distinction between "here" and "there." He is the same in Boston, Brazil, and Baghdad.

QUESTION #3:
I Thought Healing Only Happened in the Bible?

Growing up, my favorite book of the Bible was Acts. I imagined the thrill of witnessing Peter raise the dead woman to life or learning through firsthand observation what distinguished Paul's "extraordinary" miracles from regular ones (see Acts 9:40, 19:11). Unfortunately for many within the church, miracles in general and specifically healing are limited to Bible reading. A close friend of the "over there" mindset that limits *where* God wants to heal is the "only then" mindset, which limits *when* God miraculously heals. Only-then thinking, more formally called cessationism, argues that the gifts of the Spirit ceased with the death of the original twelve apostles.[31] The basis of this argument is that miracles were necessary to validate the apostles' authority and are now unnecessary due to Scripture's canonization.

It's outside the scope of this book to counter cessationism. However, it is worth mentioning that Jesus encouraged us to view miracles as validation of his identity and message. In reference to the miracles he performed, Jesus said, "Believe me when I say that I am in the Father and the Father is in me; *or at least believe on the evidence of the works themselves"* (John 14:11, emphasis added).

Yet validating Jesus, the apostles, or even the Bible is not the only reason for miracles. Jesus expressly came to destroy the devil's works (1 John 3:8), works easily identifiable by their telltale trail of death, destruction, and loss (John 10:10). When Jesus healed people, it both validated his messianic identity *and* destroyed the devil's works. This is important to us because Jesus continues to destroy the works of the devil today—through us. We are the ones who now carry that great charge. Jesus commissioned us in Mark 16:17–18:

---

31. Such as the gifts listed in 1 Cor. 12 and Rom. 12.

*And these signs will accompany those who believe: In my name
they will drive out demons; they will speak in new tongues;
they will pick up snakes with their hands; and when they drink
deadly poison, it will not hurt them at all; they will place their
hands on sick people, and they will get well.*

It doesn't matter when you live—if you've put your faith in Jesus,
you fall into the "those who believe" category. Healing is for here
and now, and it comes through you and me.

QUESTION #4:
Are Medical Healings Lesser Healings?

A few years ago, I was in the act of taking a couple of aspirin, water
glass in one hand and pills in the other, when I felt that little internal
check I've learned to recognize as God's warning sign. I halted what
I was doing and asked him the reason for the stop sign. God gently
showed me that I was taking aspirin because I had placed greater
trust in a pharmaceutical fix than I had in the Holy Spirit's healing
power. The issue wasn't the aspirin. The issue was my heart motivation in taking it—fear was my motivator. I quickly repented for my
lack of faith and then felt a green light to take the aspirin.

On the other hand (or in this case, shoulder), around the same time
as the aspirin incident, I threw a football and felt a pop in my shoulder
that caused searing pain. For two weeks, I prayed every day for healing and walked around declaring, "God's going to heal my shoulder!"
Finally my roommate confronted me. She kindly pointed out that God
provided doctors, and it was high time I saw one. Her words hit my
heart as I suddenly saw that my bold statements and prayers were *not
based* in faith or the Lord's leading, but they were an attempt to *prove*
my faith and *earn* my healing. A few months of physical therapy later,
my shoulder tendons instead of my hand kept my joint in its socket—

a huge improvement. But the fact remains that my wrong mindset kept me in agony for weeks. Again, the issue wasn't about doctors but about my motivation, heart position, and listening to God.

Our thinking surrounding doctors and medicine can limit us from receiving healing in ways God does not limit us. Often in the United States, we turn to God for a miracle only after we've exhausted our medical options. It is possible to focus solely on medical care and ignore the supernatural healing grace available to us, and it is also possible to ignore the great medical options God has provided for us because of a spiritual bias that deems a doctor's visit "less holy." Either extreme is dangerous and contrary to our heavenly Father's desire for his children.

Most of us have more experience and are more comfortable with visiting a doctor than praying for healing. Seeing a doctor is the in-grained default response when we're sick, which means seeking God first in times of sickness requires breaking old habits and creating new ones. Doing what's worked in the past (e.g., visiting a doctor or undergoing a course of treatment) is absolutely fine so long as it's in alignment with God's direction. To be very clear, medical healings are not lesser healings. Wisdom and knowledge come from God (Prov. 2:6), so doctors and other medical professionals possess knowledge and wisdom that come from God himself. Any thinking that suggests miraculous healings are holier or that seeing a doctor requires less faith effectively leads us out of grace (supernatural empowerment) and into striving (qualifying works), introducing us to a contorted, disempowering religious mindset. And religious mindsets always tell us to do more or that human effort is required in place of God doing the work.[32]

---

32. To clarify, it is not wrong to seek or continue medical treatment. Sometimes this is exactly what God leads us to do. It's not about *what* we do but *why* we're doing it. Are you continuing treatment because you're afraid you're mistaken, that God isn't good, or that the issue will return? Or are you continuing treatment because God is leading you to do so? Seek medical attention when appropriate.

Healing is not formulaic. It requires a relationship to determine where and how God is leading us, particularly when we are taking a path that seems illogical or contrary to worldly wisdom. Whenever we feel sickness knocking at the door or receive a negative report from the doctor, we have a powerful opportunity to choose our response: faith or fear. It isn't right or wrong to pursue a miraculous healing or to visit the doctor, so long as we are following what God is saying. So the first step is asking ourselves if we're being led by his voice, fear, or a religious mindset seeking to prove something. Replacing sound medical care with a spiritual formula is dangerous and sometimes can be an attempt to force God's hand, but it's equally dangerous to ignore the promises of Scripture by placing greater faith in a doctor's report than in God's healing power.

Due to the sensitivity of this subject, I want to reiterate that if you need a doctor, go to the doctor. Even though I've seen a number of broken bones healed in front of me, if I fall and break my leg, I'll pray for healing *and* go to the ER. Furthermore, while I will hold someone to a biblically defined standard or principle, I will never risk another's health or safety over my conviction. God teaches each of us different things at different times. In many cases, he may be teaching the person next to me something he isn't teaching me right now, and what's okay for her may not be okay for me. Whether I undergo a recommended course of treatment or feel led to abstain from it at the time, my decision needs to be rooted in a deep knowing of God's unwavering and unending goodness toward me.[33]

God is incredibly creative. He will bring healing through any number of options, be it a child's prayer or a surgeon's skill. When we are sick, a friend is suffering, or there are questions surrounding a child's health, we have an opportunity to lay our anger, offense,

---

33. Navigating personal conviction is Paul's subject in Rom. 14—well worth a read in light of our subject.

and fear at the foot of the cross—the place where disease was destroyed—and offer a prayer of faith that says simply, "Father, I trust you." If healing comes miraculously through prayer, God the Healer is glorified. If healing comes through a doctor, God the Healer is glorified. However healing occurs, the nature of our loving heavenly Father, *Jehovah-Rapha,* is revealed.

QUESTION #5:
Does Healing Condone My Current Lifestyle?

California has a health-conscious reputation. Maybe it was the constant sunshine or the yearlong access to fresh produce, but somehow I came to consider a detox cleanse a "fun" activity. In addition to healthier eating habits, living there for five years led me to think about health in general instead of just healing. My dream is no longer just to see people healed of cancer but for cancer to be eradicated, not just for malaria to be treated effectively but for even its memory to be forgotten, and for childhood diseases to become a thing of the distant past. Imagine with me entire regions where people don't get sick, where accidents don't happen, and where healing isn't needed.

My hopes and prayers are aimed at these dreams, but they're balanced by an awareness of current reality. As we discussed in chapter 8 regarding the origin of illness, there are natural laws that govern our physical bodies. If I jump, gravity applies; if I eat a diet high in unhealthy fats, I set myself up for heart problems; and if I don't sleep, my body becomes vulnerable to infection. God is extremely gracious and kind. He heals us whether our sickness is directly related to our own decision-making or not. Mindsets that suggest his grace gives me permission to live an unhealthy lifestyle miss the point of health and healing entirely. God's healing grace covers our mistakes and empowers us to live healthy lifestyles; it does not give us license to ignore the natural, God-created order he set in place. In other words, if God heals me of lifestyle-induced diabetes, that healing is not divine enablement to continue living an unhealthy lifestyle. It is a holy reset button that provides me with an opportunity to establish new habits and effectively steward my healing. This doesn't mean I am cut off from God's grace or mercy if I've made the same mistake dozens of times, but as I mature, I grow in my ability to steward the grace imparted to me.

In no way am I suggesting that we need to live with an injury or illness that is the result of our actions or lifestyle. It's important that we nip in the bud any thinking that says, *I deserve this,* or *This is the natural consequence.* We never need to live with natural consequences because we have a supernatural God. I needed a little help with this mindset not that long ago. After a week of extensive travel with early flights and late nights, I came home feeling a cold coming on. As I lay in bed, I heard God say, "Why don't you ask me to heal this?" His question revealed that I hadn't asked for healing because I knew the cold was a natural consequence of my choices. I repented of my self-punishing attitude and for allowing something that Jesus died to destroy to remain in my body. I went to sleep and woke up fully restored.

I love the idea of Christians leading the charge in healthy living combined with a healthy healing theology. From people like Bill and Beni Johnson, Randy Clark, Chris Gore, and Joaquin Evans, I've learned to live by the following three-point health model. This model dispels the lie that grace gives us license to live an unhealthy lifestyle, but it empowers us to seek God even if our sickness was caused by our own choices:

1. Live preventively—eat well, sleep, and exercise. Take care of yourself in the first place.
2. If a need arises, pray for and expect God's supernatural intervention.
3. Seek proper medical care when appropriate.

It's that simple. The Bible says that my body is the place where God resides (see 1 Cor. 6:19–20), and I'm committed to providing him with a stay at the Ritz.

QUESTION #6:
Does God Heal Me for My Testimony?

In the middle of a trying circumstance, it's very tempting to pray a "God, if you get me through this/heal me, I will—" prayer. I prayed for years, "God, if you heal me, I'll go to the nations." In fact, my first thought when I was healed was, *This is incredible!* My second thought was, *I really hope I like the nations.*

While this kind of bartering prayer is typically born of a good but desperate heart, it's also an attempt to regain a measure of control in an area in which we feel powerless. This prayer also unintentionally insinuates that God is not already fully invested in helping or healing us.

I'm not saying it's innately sinful to pray this way—bartering and bargaining are part of the grieving process when battling a chronic illness or when someone we love is suffering—but what is dangerous is when we begin to think that God will heal us *because* of the testimony.

A belief that says, "God will heal me so I can _____ [insert your end of the deal here]," creates a boundary around *why* God wants to heal us. It greatly downplays his compassion toward us. God will certainly turn your illness into something good, but there's a significant difference between "God uses all things for good" and a mindset that says, "He heals me so I can keep my end of the bargain."

Any belief that suggests it is better for us or for those around us that we're sick is wrong. God heals you because he loves you, not so you can more effectively witness to others.

QUESTION #7:
Does My Health Disqualify Me from Praying?

Recently, I was hit hard by a nasty sinus infection that left me in bed for several days and sent me to the doctor. Twice. In years past, being sick made me feel disqualified from praying for the sick. Who was I to pray for healing when I needed it?

The idea that our own health qualifies or disqualifies us from praying for others is both extremely common and entirely unfounded. This mindset suggests an unbiblical prerequisite to praying for healing—a concept that sounds alarmingly similar to the belief that we need to be clean and pure before we can approach God to clean and purify us. Likewise, this mindset seeks to disqualify us from something we didn't, and couldn't, qualify ourselves for in the first place. In the same way that it isn't our own righteousness that qualifies us to enter God's kingdom, it isn't our own health that qualifies us to pray for healing.

The devil wants us tired out and discouraged. When we respond to his attempts to discourage us by praying for healing even though we're sick or hurting, it's like a kick in his face.

I recently heard of a woman who is a quadriplegic and confined to a wheelchair, yet she still prays for and sees many people healed. Instead of allowing her present condition to disqualify her, she boldly demonstrates the reality that the kingdom of God cannot be stopped.

In addition, there is untold power in standing confidently, even defiantly, on the Word of God *before* we see it manifest in our lives.

Instead of allowing our own battle with illness to make us feel inadequate, we can once again trust in God's grace and power to work through us even in our weakness (2 Cor. 12:9). God qualified us. A cough, cold, or cancer can't disqualify us from praying for healing.

QUESTION #8:
Does Pursuing Healing Mean I'm Ungrateful?

"It's been a long time," I said to a friend over Skype. "How are you?"

"You know—praise God—I'm doing much better than I was. God's really brought me through that health issue of a year ago." Her reply was a veiled response for, "I'm doing okay but not great."

"I'm so glad to hear that," I answered and I truly was. It'd been a rough road and a cancer scare at far too young an age. But I knew the response I was getting wasn't the whole story. "Really, how are you doing?"

This time I got the full answer; the tumor was gone and the margins clear, but a car accident the previous year still meant chronic neck pain.

"Friend," I interrupted, "let's pray for your neck."

"No, no, *no*. Please don't worry about that. God has already done so much in my life. The cancer is gone—the neck I can live with."

My heart went out to her. The lie she believed was one I'd firmly held for years. "God won't think you're ungrateful for healing the cancer if we pray for your neck. His blood covers that, too." We prayed, and all her remaining pain, both the physical pain in her neck from the car accident and the emotional pain that came from withholding part of her heart from the Lord, disappeared.

Even if their kids already ate breakfast and lunch that day, parents aren't upset when their children come hungry to the dinner table. In fact, parents recognize a child's absence at dinner as a signal that something's wrong. In the same way that wanting dinner doesn't make a child ungrateful for his previous meals, pursuing further healing doesn't make us ungrateful for what God's already done. Ingratitude comes from devaluing or not recognizing what we've received. We live with thanksgiving for what God has done, but we continue to press on toward all our Father has for us.

QUESTION #9:
If My Pain Is Back, Did I Lose My Healing?

Several nights ago, a few friends and I sat eating *carne asada* fajitas (one of my favorite things) while talking about healing (another of my favorite things). The conversation progressed from getting healed to staying healed or, more specifically, reappearing symptoms and "lost" healings. One friend shared her own healing process with details I hadn't heard.

At age twelve, my friend's autonomic nervous system (the part of your nervous system responsible for the things your body controls unconsciously like heart rate and digestion) shut down, and by nineteen she was diagnosed with thirteen different conditions ranging from sleep apnea to several genetic diseases. Contrary to the doctors' prognosis, God promised her she would be healed in five months. After she walked through a good deal of emotional healing, the promise was realized as her doctor gave her a clean bill of health exactly five months later. However, her story didn't end there. After she'd received the all clear, her symptoms returned one by one over the next few weeks, and they felt just as real and frightening as they had before her healing. In the midst of her fear and physical pain, she heard God ask, "Are you going to believe me or the symptom?" She chose to believe God and said, simply and calmly to each symptom, "No," and it left, usually within minutes. Nine years later, she's a vibrant and healthy woman.

Many people who are healed never experience their symptoms again. Yet there are cases like my friend's when, after receiving either a measure of healing or complete breakthrough, the person begins to experience her old symptoms again. In light of familiar pain, it's easy to conclude there was a mistake, the healing never occurred, that an adrenaline and emotional high masked the problem, or that the healing happened but was somehow "lost." Our response in this moment is extremely important: Is fear allowed to direct our thoughts and actions, or do we stand confidently on God's unchanging nature in spite of how things appear?

At some level, sickness and pain are enemy territory. They are the contested areas of our lives. They are the places of great faith and trust in the midst of mystery and uncertainty, *and* they're places of doubt and fear—sometimes all on the same day. Contested areas aren't to be worried about; they are the exciting places where the full victory of the cross is being made manifest. When we are healed, it is as much a spiritual victory as a physical one. This makes our healing the strategic place for a counterattack. The place of our most recent victory is more vulnerable than ground long held and heavily fortified. It's here the enemy strikes by introducing fear and doubt, sometimes even mimicking old pains and symptoms. He will do anything to convince us to abandon our newly won territory so he can reestablish his old position.

Even more than an attack on our physical bodies, recurring pain or "lost" healing is an attack on our identity. My symptoms never returned, but my thoughts underwent an all-out assault when I experienced a normal physical or emotional low such as a post–mission trip letdown. Ever so subtly I'd begin to question if I would recover from my cold or if I was sick with something far more serious. The revelation of God's desire to heal *me* and his personally demonstrated love and power in my life were extremely threatening to the devil—even more threatening than perfect health. As I entertained these thoughts masquerading as logic and reason, they began to feel true and I'd start to believe that God never wanted to heal me in the first place. Counterattack is more about causing us to question our identity as the beloved sons and daughters of a good Father than it is about our health.

Here are a few keys to help you if you received a measure of breakthrough or complete healing, but you feel symptoms or pain returning:

1. **Ask God to remind you of what he did for you.** Start by focusing on the one who heals.

2. **Speak out loud the truth about God's faithfulness and that he finishes everything he starts** (see Phil. 1:6).

3. **Take every thought captive.** Do not entertain any thoughts or lies that are attacking your mind (see 2 Cor. 10:5).

4. **Listen to testimonies of healing.** This will encourage your heart and remind you of God's faithfulness.

5. **Spend time with encouraging friends.** Invite like-minded friends to encourage you, and borrow some of their faith. Allow their confidence in God's promises to speak more loudly than your fears.

6. **Take a break from spending time with those who do not believe in healing.** Their doubts and well-meaning advice can be harmful to us when we're vulnerable. There will be time to share with them after we've reinforced our victory but not while we're walking it out.

7. **Worship.** Worship brings us into God's presence and fills our hearts with courage. It also provides the space for him to minister his perfect love in the places of our fear.

God won't take back your healing, and the enemy can't undo it. Take heart, my friend. Resist the devil and he will flee (Jas. 4:7).

In the face of recurring symptoms, there can also be a strong temptation to return to the familiar safety of a physician's care. This is particularly true for those of us new to the concept of miraculous healing. Sometimes doctors will encourage us to treat something God healed because they don't understand the miraculous. While this may appear wise, like a nation diplomatically recognizing a rogue state, it can validate something illegally present. I'm not suggesting you ignore your doctor's advice—do not ignore your physician—but prayerfully consider the doctor's advice in light of what God has done. If you decide to continue treatment, do so with faith and confidence in God's healing grace instead of fear of your condition returning. And don't worry. The Holy Spirit will lead you to what's best. Listen to his voice *and* the doctor's.

Like a Brit in the States who regularly tries to get in on the wrong side of the car, walking out our healing takes time as we unlearn long-held habits and thought patterns. It took me well over a year to begin thinking like my physically healthy friends. It took even longer to relearn my body's signals and healthy physical limits. Just because I could surf at sunrise, stay up past midnight, and fill all available hours in between with class, work, and fun didn't mean it was a good idea. While that's probably obvious to someone who grew up with a normally functioning body, it wasn't for me. In the midst of this relearning process, a number of times fear knocked on the door of my heart. Each time I had a decision to make as to whether or not I would open that door. An essential part of my learning process was my daily prayer time, where I sat and asked the Holy Spirit, "How do we do today healthy?" I also needed the loving support of friends and family.

Battles require bravery, which isn't the absence of fear but courage in the face of it. We are all afraid at times. We all need reminding of God's work in our lives. But we are not left to figure it out on our own. Our heavenly Father is with us every step of the way. Healing is an extremely personal encounter with our perfectly loving God. We exchange the things broken and hurting in our bodies for his love and grace in the most tangible way possible. But even more than the newly functioning kidney or the freedom to bend over without pain, we receive his incredible love in an intimate, knowable meeting with his grace. We won't "lose" our healing because of fear or a bump in the road. Instead, in our moments of uncertainty, we turn to him and receive fresh grace to stand on the truth of what he's done and our identity as the beloved one for whom he did it. Jesus paid for your healing two thousand years ago. He won't take it back now.

Not everyone will experience recurring pain, but if you do, you'll be ready for it.

QUESTION #10:
When Is It Time to Give Up?

Just a couple of days ago, a friend pulled me aside at a party to talk with me about her health. After several years of medical treatment and countless prayers for healing, she's still far from 100 percent. I listened as she described the very legitimate emotional and mental pain of this ongoing process. In addition to validating her pain, the greatest thing I could offer her was encouragement to continue.

Chronic illness, particularly the kind that doesn't have a diagnosis or treatment, is extremely challenging on every front—mentally, emotionally, *and* physically. It can be easier to believe that God sent an illness than it is to live in the tension of fully believing he will heal us—despite the daily pain and reality of that illness. When the situation and God's truth are not in alignment, there is only one option: Keep going.

Holding on to the truth of God's healing power when everything else in our lives screams the opposite is not foolishness but a violent and bold act of faith. There are some days when it's easy and some days when, frankly, it's not. On the days when we're hit with another disappointing setback, miss out on yet another highly anticipated activity, or the pain is especially intense, we need to give ourselves permission to acknowledge the emotional, mental, and physical hurt we're experiencing and be very, very real with God. It's entirely permissible to be in process. But while in process, we can't give up.

Persistence defiantly says, "God is good and faithful," when every ounce of reason and logic tells us otherwise. It enables us to keep going when everything else says to stop. This is Jesus' message in the parable of the Persistent Widow (Luke 18:1–8) and his teaching on prayer in Matthew 7, a place where we are told, "Keep on asking, and you will receive what you ask for. Keep on seeking, and you will find. Keep on knocking, and the door will be opened to you" (v. 7 NLT). We do not knock once or twice politely and then walk away. No! We knock until the door is opened. Don't stop praying for and believing in God's extreme goodness and desire to heal *you*. Speak out the truth and promises of Scripture even when they don't seem true. Read the Psalms until you hear your own voice expressed in one of those prayers, and then read that psalm out loud over yourself daily. Invite others to remind you of the truth and encourage you when you forget. And be careful not to accuse God—our heavenly Father is on our side and is the one who releases the necessary grace to keep going. Remember, if it's not too good to be true, it's not the end of the story.[34]

We live in the very real and mysterious pressure of the kingdom of God here and on the way. Pursuing our healing is part of bringing heaven to earth and living a life that fully glorifies God. Persistence in prayer is powerful spiritual warfare. It's far from easy, but you weren't made to accomplish easy things. You were made to do the impossible.

---

34. Not surprisingly, Bill Johnson taught me about persistent prayer. He has some great teachings on the subject, and I recommend checking them out.

CHAPTER KEYS

Our heavenly Father loves to see us living abundant, full lives, which by definition means they are healthy ones. Any restriction we've placed on healing that God hasn't needs to go. He heals because he loves us and hates disease. He heals in New York and New Delhi. He heals fiery, committed Christians and those who don't believe in him and may never believe in him. God is much more concerned with healing and health than he is with receiving credit. He heals through doctors and medicine and through declarations and prayers. He heals whether we brought the pain on ourselves or not. And he will work through us regardless of our current state of health. What God does is an extension of his character, which is both permanent and unchanging.

An interesting aspect of human nature is that it's often easier to believe the negative things said about us than the positive ones. We have to consciously train ourselves to receive compliments and encouragement. Likewise, we can actively train ourselves to think about healing the way God thinks about it.

Get healthy however he leads you. Stand confidently in faith instead of fear. Pray for healing expectantly. Don't get weary in coming before the Lord or believing today is the day. Our mighty heavenly Father is for us—what could ever stand against us?

MINISTRY

This chapter contained many mindsets that I had to work through myself or that I'm frequently asked about. It is in no way exhaustive, nor does it provide an answer for every question. Instead, I hope it starts a conversation between you and the Lord about any areas where something you believe may be keeping you from pursuing healing as Jesus modeled it. I encourage you to stop and take a minute to ask the Holy Spirit, the one who searches the mind of Christ and reveals all things to us (1 Cor. 2:10–16), to shine light on any remaining mindset or thought that limits you. It really comes down to this: Which of us would knowingly choose to think something about healing that Jesus doesn't think?

Father, thank you so much for your unequalled heart for me, passion for healing, and commitment to see me become the person you created me to be. I want to think like you do about healing. Right now, I invite your Holy Spirit to come illuminate any thoughts that limit me from walking in the full healing grace Jesus made available to me. Lead me in paths of truth and righteousness that bring honor to your name and freedom to your children. Amen.

If you've received healing or a measure of healing but old symptoms have returned, I encourage you to ask the Holy Spirit to help you stand confidently on Jesus' finished work. Tell the symptoms to leave and recite out loud God's promises. He always finishes what he starts.

13

THE QUESTION OF
HOW: PART 1

...

"All right, can everyone who isn't standing for healing please raise their hand?"

Arms go up across the crowded room. After two hours of teaching about healing, a new subject for the majority of those present, I am pleased to see an engaged and ready response. "Awesome! Thank you for volunteering to be the ministry team."

Nervous laughter flits through the room, but it can't dampen the group's growing anticipation.

"God's here and loves healing. It's going to be so easy. Don't worry if you've never done this or don't know what you're doing. If you love Jesus and have compassion for the person in front of you, you're qualified and ready.

"Don't pray yet. The first step is to ask the person receiving prayer a couple of questions; we need a target for our prayers. Ask the person in front of you what hurts or his or her current pain level from one to ten—one is little pain; ten is excruciating pain. That's all the information we need right now. No medical histories. We will rein-terview the person after we pray to find out what God's doing."

Conversations buzz as people form groups of threes and fours, enthusiastically following my instructions.

Observing the controlled chaos, I smile from ear to ear. I love watching the transformation that occurs in believers over the course of a few hours of teaching and testimonies. We want to be used by God, to see the kingdom come, miracles happen, and the sick healed through *our* hands. As we hear biblical teaching that gives us permission to heal the sick, testimonies that encourage and inspire us to do it ourselves, and finally are given an opportunity to act, the results are nothing short of miraculous. In fact, James tells us that the prophet Elijah was just like us. Elijah believed his prayers would impact the world, and they did (see 1 Kings 17; Jas. 5:17–18). So, too, our prayers bring heaven to earth and work powerfully among us.

"Okay," I tell the eager group. "Now that you know where to aim your prayers, you have ten seconds to pray. Remember, you don't need to convince God to do something he wants to do. Declare healing. Invite the kingdom of God to come into that knee, or back, or whatever it is in Jesus' name. Ready? Pray!"

I don't give them ten seconds to pray. I give them eight. "Ask the person what he or she is experiencing—maybe heat, electricity, or a decrease in pain? We want to direct our focus onto what God is doing. Ask them to test it out. If it was a hurt knee, have them squat; if it was their back, have them bend over."

Throughout the room people test their injuries and ailments. Several people bend over to touch their toes. One girl starts doing push-ups, and a young man bolts out the side door to run laps around the building to test his exercise-induced asthma. Cheering erupts from several groups. Others cry and laugh, overcome by the awareness of God's love and the absence of their pain. I ask for every group who saw an improvement of at least 80 percent to wave both arms. Across the room, arms wave.

"That's so incredible! Thank you, Jesus!" I shout, unable to contain myself. "Let's go for another round of healing. If there's any pain remaining, pray again."[35]

Again, the groups pray for about ten seconds before testing the injury or ailment. (Of course, some things cannot be checked on the spot. In these cases, time and doctors validate a healing.) This time I bring the microphone around to different groups so everyone can hear what God did.

Newly returned from his laps around the building, the guy who suffered from asthma is eager to share: "They prayed for me and the only way I'd know is by running. So we—" He points to a man thirty years his senior who was part of the team praying for him. "—went on a little jog. Normally I'd be wheezing after one lap, and my chest would start getting tight, but I didn't feel any of that, so we ran three more. I feel great!" The room erupts in cheers as we corporately celebrate his healing.

Even more than I love seeing people healed (which is a lot), these are my favorite moments. The audience that evening underwent a massive transformation from passive, even skeptical, observers to a unified group actively participating in healing, celebrating one another's victories, and corporately enjoying God's presence. The apostle Paul's words to the Ephesians became real right in front of us as we were equipped "for works of service, so that the body of Christ may be built up until we all reach unity . . . attaining to the whole measure of the fullness of Christ" (4:12–13). After a few more

---

35. While we encourage people to test the body part that was prayed for so we can identify a change, we never risk someone's safety or pressure a person into doing something he or she is uncomfortable with. The Holy Spirit often leads people in faith to courageously do something that used to cause pain or a reaction, but that's his job, not ours.

testimonies, I officially end the evening, but that doesn't stop the party. People continue praying for one another, calling people who need prayer, and lingering in the unified, joyful atmosphere that comes with the Holy Spirit's presence. We are there until the maintenance crew kicks us out.

• • •

Long before I led others to pray for healing, I was like most of the people in the room that evening: committed to Christ but completely unaware of their God-given authority over sickness or the effectiveness of their prayers to bring the manifest presence of the kingdom. The last hurdle for me to jump when it came to praying for healing was the most practical one: how to do it. In the next few chapters, we will look at a basic healing model as well as keys that will help us before, during, and after we pray.

This chapter will help us grow in confidence and effectiveness before we say a word in prayer. But first, a word of warning: It's very likely that after you finish reading the next couple of chapters, you will want to pray for every person you see.

PRIVATE DEDICATION WINS PUBLIC VICTORIES

I love the Olympics. It doesn't matter if it's a sport I regularly follow, like tennis or basketball, or something I've never watched in my life, like field hockey or handball. If it's on, I'm watching. During the last Summer Olympics, a sportswear commercial featuring swimming legend Michael Phelps stuck with me. The commercial consisted of darkly lit scenes of Phelps training by himself in a pool or gym. Sounds of cheering and an announcer calling another Olympic win could be heard in the background as words flashed on the screen: "It's what you do in the dark that puts you in the light."

There's no shortcut to an Olympic medal. We may witness the shining moments of success, but they occur only because of the countless unseen hours of preparation and training. The same is true of healing. Healing flows from intimacy. There's no shortcut to intimacy; intimacy requires time. Jesus said it this way: "But when you pray, go into your room, close the door and pray to your Father, who is unseen. Then your Father, who sees what is done in secret, will reward you" (Matt. 6:6). Our time in the secret place is where we grow in relationship with the Father, learn to believe like Jesus, sharpen our hearts to recognize what the Holy Spirit is doing, and win victories over back pain, cancer, and hepatitis before we pray for a single person. What happens in public is because of our time in private.

To be clear, we can't "earn" more healings in our personal quiet times, nor can we earn something Jesus freely gives. There is no formula for breakthrough. Instead, time in the secret place renews our minds, encourages our hearts, and imparts the necessary strength to live in the tension of the kingdom of God here and on the way. It's where we are reminded of God's goodness when we face defeat and where we celebrate our victories. It's the place we learn to believe like Jesus does about healing. The most important prayer to heal the sick doesn't actually involve a person who needs healing. It's not in front of a crowd or with a microphone at a church meeting. The most important prayer to heal the sick is offered alone on our knees with no earthly witnesses.

ACCORDING TO YOUR FAITH

The second thing to remember when praying for healing is that God responds to faith. Faith can work both for us and against us. In his hometown, Jesus "could not do any miracles there, except lay his hands on a few sick people and heal them. He was amazed at their lack of faith" (Mark 6:5–6). To clarify, this does not mean there were some people Jesus couldn't heal, but the lack of faith in his hometown prevented people from coming to him for healing (see Acts 10:38). If faith opens the spiritual environment and turns the tide in spiritual warfare, then the absence of faith can have the opposite effect. Without faith, we can unintentionally close off our hearts to what God wants to do. Lack of faith shuts down our prayers before they're ever offered.

This doesn't mean healing is impossible in situations where there is little or no faith present—Jesus still healed people in an environment characterized by an extreme lack of faith. It means that what we believe becomes the limit to how we think God wants to act. Let's call that limit our *faith ceiling.*

Our faith ceiling dictates what we will and won't go after and hinders us from praying boldly or even praying in the first place. Our faith ceiling will keep us from stepping out in places where God has called us to take risks, and we often won't even realize that it's happening. The good news is that the Holy Spirit is fully equipped to break through our faith ceiling.

To be entirely honest with you, I have a ton of faith to pray for someone to be healed of a backache or a headache because I've seen it happen so many times, but I have less faith to pray for a cold to be healed, something I haven't seen healed very many times. Since I know that my faith level affects my prayers, I actively work out my faith muscle so it grows. Here are a few practical steps I take to increase my faith:

1. **Ask God for more faith.** This is entirely "legal" and a smart first step (see Luke 17:5).

2. **Fast and pray.** Fasting is terrific at bringing areas of unbelief to the surface. I also spend time asking the Holy Spirit to search me

and reveal any areas of unbelief in my heart. When I do this, I am careful not to become introspective; I listen for about twenty seconds and then move on. God will reveal things at the right time, and I don't need to go digging for them.

3. **Study the Bible.** Nothing imparts faith like reading his Word.

4. **Read and listen to healing testimonies.** I particularly focus on whatever I want to see breakthrough in at the moment. In other words, if I want to see more colds healed, I intentionally listen to testimonies where colds were healed.

5. **Read about/study great healing revivalists.** Two of my favorite healing revivalists to read about are John G. Lake and Smith Wigglesworth. Modern history is full of amazing men and women of God who saw incredible breakthroughs in the realm of healing.

   Unfortunately, some of these men and women fell into error and sin. In the past, I let this keep me from gleaning from their insights and incredible testimonies, but I've since learned it's important to eat the meat and spit out the bones. I can learn from what is good and true *and* from their mistakes and pitfalls so as to avoid them myself.

6. **Thank God for growth before seeing it manifest.** I know that I receive whatever I ask for (Mark 11:24), so I make a conscious decision to thank God even before I see the breakthrough in my life.

7. **Pray for the sick whenever possible.** This is where the rubber meets the road and where I get to see the new strength of my faith muscle.

Talking about faith helps explain what's happening in the spiritual realm when we pray. However, I know how easy it can be to accuse ourselves of having too little faith when we don't see immediate healing. If this discussion brought accusation or self-condemnation to our hearts, we don't have to worry—we just discovered the place where God wants to encounter us with his love. The Holy Spirit wants to crash in on our hurt, anger, and guilt, restoring us to who we were created to be, so we can continually grow in our faith.

It's also important to recognize that not everything that happens when we pray for healing is directly related to us; there are things happening in the spiritual realm that we don't see or understand. God responds immediately to our prayers, but sometimes there is spiritual "interference" or warfare that delays the response from being made manifest on earth—warfare that has nothing to do with our faith ceiling (see Dan. 10). In those instances, our faith protects our hearts from disappointment and discouragement as we eagerly await the answer to appear.

In addition, faith that does not wane in the face of conflicting evidence is called perseverance, and perseverance always breaks through. Undeterred faith is a violent act that turns the tide in spiritual warfare and creates an opening for something that likely wouldn't occur otherwise. This is exactly what happened when Jesus healed the Canaanite woman's daughter:

> Leaving that place, Jesus withdrew to the region of Tyre and Sidon. A Canaanite woman from that vicinity came to him, crying out, "Lord, Son of David, have mercy on me! My daughter is demon-possessed and suffering terribly."

> Jesus did not answer a word. So his disciples came to him and urged him, "Send her away, for she keeps crying out after us."

> He answered, "I was sent only to the lost sheep of Israel."

The woman came and knelt before him. "Lord, help me!" she said.

He replied, "It is not right to take the children's bread and toss it to the dogs."

"Yes it is, Lord," she said. "Even the dogs eat the crumbs that fall from their master's table."

*Then Jesus said to her, "Woman, **you have great faith!** Your request is granted." And her daughter was healed at that moment.*

MATTHEW 15:21-28 (EMPHASIS ADDED)

The Canaanite woman was absolutely desperate. The trauma and horror her daughter regularly experienced must have been excruciating for her to watch. How many nights did she lie awake listening for another attack on her child? How many hours did she spend holding her baby girl and hoping against all hope for her freedom and healing?

In the same way that a bodybuilder needs something to lift in order to demonstrate strength, persistent faith is demonstrated in the face of opposition. If faith is revealed through persistence and risk-taking (stepping beyond our comfort zones), then the Canaanite woman operated at an extremely high level of faith. Mark added that "as soon as she heard about him, a woman whose little daughter was possessed by an impure spirit came and fell at his feet" (7:25). When this mother heard that Jesus could deliver her daughter, she knew her job was to find him and not leave until her daughter was free. And Jesus, who did only what he saw the Father doing, recognized the woman's great faith as evidence of the Father at work and granted her request.[36]

---

36. Interestingly, the only other person Jesus described as having "great faith" was another Gentile whose faith also opened the door to healing (see Luke 7:1-9).

That is an incredible story. Jesus was a man full of compassion and kindness; he cried over the death of his friend, mourned for the fate of Jerusalem, and even raised a dead boy to life because he felt compassion for the mother (see John 11:35; Matt. 23:37-39; Luke 7:11-17). Yet here Jesus seemed to ignore and then insult a desperate mother—a conclusion that must be wrong because it contradicts what we know about Jesus' character and nature. The word commonly translated as "dog" in English is *kynarion,* which is better translated "puppy" or "house pet."[37] It's a term of endearment, not a slur. And as anyone who's had a dog knows, they do indeed gobble up crumbs spilled under the table. What appears to be an insult is actually an invitation. Jesus' comment provoked a response of faith that created an opening in the spiritual realm for a miracle to occur. The mother's faith facilitated her daughter's healing.

Numerous times throughout the Gospels, Jesus declared that someone's faith brought healing (see Mark 5:34, 10:52; Luke 17:19). This doesn't mean that someone's faith changed God's mind—God had already made up his mind to heal from the very creation of the earth (Rev. 13:8)—but that Jesus recognized the spiritual condition altered by the person's faith and commended him for it. As demonstrated by the people seeking Jesus on behalf of their friends or family, our faith can radically impact the lives of those we love. In fact, it isn't necessary that the person in need of healing demonstrate any faith; people with little faith to be healed are often healed. The man who confessed his unbelief saw his son healed (Mark 9:23-25), while Lazarus operated in no faith at all when he was healed—he was dead.

God still heals in spite of a lack of faith. In fact, it's often a healing that releases the faith necessary to believe in God, not the other way around. On the other hand, faith attracts heaven and is one of our

---

37. Strong's 2952.

most powerful weapons to counter the demonic forces that seek to discourage and harm us (see 2 Chron. 16:9; Ps. 34:15). While faith is an extremely important component of our Christian walk in general, and in healing specifically, we should never accuse someone of not having enough faith to be healed. Accusations and assumptions about another person's faith level have the potential to cause the greatest harm when we're praying for healing.

God is obviously able to heal when faith is not present, but our faith empowers us to believe like Jesus, persistently stand in the face of opposition, and partner with God in bringing heaven to earth. Before we pray for someone, we want to direct our attention to the things that build faith. Practically speaking, this can mean respectfully cutting people off if they begin to tell us the reasons they believe they won't be healed. It may seem counterintuitive, but people often share why they think our prayers *won't* bring healing—be it a doctor's prognosis, the years they've suffered from the disease, or the number of times they've been prayed for previously. It's good to draw their attention back to the Lord Jesus and his ultimate victory. We can remind them they don't need to do a thing because Christ did it all already.

Understand that just by your stepping out to pray for someone, the door is already open for God to move mightily.

THE POWER OF THE TESTIMONY

The first two pre-prayer points set us up for the following: Before praying for someone, grab hold of a testimony of a similar healing, and share the story with that person. Testimonies are much more than a faith-building exercise before we pray; they are one of our mightiest weapons of spiritual warfare. We triumph over the enemy "by the blood of the Lamb and by the word of [our] testimony" (Rev. 12:11). When we share a testimony, it's not just a nice story—it's an all-out assault against demonic strongholds. Furthermore, celebrating what God has done actually prophesies what will happen. "For the testimony of Jesus is the spirit of prophecy" (Rev. 19:10 NASB). Like faith, testimonies are powerful in the unseen spiritual realm and create an opening for heaven to come to earth.

Sharing testimonies inspires us, releases faith, and imparts the courage to do something we may have been too afraid to attempt only minutes earlier. One of my favorite testimonies is when Jesus healed the woman subject to bleeding. Mark described the woman as one who "had suffered a great deal under the care of many doctors and had spent all she had, yet instead of getting better she grew worse" (5:26), a story all too familiar to scores of people today. The woman had nothing left and nothing to lose. So when she heard about Jesus, she did the culturally unthinkable. "She came up behind him in the crowd and touched his cloak, because she thought, 'If I just touch his clothes, I will be healed'" (vv. 27–28). And she was. This was the first time a healing from touching Jesus' clothes was recorded in the Bible, but after the woman's healing and her story's inevitable retelling, wherever Jesus went, the sick "begged him to let them touch even the edge of his cloak, and all who touched it were healed" (6:56). The testimony of one woman's healing inspired and emboldened many, many more to be healed in a similar fashion. Hearing a testimony is often all it takes to fill us with the courage to pray expectantly, either again or for the first time. That is a large part of why I love sharing my own healing testimony. If God healed me of an autoimmune disease, he will heal others.

Personally, I have not yet seen a childhood developmental disorder healed. That could make praying for a developmental disorder extremely intimidating for me. It could hinder my expectation, decrease my hope, and lead to a prayer offered with little faith attached to it. All of that *could* happen, but it doesn't happen, and that's because of the power of the testimony. A friend of mine *has* seen substantial improvement in a child he prayed for who had a developmental disorder: The child went from struggling in a special education class one year to catching up to her grade the next, and then she was placed in an advanced class the following year—what an incredible miracle and wonderful testimony to impart hope. Instead of feeling intimidated when presented with the opportunity to pray for someone with a similar condition, I remind myself of the breakthrough my friend witnessed and receive the courage necessary to pray with confidence and boldness.

If you've seen this particular disease healed, share that testimony before you pray for the person. If you haven't, borrow a friend's testimony. And if you don't know a similar testimony offhand, recount some of Jesus' healings from the Bible—he never met a person he couldn't heal. If God has done it before, he'll do it again, and he'll do it through you and me.

FIX YOUR EYES ON THE ONE WHO HEALS

It's the end of the second night of a two-day event in South America, and my team and I can't pray fast enough. Literally. People are healed before my prayer partner/translator can translate for me. Deaf ears open. Pain disappears. People are delivered and set free. It all happens faster than I've ever seen, often before we even say a word in prayer—which is good news for us, if we want to see the end of the line of people waiting for prayer that evening. Longingly I glance over at the front of the stadium where a celebratory worship dance party is underway.

"Pray *más rápido!*" I encourage my partner, who turns his gaze from the ecstatic worshipers and eagerly agrees.

In the midst of our rapid-fire prayer, I feel a tap on my shoulder. I turn and see a woman holding her seven-year-old daughter's hand. Pain distorts the girl's face and her free hand clutches her stomach.

The mother explains that her daughter suffers from terrible stomachaches that make eating extremely painful. The look on the little girl's face breaks my heart. Maybe it is because of the fear in the mother's eyes or maybe it is because I see myself in the girl; whatever the reason, my attention shifts off of Jesus and onto the problem. *Oh, God,* I internally plead. *You have to do this. You have to heal this little girl.*

We pray. The girl's condition doesn't change.

I am shocked. Every person we've prayed for this evening has experienced breakthrough, and here is the one who affects me the most, the person I most want to see healed, a child, and nothing changes. We pray again as desperation rapidly grows inside of me. Again, nothing.

Suddenly the Holy Spirit points out the trap I've fallen into: I've stopped focusing on Jesus and am instead focusing on the problem. The more I fixate on the problem, the bigger it becomes, growing in size until it surpasses my awareness of Jesus' love and power. Though the change is likely imperceptible to anyone watching, I shift my focus back onto Jesus and begin to praise him out loud. "God, thank you that you are so kind and unquestioningly good. Thank you that you already paid for this precious girl's healing. You are her perfectly loving Father. Your name is truly greater than any other."

As I praise God, the girl's face relaxes, the arm once holding her stomach lowers to her side, and she interrupts us to ask her mother for something to eat.

• • •

Faith and fear are opposite sides of the same coin. Both say that something that has not happened will occur. One is belief in what God says, while the other is belief in what the enemy says.

Whatever we grace with our attention graces us with its presence and grows in authority in our lives. In other words, what we focus on gets bigger. The more aware I was of the problem in front of me, the bigger it became. But as I focused on Jesus, the healing that at first seemed so difficult manifested in front of us. When you pray for healing, keep your focus on the Healer instead of the one in need of healing.

Some heavy words lurk out there, waiting to jump on and crush the hearer's hope. Words like *inoperable, malignant, terminal.* While it's unwise to bury our heads in the sand and ignore the problem, it's an equal if not greater problem to lose our sense of perspective by concentrating on the problem instead of on the one who is the solution. We have a big God and a little devil. To live fearlessly, we keep our eyes on the fearless one.

The more attention we give Jesus, the more the things that once seemed so formidable—be it a healing we are desperate to see or a situation that frightens us—lose their power to terrorize and intimidate. Instead of letting sickness set the tone of our prayers, we allow the reality of the resurrected Christ inside of us to lead the way.

VICTORIOUS PRAYERS

Finally, when praying for healing, remember that Jesus already won. God does not need to be convinced to heal. There's no need to beg, plead, or bargain for healing because he already said yes. Christ's victory was sufficient, lacking nothing. We know the ending—God's perfect will shall be accomplished as all things are reconciled in Christ (see 2 Cor. 5:18; Col. 1:20). We're placing a bet on a race that's already run. We have the privilege of praying from a place of absolute victory with all the confidence, boldness, and authority that come with it. This is the last, but in no way least, key to hold on to before praying for healing: Pray from victory, not for victory.

CHAPTER KEYS

Someone once came up to me after a meeting and, in all seriousness, said, "Wow—Christians are the superheroes of people!" I think that sums it up nicely. Of course, there are a few differences between comic book superheroes and Christians, not the least of which is that superheroes are fictional. But like the heroes in our comic books and movies, we are equipped and empowered to see the impossible happen—the very same Spirit who raised Jesus from the dead is alive in us (Rom. 8:11).

When it's time to pray for healing, we will find it a lot easier if we hold on to the keys offered in this chapter. Our private times with the Lord are where we win public victories over sickness and disease. Faith empowers our persistence when everything else tells us to quit. God responds to faith but isn't dependent on it, and we never assume—and never suggest—it was the person's lack of faith that prevented her healing. Instead, we encourage faith through the retelling of testimonies, which inflicts heavy damage on the enemy in spiritual warfare. With an unflinching gaze, we keep our focus on Jesus instead of the problem. And finally, we do all of this from a place of victory. The person who prays with these things in mind is the woman unshaken and confident in her heavenly Father's desire to act on her behalf. It's the man who knows Christ's victory will be evident in every place where the knowledge of the glory of God has yet to shine. It's the Christian brimming with contagious and powerful kingdom life.

I'm not that person all the time. Too often I forget one or two of the truths I've presented in this chapter, and my hope and faith levels ebb and flow more than I'd like. My mind is not fully transformed; I don't yet believe like Jesus in every single area. But I'm getting closer. Today I'm one day nearer to believing like Jesus. I have one more day's experience of God's personal love for me, a love I'm committed to knowing more by the time I crawl into bed than I did this morning. That doesn't make me perfect, but it does make me dangerous to the enemy. The same is true of you.

It's our joy and privilege to partner with God to see his kingdom come. Like Jesus, we get to do the work of our Father. As we learn and grow from experience, we find things that help and hinder that work. I hope these keys encourage you as you pursue a lifestyle of healing. But most important, remember that whenever we pray for healing, our primary aim is not to see a miracle occur but to love, value, and honor the son or daughter of God in front of us.

MINISTRY

You're ready. Even if you don't *feel* ready, you get to see the sick made well when you pray. All that's left to do is praise God for choosing you to live at this unique time and point in history.

Father, thank you for creating me for a time such as this. Thank you that I'm alive at a point in history when the church is waking up to her identity in Christ and the reality of the kingdom here and now. Thank you for not leaving us alone to figure this out but sending us the greatest treasure in heaven: your Holy Spirit. Father, thank you that the sick will be made well when I pray for them, your kingdom will advance, and lives will be transformed. Let heaven come and your will be done in and through me. I pray these things in Jesus' mighty name. Amen.

14

THE QUESTION OF
HOW: PART 2

...

"The kids are asleep," my friend Bryan announces as he returns to the kitchen, where his wife and I are finishing up the dishes. "How about some coffee and a little something sweet?" With a twinkle in his eye, he slyly reaches for a chocolate bar hidden away from small hands.

"Sounds great," I say, folding the dishtowel and watching his precise technique of weighing and grinding the coffee beans.

Within a few minutes, the pleasant aroma of brewing coffee drifts into the living room where Sara and I sit chatting. It's been almost a year since I was with these dear friends, and we quickly bounce from topic to topic, catching one another up on our lives.

"Here you go, ladies," Bryan says, setting a plate of dark chocolate squares on the coffee table and handing each of us a coffee mug. "So has she told you yet?" he asks me.

"I was waiting for you," Sara responds excitedly.

"Told me what?" I question, looking at their smiling faces.

"Well, do you remember when you taught on healing the last time you visited?" Bryan begins, taking a sip of his coffee. "I never heard anyone explain healing like you did, but I figured if you can pray and see people healed, I can, too." He pauses to take another sip, allowing the suspense to build. "Honestly, the idea intimidated me at first. I'd never done anything like that, not in a Bible study or church service and definitely not outside of our Christian circle. But obviously, we've known you for years and saw the transformation in your life."

"Get to the story!" Sara interrupts.

"Oh, right. Sorry." Another sip. "Well, a few months ago, I heard a coworker complaining that his ankle hurt. I just kind of noted that he was talking about it, and then a week or so later, he mentioned it again after work. So I prayed for him just like we did that night you taught, and all of his pain went away!"

"That's awesome!" I say. "Way to go. Way to step out."

"But that's not all," Bryan responds with a smile. "His pain left that day, and two days later he shows me his workout app that recorded how many flights of stairs he ran, all without any pain in his ankle."

"Come on, Jesus!" I excitedly exclaim.

"And then," he continues, "he started telling some of our colleagues how Jesus healed him."

"Isn't that incredible?" Sara interjects. "This guy who isn't even a Christian goes around testifying about what Jesus did for him."

Bryan continues, his enthusiasm growing, "Now I have coworkers come to me and ask for prayer, and they're getting healed! I've gotten to pray for several of my colleagues because the first guy was so blown away by what God did for him."

"I love this," I say, the coffee and chocolate momentarily forgotten. "Way to take a risk and go for it. That's amazing."

Fueled by our excitement (and maybe a little post-dinner caffeine), the three of us talk well into the night about all that occurred and what it will look like when believers everywhere realize the power and authority we have to heal the sick everywhere we go. My friend's observation about how easy it is to see people healed is one of the most important things to take away from this book: Praying for healing is easy. In fact, it's so easy (and so much fun) that once we learn how to do it, it's hard *not* to pray for people.

My friends shared that the two main things that used to keep them from praying for the sick were a lack of understanding about God's desire to heal and ignorance about their own authority to bring healing. The first time they saw healing prayer taught and modeled was in our short training. An hour-long teaching, a few testimonies, and one demonstration later, they couldn't help but pray for the sick. You've read an entire book about praying for healing—think of how well positioned you are for success!

In this chapter, we'll walk through a prayer model and clear up any remaining questions regarding how to pray for healing. Bear in mind there is still much to learn and discover about healing—this book is only an introduction to a life of miracles.

CREDIT AND RESPONSIBILITY

Last night a certain Northern California baseball team allowed four runs in the top of the ninth inning to blow a three-run lead. (To those unfamiliar with baseball jargon, my team went from almost assured victory to a very uncomfortable position that required us to score to stave off elimination.) Though separated from the action by hundreds of miles, I did what any self-respecting fan would do when my team came up to bat in the bottom of the inning: I put on my rally cap. The rally cap, worn to "help" your team score runs when behind in late-inning play, is fashioned by turning a regular baseball cap inside out. In this particular instance, it didn't work. I was left watching the opposing team's celebrations in disbelief.

A rally cap may be a silly example, but we sports fans are well known for having an endless list of crazy things we do to "help" our teams win. Even though I unblinkingly wore a rally cap last night, deep down I understood that my actions wouldn't really cause a sharply hit ground ball to find a gap through the middle infielders. When my team wins, I enjoy the victory and relive the highlights, but I can't (and don't) take credit. Likewise, when they lose I discuss what could have been done differently and hope for a win next time, but I don't take responsibility. As much as I might shout in my living room, I know that both credit and responsibility lie with those on the field.

Growing in my ability to recognize what the Father is doing, stewarding the measure of breakthrough I've experienced, and actively taking risks outside of my comfort zone—these decisions impact my prayers. But in the same way a fan can't take responsibility for a team's performance, when we pray for healing, ultimate responsibility must rest with the one ultimately responsible: Jesus. God graciously gives each of us a role to play, but he is the one who heals, and Jesus gets all the credit and responsibility.

For most of us, it's relatively easy to avoid taking undue credit for healing. This usually isn't the dangerous side of the coin; we are well aware of our inability to work a miracle and consequently have no problem directing the credit and praise to Jesus where it belongs. Yet for some reason, we're quick to blame ourselves if things don't go according to plan and someone isn't healed immediately. Wrongly taking responsibility for an unwanted outcome is a common pitfall.

Even as I write this, I know there are many who, when faced with a situation where the healing is yet to come, will go home and think about what they did "wrong," even justifying their self-accusations by assuming this section of the book wasn't written with their particular scenarios in mind. But that isn't true. It's for these people that this section exists. Blaming ourselves for not "doing" enough—be it praying hard enough, fasting long enough, or praying the "right" things—is harmful *and* contrary to Scripture (see Gal. 3:1-5). And it's not how Jesus thinks about the situation. This kind of self-accusation agrees with a spirit of religion that promotes form over power and a humanistic spirit that suggests our efforts will save us. The Holy Spirit is the one working the miracle. He deserves all the responsibility, both when the healing occurs and when it is yet to come.

Taking credit for something Jesus deserves is dangerous territory. The times when we have yet to see the healing take place are great opportunities to go before Jesus and exchange any wrongly assumed responsibility. Jesus gets our praise and questions, our thanksgiving and our fears. The burden to heal is a heavy one, far too weighty for us. We must leave the responsibility to heal squarely on Jesus' shoulders lest it crush us.

IF AT FIRST YOU DON'T SUCCEED, SPIT, DECLARE, AND TRY AGAIN

His pleas for bread unanswered, the man coughed and wiped the dust from his face as another wagon kicked up dirt. For many, he was like a mile marker or tree stump, a part of the road itself. Hot and dusty after another long day begging near the city, the man held out his hand, this time not for a coin or a piece of bread but to judge the warmth of the sun. The shadows were beginning to creep across his body, and he knew by feel that soon people would be along, their work finished for the day. *How many years have I held watch over this strip of road?* he thought to himself and then snorted. *Watch. If only my eyes could see again.* He sighed, remembering the days before the accident took his vision and his world went dark.

The sound of people approaching pulled him from his memories. "Soldiers," he said aloud, recognizing the distinct clanking made by their armor. Roman soldiers often passed by the blind beggar and frequently unleashed their pent-up frustration and anger on the man. The soldiers' jeers were relatively easy to endure and, in some cases, he found them almost amusing. One particular soldier took it upon himself to learn disparaging remarks in the blind man's vernacular. No, the man expected nothing but insult from the soldiers, and their words were easily ignored. The comments that cut deeply were the ones shouted by his own countrymen, their remarks reminding him that he was cursed and unfit to be part of their society.

But today, the soldiers came and went without a word. *What's gotten into them?* the man thought. Soon he began to hear excited voices farther up the road. It sounded like some sort of wedding party or celebration was approaching. *What could this be?* he thought.

Quick footsteps and the sound of youths shouting to one another descended on his position. "You there," he shouted in the general direction of the road. "Tell me—is there some celebration today? A wedding perhaps?"

"No!" a boy shouted back with a laugh. "It's Jesus of Nazareth."

"Jesus of Nazareth?" the man repeated. The name was familiar to him. Stories of Jesus healing the sick and teaching with great wisdom and authority were commonly discussed along the road. Some said he was a prophet, while others said only God could perform such miracles. A warm feeling flooded the man's tired frame as hope began to blossom in his heart. *If Jesus is truly the Son of David, the Messiah . . .* His thought trailed off. His heartbeat quickened, his pulse beginning to shout more loudly than his fears. Unable to contain himself, he imagined what it would be like if Jesus noticed him. *Maybe Jesus will heal me!*

"Here he comes now!" another boy shouted.

"Jesus, Son of David!" the man yelled. The sound of a great crowd walking on the road drowned out his cry, so he shouted all the more loudly, "Mercy, Son of David! Have mercy on me!"

"Be quiet, you!" came a gruff response.

"Allow the teacher to pass in peace," shouted another.

Their stern rebukes could not stifle the overwhelming hope within him. With all his might, the man cried, "Jesus, Son of David, have mercy on me!"

The crowd stopped their march toward the city and grew quiet. Before he knew what caused the sudden hush, he felt himself raised by a pair of strong arms and led through the throng of people.

A kind voice addressed him: "What do you want me to do for you?"

The voice needed no introduction; the blind man knew it was Jesus. His cries for mercy had fallen on compassionate ears. "Lord," the man replied, falling to his knees, "I want to see."

"Receive your sight; your faith has healed you," Jesus replied.

Immediately, sight returned to his eyes. He covered his face with his hands, overwhelmed by the sudden flood of light. "I can see," he said slowly, pulling back his hands and looking around at the stunned crowd, many of whom regularly passed him on the road. His gaze rested on the man in front of him. Surely this was Jesus. "I can see," he repeated.

"Yes, you can," Jesus replied, smiling.

"Praise God, the mighty one of Israel!" the man shouted, arms and face lifted to the sky. "Oh, God of my fathers, there is no God like you in all the earth, for you are mindful of the low and the meek. You bring light to those lost in darkness." And turning to Jesus, he said, "Thank you, Jesus, Son of David! Thank you!"

The crowd, amazed by what they witnessed, joined the man in praising God. Even those who only moments before had attempted to silence the man picked up his refrain of praise. "Surely only God can make the blind to see!" they exclaimed.

• • •

That is how I imagine the scene described in Luke 18:35–43. The Bible tells us that the blind beggar called out as Jesus passed by, and though rebuked and told to be quiet by those in the crowd, the man continued his shouts until Jesus heard him. I love that even though he was blind, the man could "see" Jesus' true identity, and his spiritual vision opened the door for him to receive his physical sight.

While there are a number of lessons we can glean from this passage, I want to focus on how Jesus healed the man. Scripture states that Jesus spoke declaratively: "Receive your sight," and the man's blind eyes opened (vv. 42–43). Commanding or speaking a declaration is one way of praying for healing, but it's not the only way. A quick look at the different ways Jesus healed blindness in the Bible reveals multiple prayer methods:

- Spitting in the man's eyes, touching them, praying, and then touching the eyes a second time when the first prayer did not bring perfect vision (Mark 8:22–26)

- Touching the eyes and speaking declaratively (Matt. 9:27–31)

- Casting out a demon (Matt. 12:22–24)

- Touching the eyes without speaking (Matt. 20:29–34)

- Making mud with his saliva, putting it on the man's eyes, and telling him to wash in the pool of Siloam (John 9:1–6)[38]

Sometimes Jesus touched the person, and sometimes he didn't. Sometimes he healed in front of a crowd, and sometimes he healed away from others. Several times he spit, either on the ground to make mud or directly into the person's eyes. And at least once Jesus

---

38. I like to call this the "jump in the lake" prayer method.

exorcised a demon that caused blindness. Clearly, Jesus did not find one way that "worked" and stick to it, but he actively listened to the Father to partner with what he was doing *this* time.

God brings healing in many different ways. It's never about following a formula, and it's always about relationship. As long as the person we pray for is loved, valued, and honored, there is no right or wrong way to go about it. The key is to focus on what God is saying now, in this moment, for this situation. Sometimes it looks like a declaration ("Receive your sight"), while other times it looks like the laying on of hands. Still other times it requires the person we are praying for to partner with our prayers in some way—to act in faith and wash in the pool.

While I've never asked anyone to jump in a pool (not yet, anyway), I have been led by the Lord to some creative, nontraditional ways to pray for healing. In fact, to keep any of us from getting stuck in a "prayer box," sometimes when I teach on healing, I ask the groups to pray in a way they never have before. This forces us to trust the Holy Spirit's leading instead of a formula, *and* it encourages us to trust our ability to recognize God's voice. We've seen God heal through shadows (see Acts 5:12–15), as we've counted backward from ten to zero, and through cell phone flashlights shone on an injury like a healing spotlight.

In the same way that power doesn't depend on the precise words we say, our actions don't cause the healing. Instead, our words or actions require us to exercise our faith while drawing a target for the Holy Spirit's power. Actions are also convenient ways to *demonstrate* our faith; sometimes the water parts as we stand on the shore (Exod. 14:21–22), but other times we must get our feet wet in the river before it stops flowing (Josh. 3:14–17). Regardless of what we say or do, if we seek to love the person in front of us and partner with God to see his will done on earth as it is in heaven, we are already successful.

PRAYER MODEL

Even though we are about to discuss a prayer model, I want to be profusely clear about one point: This is not the only way to pray for healing. As Jesus demonstrated throughout the Gospels, there are many different ways to pray for healing. He explicitly stated that he did only what he saw the Father doing (John 5:19), so it's our aim to stop, look, listen, and partner with what God is already doing—even if it's different from the following model. This isn't a formula that indiscriminately fits every case and scenario, but it's a helpful tool to get us started. Personally, I follow this model the majority of the time I pray for healing.

Whether we follow this model or not, love is our green light every time we pray. It's always our aim to honor the person in front of us, demonstrate the power of Christ's love, and see Jesus get his full reward. With that said (and resaid), it's time to proceed.

Ask a Couple of Questions

The first step in praying for healing is to respectfully question the person about what needs to be healed. We don't need a detailed description, just a target for our prayers. Ask the person about his current range of motion (or eyesight, hearing, etc.) and pain level on a simple one-to-ten scale, with one being little pain and ten being extreme or debilitating pain. This gives us a pre-prayer baseline so we can easily recognize what God is doing after we pray.

Another reason we question the person before we pray is that sometimes the simple act of coming forward or asking for prayer is enough of an open door for God. People are regularly healed before we even pray for them, but they don't realize it until we ask them what hurts.

Stop and Listen

Pause and ask God how he wants to heal *this* time. What is God already doing and how can you partner with him? Are you being led to pray with words or some other act of faith? Often the risk (act of faith) necessary to obey the Holy Spirit's leading releases the miracle (see 2 Kings 5:14; John 9:7).

10-Second Prayers

Always pray as the Holy Spirit leads you and remember you're not asking God to do something—you are declaring or commanding in agreement with what he's already done.

- Speak to whatever needs healing, commanding it to be healed and the pain or illness to go. If the person has a hurt shoulder, you could pray something like, "Shoulder, be healed. All pain leave in Jesus' name."

- Invite God to intervene and the person's body to come into alignment with heaven. You could pray, "Body, be here on earth as you are in heaven." Or "Jesus, come touch this shoulder."

- Keep your eyes open. You want to stay aware of the situation and see what God is doing.

- Keep the entire prayer under ten seconds. Eight seconds is even better. When we pray for healing, long prayers are almost always due to a lack of faith. We're worrying about the words we're using or questioning whether God will really work through us when we need to be listening to the Holy Spirit's leading.

Don't worry if you don't fully understand what needs healing or can't name the knee ligaments that need replacing. I've seen God heal people from diseases I can't pronounce, repair ligaments I didn't know existed, and—on multiple occasions—heal people who simply told me they needed healing without supplying any further information. God is the Great Physician and understands better than any of us what needs to be repaired, replaced, or recreated. The power isn't in the words we say but in releasing the one within us.

If you feel bold, pray boldly. But if praying for healing requires every ounce of your faith, there's no need to fake confidence. Humility and honesty go much further in the kingdom than false bravado. Remind yourself of Christ's total victory already won for *this* person, and then invite the Holy Spirit to touch the one in front of you. There's no such thing as a wrong prayer so long as we honor the person in front of us, remembering that Jesus wants to see her healed more than we do.

Sometimes I feel God leading me to *do* something instead of *say* something. In that case, after interviewing the person, I'll do whatever it is I feel led to do. For example, when praying for one young woman who suffered terribly from chronic back pain caused by a car accident, my friends and I felt like God was leading us to use my shadow to bring healing (see Acts 5:15).

We explained what we thought God was directing us to do, and without touching her or saying anything else, I waved my shadow down the length of her body.

Immediately she burst into tears and told me that as soon as my shadow touched her body, the pain left. It was her first pain-free moment in five years.

Ask a Few More Questions

After praying, ask the person what is happening. Sometimes people aren't aware that God is at work until we ask them what they are experiencing.

- Are they sensing anything? People often experience a low-level sensation of electricity or heat or a strong sense of love, joy, or peace when God is at work. One time a woman I was praying for told me she felt nothing when I prayed for her broken wrist. I mistakenly interpreted this to mean nothing happened. She further explained that she literally felt nothing—the whole area was numb. She took off her splint to find she had full mobility, and the swelling and egg-sized bump were gone. It isn't necessary that people feel something, but it is good to know about anything that occurs.

- Did the pain move or worsen? This often means there is a demonic element involved. There's no need to worry or be frightened, nor do I recommend sharing that tidbit with the person you are praying for. Telling someone there might be a demonic element present can introduce fear and probably won't leave the person feeling loved and encouraged (and it's also possible we're mistaken). Instead, moving or increasing pain is useful information for us and gives us a target at which to aim our prayers. Simply tell the demon to go to Jesus—he'll deal with it. You could say something like, "Spirit of Pain, go now in Jesus' name."

- If the injury or illness is something that can be tested on the spot, encourage the person to check it out to see what changed—but never force someone to do something he's uncomfortable doing. If you prayed for back pain, have her bend over and touch her toes; if it's knee pain, have him do squats. Often the healing manifests when we partner with God in faith.

- Ask the person for a current pain level or for her current range of motion, and compare this to the pre-prayer number or range of motion. Reinterviewing the person this way lets us know if we need to pray again and helps us focus the attention on what God is doing instead of what hasn't occurred. Sometimes people will say they aren't healed when they mean they're not *completely* healed. If his pain was a level five before you prayed and now it's a level two, give thanks. If she can raise her arm another fifteen degrees without pain, God is at work and you are witnessing a miracle.

Pray Again (If Necessary)

Jesus prayed for the blind man in Mark 8 two times before the man saw perfectly. If even Jesus prayed twice for a complete healing, it's definitely okay for us to pray more than once. I've witnessed breakthrough occur on the eighth time I prayed for someone, and that's nothing compared to one of my friends who prayed for a man more than fifteen times (they lost count) before seeing the miracle occur. Our prayers, declarations, and acts of faith wage war in the spiritual realm; sometimes it takes more than one prayer before we see the breakthrough. We remain sensitive to the person we are praying for, but if she's up for it and we feel the Lord leading us to pray again, we pray again.

Have Fun

God loves to break down the boxes we put him in and surprise us with his goodness, love, *and* his sense of fun. While the need for healing is often grave and serious, healing itself needn't be. Moreover, I think there's a strong correlation between Jesus being anointed with the oil of joy more than anyone else and his seeing everyone he prayed for healed (Heb. 1:9; Acts 10:38). Laughter helps break us out of mindsets that unintentionally limit our hope for heaven to come and God's will to be done. Of course, there are times when laughter is inappropriate, but the rest of the time a joyful heart is good medicine (Prov. 17:22). You have permission to have fun and enjoy yourself when praying for healing—it's possible that a little laughter is exactly what the situation calls for.

Stay Positive

Healings can take time to manifest. Just yesterday I received a text about two women I prayed for a few weeks ago. Both women dealt with uncomfortable skin conditions, both noticed no change when I prayed, and both women woke up the next day healed. Healing was released the moment we prayed, but it didn't manifest until the next morning. Even if you didn't see a change in the moment, it's impossible to pray and have nothing happen. Don't be discouraged by an apparent lack of change or an incomplete healing. Often it takes time for the natural body to catch up to what's occurred in the spirit. This makes what we believe *after* we pray arguably more important than what we believe before or during our prayers. Is God still good and faithful, and does he still desire to see his will manifest on earth? There is no doubt about it—the answer is yes. Therefore, don't allow an outcome to change your mind. We can rest in complete confidence that "he who began a good work in you will carry it on to completion" (Phil. 1:6). He finishes what he starts, even if we're not around to see it.

Through every step of this prayer model, remember that the God of heaven and earth, the Creator and Great Physician, is at work. People will get healed when you pray. Relax, have fun, and go for it. The God who "heals all your diseases" (Ps. 103:3) is with you.

CHAPTER KEYS

My own healing left me with a great desire to see others healed, but I had no clue where to begin. As I was exposed to more and more testimonies of God healing through people like you and me, my hunger to see the sick made well when *I* prayed bubbled over into frustration because I didn't know how to do it. I didn't know then what I know now—praying for healing is remarkably easy and flat-out fun.

An old maxim states it's easier to steer a moving ship than one stuck in port. The same is true when praying for healing. God will lead and teach you as you step out in faith. While it may feel intimidating to imagine yourself praying for someone, I strongly urge you just to do it. Don't hesitate. If you're nervous, grab a friend to go with you or get a few friends together and practice on one another. Begin somewhere. Begin today. Whether it's through declarations, the laying on of hands, or something out of the box like shadows or squirt guns, go for it. It's just possible that God will use you to answer someone else's prayer.

MINISTRY

With a biblically solid theology of healing and a prayer model in hand, it's time to pray for the sick. Jesus is your example and love is your green light.

Father, please set me up. Arrange divine appointments for me to heal the sick. Give me the eyes to recognize the opportunity to demonstrate your kingdom and the courage to take a risk in love. Embolden and enable me now through the power of your Holy Spirit to see the sick made well wherever I find them, to the great glory of your Son, Jesus. Amen.

15

THE QUESTION
OF INCREASE

...

About a year ago, I had the opportunity to pray with a woman who had used up all her medical options and desperately needed a breakthrough. She came with a long list of ailments, including a frozen shoulder that had been operated on more than half a dozen times. It was readily apparent that asking for prayer required all the emotional energy she could muster.

Here's what happened.

"What are you experiencing?" I gently ask after praying.

"Nothing. I didn't feel anything. I'm not healed," she replies tersely, reaching for her purse with her good arm. "Thanks for your time."

"How's the shoulder doing?" I ask, smiling politely and sidestepping her glare. She looks at me like she can't believe I'd ask such a question.

She sighs heavily and sets down her purse. Slowly she attempts to raise her arm from its protected position at her side. Her eyes grow large as she raises it higher and higher. Her arm is about parallel to the ground before a twinge of pain shoots across her face. Immediately, she pulls her arm back to her side. Disappointment replaces her surprise, her hopes yet again proven false. Or so it seems. "It's not healed," she says.

I try to redirect her. "Before we prayed, how high could you get it without pain?"

"Well," she stammers, "I couldn't raise it at all without pain."

"And how high can you get it now?"

"About here." She again raises her arm until it is parallel to the ground. "But I can't get it any higher than this. It's not healed."

"Let me get this straight—before we prayed you couldn't lift your arm at all without pain, and now you can lift it parallel to the ground?" When she nods, I tell her, "That's a miracle. God is healing your shoulder."

Hope glimmers faintly in her eyes.

"Let's just thank God for what he's done and not worry about anything else right now."

She agrees and slowly joins me in thanking God for the increased mobility and decreased pain. Without praying again, I ask her to check her shoulder. Cautiously she raises her arm about fifteen degrees higher than she could before we gave thanks. She looks at me questioningly.

"He's a good Father and always finishes what he starts. What we give thanks for increases," I explain. "Let's thank him for another fifteen degrees."

Dazed, she again thanks God for what happened and again checks her arm. She finds she's gained another fifteen degrees of pain-free mobility. We repeat the cycle of thanksgiving and testing out the joint until she can extend her arm almost completely above her head without pain. After this incredible breakthrough—which is the first positive physical change in her life in a very, very long time—I ask if we can pray for the other ailments on her list.

Overcome by God's love, the woman can only nod her agreement as once again we pray for her healing, albeit this time from a place of thanksgiving and expectation.

. . .

It was a great privilege to share this moment with this woman as the love and power of God slowly disarmed the barriers built by chronic pain and disappointment. Breakthrough brings fresh life to faith and permission to hope. As we focused on what God was doing, faith was released that allowed us to hope for his will to be accomplished in a way we weren't capable of only minutes earlier. This encounter proved yet again that thanksgiving is a powerful weapon to fight the destructive forces of disappointment, discouragement, and disease. Thanksgiving is a key to increased breakthrough in our lives and the lives of those around us.

AN INCREASING KINGDOM

Defense is fundamentally important, but it won't score you any points. (Except in football, where it can get you two.) For many years, I possessed a defensive mindset regarding my role in divine health and healing. The only thing I knew to pray for was protection. I was ignorant and untrained regarding my offensive role in taking the fight to the enemy—I didn't know how to actively confront pain, sickness, and disease. In other words, I didn't understand that God intends for the rule and reign of his kingdom to come through *me*.

Seeing the kingdom's territory increase is both our original God-given task and our current objective (Gen. 1:28; Matt. 6:10). We are God's "plan A" for his perfect will to be accomplished on earth as it is in heaven. Everything we know about healing right now is a great beginning, but we can't stop here. We need to press on and continue to learn, grow, and advance in our understanding about healing as our lives continue to become aligned to the one-way growth pattern of God's ever-increasing kingdom (Isa. 9:7 NASB). Our heavenly mandate is unidirectional and can be summed up in one word: increase.

THANKSGIVING

The opening story of the woman's (formerly) frozen shoulder demonstrates our first key to increase: What we give thanks for grows. Jesus modeled this for us when he fed the five thousand. He chose to give thanks for the few loaves and fish available to them instead of focusing on the missing ingredients necessary to feed the crowd. This effectively set the table for a great miracle (see Matt. 14:13–21). When we give thanks for what God has already done and provided for us, we align our hearts with heaven, a place that knows no lack and sees problems from the perspective of already being answered. Jesus wasn't unaware of the physical needs the crowd presented; instead, he was *more* aware of heaven's reality of abundance accessed through thanksgiving.

It's easy to joyfully give thanks when the man gets out of his wheelchair or the blind woman sees (actually, it's hard *not* to get a little crazy when that happens), but it's far more challenging to give thanks before we've seen the miracle. Yet we have insider information that enables us to offer thanksgiving before we see the breakthrough. We know the character of our God, his will to heal, and his unchanging plan for every person to experience him as a loving Father. We know that sickness, disease, and death were defeated once and for all at the cross. That is why we can always give thanks to the Father for everything (see Eph. 5:20).

Like tuning the radio to a frequency without static, thanksgiving positions our hearts to hear the Lord regardless of whether or not the healing has occurred. It refocuses our attention on what's truly important. We look at what God has done instead of becoming overwhelmed, distracted, or discouraged by what hasn't happened yet. And what's more, it's incredibly powerful to offer thanksgiving before we see a complete breakthrough. Thanking God before we see the healing manifest is a violent act of spiritual warfare. Pre-breakthrough thanksgiving is a kick in the enemy's teeth.

Thanksgiving brings increase, aligns our hearts with the Lord's, and is one of the most practical acts of obedience available to us—and that's just for starters. In fact, it is *the* start, or better said, the entrance: Thanksgiving is our entrance point to the presence of God. King David wrote, "Enter his gates with thanksgiving and his courts with praise" (Ps. 100:4). It is in God's presence that we are reminded of our true identity as daughters and sons of a perfectly good, loving Father who has won absolute victory. It's where we are filled with joy (see Ps. 16:11), the grace to stand firm in the faith, and the encouragement to press on when everything else tells us to quit.

Our God is not careless. He does not get distracted, forget, or change his mind. He's extremely intentional and does everything with excellence. Whether we're dealing with a frozen shoulder or a few loaves and fish, thanksgiving brings increase as we align ourselves with the constant, consistent nature of God. A thing begun is as good as done. He will finish what he starts. Therefore, whatever we do, whether in word or deed, we "do it all in the name of the Lord Jesus, giving thanks to God the Father through him" (Col. 3:17).

PRAISE

If thanksgiving is the gate to God's presence, then praise is the door and, not surprisingly, our second key to immediate increase. Let's take another look at Psalm 100:4: "Enter his gates with thanksgiving and his courts with praise; give thanks to him and praise his name." Praise, like thanksgiving, ushers us into God's presence, wages spiritual warfare, and brings breakthrough. Though praise is intricately linked to thanksgiving, it's not quite the same thing; thanksgiving is grateful acknowledgment of God's actions—what he's done, is doing, or will do—while praise is grateful acknowledgment of God's character and nature. One is our response to how he acts, and the other is our response to who he is. When we offer praises to God, particularly in the midst of circumstances where we don't feel like praising him, we place ourselves in a position where he is justified to act on our behalf (see Ps. 91:15).

We praise God in spite of our circumstances because we know the ultimate outcome, not because we are ignoring the problem. We praise him because Jesus foresaw our situation and already provided our solution. We praise him because perseverance, character, and hope are growing within us (see Rom. 5:3–4). Praising God takes us from the problem and places us before the one who is the answer. It doesn't make any difference *what* is healed. Whether it's a cold, cancer, a headache, or heart failure, God the Great Physician is glorified, the Holy Spirit's manifest presence is with us, and Jesus receives the reward of his suffering—yet another reason to give him thanks and to praise his mighty name.

It can be surprisingly easy to miss what God is doing because of the shadow cast by what hasn't happened yet. Pain and disappointment can blind us from recognizing God's hand, while thanksgiving and praise open our eyes to his activities. As we give thanks for what has happened, we create space for immediate increase. Praising God for who he is before we've seen the fullness of his promises shouts loudly in the heavenly realm that we place greater confidence in his character than in our circumstances. So, too, a lifestyle of praise and thanksgiving at all stages of breakthrough—after, during, and before a healing manifests—puts us in great company with those who dared live by the Word of God instead of their experiences. They walked by faith instead of sight (see Heb. 11:13–16; 2. Cor. 5:7). Thanksgiving and praise attract heaven's attention and increase.

A LIFESTYLE OF INCREASE

At the end of *The Last Battle,* the final book in the Chronicles of Narnia by C.S. Lewis, the children enter the great lion Aslan's country. There Aslan shouts an invitation: "Come further in! Come further up!"[39] Unlike the physical world, the deeper into Aslan's country they went, the bigger and more beautiful it became.

As a child reading these stories, I struggled picturing a place that got bigger the farther into it I went—I didn't have much understanding of physics, but I knew that the more of a woods or a house I explored, the less of it there was to discover. I brushed the idea aside as pure Narnian fantasy, something not of this world. Little did I know how close I was to a great theological truth: The more we encounter God, the more beautiful he becomes and the more of him there is to discover. God paradoxically grows in beauty and size as we run "further in and further up" to him and his kingdom. We will never come to the end of this journey of discovering, knowing, and experiencing him—not for all eternity.

It should come as no surprise that as we learn about healing, we discover it's a thread we could pull on for the rest of our lives without fully unraveling the blanket. Healing isn't a one-time sermon series, book study, or event; it's a lifestyle.

Thanksgiving and praise are only the beginning. In this chapter, I want to talk about a few tools to help us continually grow in our understanding and practice of healing. It's our great privilege as the

---

39. Lewis, C.S., *The Last Battle* (New York: HarperTrophy, 1994), 197.

body of Christ to walk in intimacy with God, discover more about him, and continuously see his kingdom come through us. As you continue to learn and experience more, and the deeper into him you run, I pray you encounter more of his profound love for you and that it is (at least partly) demonstrated in radical healings through you.

EAT TO STAY HUNGRY

My first trip to a Brazilian steakhouse stands out as one of my all-time favorite dining experiences. A mission trip to Rio de Janeiro concluded with a day off to tour the city's world-famous sites: We took Jeeps through Rio's jungles, cruised by snowy-white beaches, and climbed the steep mountain to the famed Christ the Redeemer statue. Even though we stood at the top of Corcovado, the summit was not the pinnacle of our day. Our final stop was at a local *churrascaria,* which turned out to be an experience unlike anything I'd ever had. Waiters carrying an unending parade of different cuts of steak met us as we walked through the door. It seemed this was exactly what the prophet Isaiah foresaw when he described heaven's banquet of "the best of meats and the finest of wines" (Isa. 25:6). A Brazilian friend, immune to the shock of a *churrascaria,* offered me some advice: "Skip the bread, eat only your favorites, and pace yourself."

The reason a dining strategy is so crucial when eating at a Brazilian steakhouse is simple: The more we eat, the less hungry we become. It's the basic cause and effect of hunger and eating. But as we briefly discussed earlier in this book, things work differently in the kingdom of God. The natural law of hunger and consumption is reversed. To maintain a lifestyle of increase, we eat to stay hungry.

The more we feed ourselves the things of God, the more we crave them. We've all experienced this at one time or another—the worship song we can't help but play on repeat, the Bible study that creates a yearning for more of the Word, the desire to spend more time with those friends who encourage us to believe like Jesus. The more we do those things, the more we *want* to do them. A steady diet of testimonies recalibrates our thinking, expands our expectation to see God move, and lifts our eyes back to Jesus and away from any problems or distractions that may have unknowingly crept into our thought lives. To keep growing in a lifestyle of healing, feed yourself healing testimonies.

Testimonies also help right the ship if we feel out of sync or otherwise off our game. Contrary to how it may sound, there are plenty of days when I don't pray for anyone's healing. Ironically, I've prayed for fewer people than usual while writing this book, as I've spent a large amount of time alone in an office to ward off distraction. When I realize it's been a while since I've prayed for someone, I start dealing with fears that I'm being hypocritical, that I've lost my passion for healing, or that I am generally unworthy to write this book. Instead of worrying about the merit of those fears, I've learned the best thing to do is read or watch healing testimonies. In fact, before I sat down to write today, I watched an incredible testimony of a little girl born with an incurable disability that affected her growth, development, and lifespan. She was radically healed and is now fully functioning and healthy. This made me praise God and encouraged my heart to do the work in front of me. As I feed myself with what God is doing, something incredible happens: Life, excitement, and energy return to the part of me that felt under attack.

An heir must take possession of an inheritance to benefit from its value. King David wrote, "I have inherited Your testimonies forever, for they are the joy of my heart" (Ps. 119:111 NASB). Testimonies in Scripture and throughout history are an extremely valuable part of the believer's inheritance as they reveal an aspect of God's unchanging nature and his incredible love, creativity, and power. When we fill ourselves with testimonies of what God has done, we feed our expectation for him to be that again in us, through us, and to us. To see more healings through *you,* fill yourself with testimonies of healings through others. Eat to stay hungry.

ASK QUESTIONS

I have it from a reliable source that when I was a child, I seldom spoke, but whenever I did, the sentence typically began with "Why—" and ended with a question mark. From the reason for the sky's blue color to what makes the grill hot, every topic was fair game. Like many children, I was naturally curious about the great big world around me. Asking questions is a child's way to engage with a world that's still a size or two too large for her. It's also one of the very best ways to learn. Regardless of age, asking questions helps us understand our own thoughts and pull on the experience and knowledge of others.

When I have the opportunity to be with those who walk in a lifestyle of healing and miracles, the inquisitive side of me comes out. I love asking about their latest breakthroughs, different things they've learned, what biblical insight they're chewing on, and just about anything else I can think of on the subject. Amazingly enough, our question asking isn't limited to those sitting across the table from us. We have access to the person who "searches all things, even the deep things of God . . . so that we may understand what God has freely given us" (1 Cor. 2:10–12). He is a resource I highly recommend we utilize.

Often after praying for healing, I spend time debriefing with Jesus. This usually looks like sitting on my bedroom floor and asking him questions. During this time, I celebrate healings or taking new risks, *and* I bring up anything that confused or disappointed me. I ask him what he thought went well and what I could have done differently. I ask him what he saw that maybe I missed, how he feels about what occurred, and what he would do next. Sometimes my excitement over the initial healing keeps me from noticing something else the Father was doing, such as ministering to the friend watching, connecting someone to a local church, or even telling the person about the Jesus who healed her. As I debrief with the Lord, I receive his affirmation and loving correction.

I highly recommend two-way conversations with Jesus—speaking and listening like you would with a friend over coffee. He's ever present, incredibly smart, and a great conversationalist. As we learn to hear God's voice and become more sensitive to the moments when he's trying to get our attention, we realize he's constantly speaking. Jesus is never critical. He's never harsh, nor are his words accompanied by guilt or shame. Never. If I see an opportunity I missed, a move of his Spirit I didn't catch, or I begin to feel guilt or shame, I know that I've stopped listening to Jesus and am giving airtime to something far more accusatory in nature. When Jesus speaks, even when he corrects me, it is kind and imparts the grace to change. His voice sounds like home.

Asking Jesus questions and listening to his answers provides understanding for what has occurred, and it takes us beyond past events and into the realm of things yet to come. Asking Jesus about future events and then using my God-given imagination to picture myself actually doing those things allow me to "practice" praying for people and has helped me overcome the fear and anxiety that used to freeze me in place. Practically, this means that before I ever prayed for the cashier at the grocery store, I sat in my quiet time and asked Jesus to help me "see" myself doing it, complete with the nervous emotions and how to respond to possible outcomes. Likewise, before I ever stood at the front of a church prayer line, resolute in the face of words like *terminal, incurable,* and *malignant,* I prepped by asking Jesus his response to those words. If Jesus isn't startled, scared, or hopeless (and he's not), I needn't be either.

Studying the Bible, reading books, and attending conferences and events are all wonderful ways to continue to grow in a lifestyle of healing and miracles. But in the midst of all these great options, we can't forget that we have unlimited access to the great Healer himself. Taking time to sit and converse with the Holy Spirit—allowing him to speak to us, upgrade our perspective, or breathe on Scripture—is one of the greatest keys available for walking in a lifestyle of increase.

THE LAYING ON OF HANDS

I liked math when I was growing up. I appreciated that if you knew the right formula, you could follow the steps and find the solution. Unfortunately, I missed a lot of school due to my health, and there was nothing more frustrating than sitting in math class attempting to follow the lesson without understanding the preceding concept. Math builds upon itself, making it essential to comprehend lesson A before moving on to lesson B. Can you imagine the sheer torture of attempting to solve a basic algebra equation without a solid grasp of arithmetic? It might be doable, but it would take a long time—with many wrong answers and probably a few tears.

Now picture the opposite. What if, instead of attempting to solve an algebra problem with shaky arithmetic, every math class from elementary school through high school repeated the same material? Maybe it was taught in different ways, or the numbers were given in Latin instead of English, but every class covered the same basic lesson. While math can certainly be frustrating when we don't understand a concept, it can bore one to tears if it's not challenging. After comprehending something, we need to move on or we risk quitting from boredom.

Believe it or not, all this math talk adds up to an important point: Basic principles (arithmetic) have to be thoroughly understood but then built upon (algebra and more advanced mathematics). An unstable foundation makes for an unstable structure, but if all your time is spent perpetually perfecting the foundation, you won't have a building. When it comes to our Christian walk, the basic principles need to be rock solid, and then we build upon that foundation. This is what the author of Hebrews recommended to the early church:

> So let us stop going over the basic teachings about Christ again and again. Let us go on instead and become mature in our understanding. Surely we don't need to start again with the fundamental importance of repenting from evil deeds and placing our faith in God. You don't need further instruction about baptisms, the laying on of hands, the resurrection of the dead, and eternal judgment.

HEBREWS 6:1-2 NLT

Most of these basic teachings are familiar to me; they were the subject of childhood Sunday school classes and are now the topic of podcasts I listen to as an adult. Yet there at the beginning of Hebrews 6 was an entirely unfamiliar concept: the laying on of hands.

I couldn't recall a Sunday school teaching on the subject, and I knew very little about it as an adult, but since the author included it with such bedrocks of Christian life like faith in God and the resurrection, I assumed it was well worth investigating. I turned to Scripture to learn about this simple-sounding Christian pillar and was genuinely surprised by what I found.

Blessings, spiritual gifts, and heaven's greatest present—the Holy Spirit—are bestowed or imparted through the laying on of hands. And what's more, it's not just a God-to-human impartation but a person-to-person release as well. In other words, if I have a grace or special gifting in a particular area, I can impart that breakthrough or gifting to *you* through the laying on of hands.

Twice the apostle Paul admonished his spiritual son Timothy to make good use of the spiritual gift he received through the laying on of hands (emphases added):

> *Do not neglect your gift, which was given you through prophecy when the body of elders **laid their hands on you.***

1 TIMOTHY 4:14

> *For this reason I remind you to fan into flame the gift of God, **which is in you through the laying on of my hands.***

2 TIMOTHY 1:6

In fact, the laying on of hands was so powerful that a sorcerer offered to pay Peter and John to lay their hands on him (Acts 8:14–24). In other words, the laying on of hands is a big, *big* deal. Though it may be a new concept for some of us, it is an important one. Through it we receive the blessing, gifting, and impartation we need to advance in our faith.

Since learning this, I've become a glutton for the laying on of hands. Everyone carries some aspect of the Lord I've yet to internalize, has experienced God in a way I haven't, or possesses a gifting and grace I don't—and I want it. Particularly when I'm around those who have seen many people healed, I make it a point to ask them to lay their hands on me and pray for me. The laying on of hands is an important basic principle of the faith through which we can shore up our foundations and advance the kingdom. It is yet another key to a lifestyle of increase.

GIFTING BY ASSOCIATION

If increase through the laying on of hands sounds like an exciting way to receive an impartation, then read on, because our next key to a lifestyle of increase is another way to receive from and impart to others.

Jason, my dear friend and mentor, walks in radical love and prays for healing everywhere he goes. The first time we hung out was in a coffee shop. I grabbed my drink and headed over to our table. But Jason picked up his coffee and headed straight for an elderly woman I hadn't noticed. A few minutes later, an ecstatic Jason rejoined our group and told us how God had removed all the woman's arthritic pain. He was overjoyed by the woman's new pain-free existence and the privilege of being the one who got to pray for her. I knew then that this was a guy I wanted to hang around with.

Interestingly, the more time I spent with Jason, the more I began to notice similar traits in my own life, including an increased love and awareness for people that moved me to stop, talk, and pray with them. Of course, some of this was because I regularly watched him pray for people and so I asked him questions, but the increase in love and miracles in my life was from more than just observing and copying him. Something else was occurring, something in the unseen spiritual realm. While just hanging out with him, I received an impartation of his breakthroughs, victories, and giftings.

The idea of impartation was a foreign one to me, so I started asking God about it and searching for it in Scripture. Jesus made an incredible statement about the people with whom we associate: "Whoever welcomes a prophet as a prophet will receive a prophet's reward, and whoever welcomes a righteous person as a righteous person will receive a righteous person's reward" (Matt. 10:41). My close association with Jason unintentionally positioned me to receive from his breakthroughs. Part of this is natural as we become like the people we spend time with through shared experiences and conversation, but another part is a God-designed supernatural blessing. God has so many gifts and blessings he longs to give us, and he finds numerous ways through which to do so. Honor and association position us to receive from others. In the world, we are guilty by association, but in our too-good-to-be-true kingdom life, we are blessed by it. Spending time with others who burn for Jesus and walk in a lifestyle of healing and miracles leads to a life of increase.

USE WHAT YOU HAVE

A couple of years ago, I heard a man speak to a small group of people. There was nothing flashy about him; he was a kind, fatherly, and perhaps slightly boring man of middle age. It was the content, not the trappings, of his message that kept me on the edge of my seat. He shared story after story of the most wonderful miracles: of the blind seeing, deaf hearing, and lame walking—even testimonies of leprosy (Hansen's disease) being instantaneously healed. The people had new fingers, toes, and noses in place of missing digits and blank spaces. As he finished speaking, he offered to lay hands on and pray for anyone interested. Without the smallest hesitation, I ran to the front.

Though impartations can be accompanied by sensations like heat or low-level electricity, that's rarely been my experience. I usually don't feel much physically. This time, however, was different. When he placed his hand on my shoulder, it felt like a hot metal glove punched me in the stomach. Sometime later I got up from the floor and asked, "Who wants to go pray for people at the hospital?"

Even if the most gifted and respected men and women of God prayed for me, whatever grace or gift they imparted would forever lie dormant if I never stepped out and took a risk in faith. The laying on of hands is of the utmost value, but it has to translate into action.

Praying for healing is an absolutely necessary step to activate what God deposited in us through teaching, impartation, or the laying on of hands. Furthermore, using what we receive falls under the principle of stewardship as Jesus described (see Matt. 25:14–29). When we use what's been given to us, we get more.

Healing works like a muscle. The more we use it, the stronger it gets. Impartation is a divine accelerant that adds immediate strength to that muscle, but we still have to use it. The more we use what we have (and the more we give it away through teaching, praying for, and imparting to others), the more we will receive. The second-to-last key to walking in a lifestyle of healing is simple: Use whatever measure of gifting and faith you currently possess and expect more.

EVER EXPECTING

We've come to the final key to walking in an ever-increasing lifestyle of healing and miracles. Don't let this section's brevity suggest it's of little importance because the opposite is true. In fact, I think it's the most important ingredient in the recipe for a lifestyle of increase: Expect God to do great things.

We are confident in God's nature—he is an incredibly loving, kind, and perfectly good Father. We know his unchanging and unquestionable will to heal. We know the inconceivable price already paid for his will to be done on earth. We know what the Bible says, what Jesus did, and the limitless power of the Holy Spirit in us. When it comes to praying for healing and walking in an ever-increasing lifestyle of miracles, we can rest assured that God's Father heart will withstand the full weight of our expectations and faith. He will go beyond all we can ask or imagine. He will show up and show off. His glory, love, and goodness will be made known throughout the earth. Expect God to do great and wonderful things through you and then stand back and watch it happen.

CHAPTER KEYS

The keys to increase listed in this chapter are not comprehensive, but they are a good start. Thanksgiving and praise usher us into God's presence, assault demonic forces, and release greater breakthrough. Feeding on testimonies encourages us, emboldens us, and makes us hungrier for more of God. Asking questions, both of others and of Jesus, is a great way to learn from the past and prepare for the future. Impartation through the laying on of hands releases gifting, breakthrough, and grace. We become like those with whom we associate.

Find others who know more, have experienced more, or who burn brightly for Jesus and hang out with them. Don't compare, don't belittle, and don't assume whatever measure of faith and gifting you have isn't enough; use what you have and receive more. And always expect God to be God—bigger, more beautiful, and better than your wildest dreams.

I am overjoyed as I picture people getting healed when *you* pray for them. I can see God's will being done, his kingdom advancing, and the sick being made well when you pray. You know that God wants to heal and that he wants to heal through you. The kingdom of God cannot and will not be stopped. We cannot and will not be stopped. Just a little yeast mixes through the whole batch of dough and causes it to rise to heights previously unimaginable. Never stop taking ground. Keep growing. Keep pursuing the Lord. Pray for the sick and watch as your life is set on an upward trajectory of increase.

MINISTRY

On the night Jesus was betrayed, he told his disciples that even though his time with them was ending, their instruction and growth were not:

I have much more to say to you, more than you can now bear. But when he, the Spirit of truth, comes, he will guide you into all the truth. He will not speak on his own; he will speak only what he hears, and he will tell you what is yet to come. He will glorify me because it is from me that he will receive what he will make known to you.

JOHN 16:12-14

What a great gift the Holy Spirit is to us. Through him we can expect to perpetually grow and increase, for our minds to be transformed until we think and believe like Jesus.

Father, thank you that you are eternal and unending and that I have forever to learn more about you and know you more. Thank you for all that you've taught me, all that I've learned and experienced, but I must have more. Lord, empower me by your Holy Spirit to pursue greater breakthroughs and to live a lifestyle that ever increases with signs and wonders, miracles, and healings. I pray this in Jesus' name and for the sake of his kingdom. Amen.

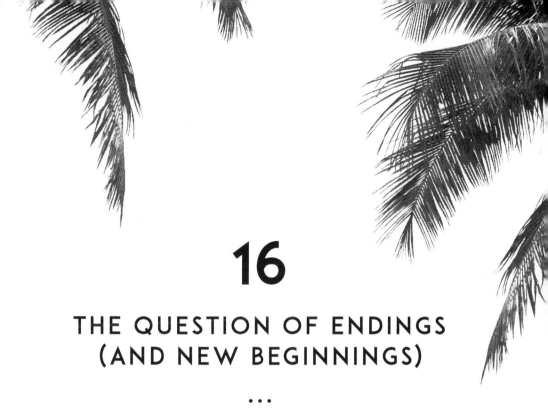

16

THE QUESTION OF ENDINGS (AND NEW BEGINNINGS)

...

It is a beautiful sunny day, the sort of day that beckons to me to come enjoy it. As is often the case on such days, I slip on my running shoes, insert my earbuds, and head outside. As I run, I recount the numerous times throughout the past year when my regular jogging habit turned into a divine encounter.

This day is no different, even though I'm not in the small town where I go to ministry school but visiting my parents. With each memory of God radically touching someone, anticipation builds inside of me—it could happen again on this run.

I turn the corner and see a woman walking twenty yards ahead of me. My excitement peaks. *I can share God's love with her,* I think, slowing to a walk and pulling out my earbuds. *God, is there anything you want to say to this woman?*

A slight twinge in my own hip draws my attention to the woman's hip and lower back.

Before I can say anything, the woman turns and approaches me. My heart leaps as I see her coming. The approach is often the hard part for me, but here she is doing it for me.

"Excuse me. Do you know how far this path goes?"

"I don't know the distance," I reply with a smile, "but do you have any hip pain?"

The woman is clearly taken aback. She pauses before cautiously responding, "Yes. Why?"

"This may sound a little strange, but I was just praying, and I feel like there is something wrong with your hip and back, and I believe God wants to heal it. May I pray for you?"

"I believe in the power of prayer," she admits slowly before telling me of her uncertainties about God and her background at Catholic school.

"Would it be okay if I prayed for you?" I ask again. She looks at me a little suspiciously, so I point to the spot in my right hip where I'd felt the slight twinge. "Is this where you have pain?"

"Yes!" she says, surprised. "You can pray for me."

I pray for her right there on the sidewalk. "In Jesus' name, I command all pain to leave right now. Father, I welcome your love and the reality of your kingdom into this hip and back. Amen."

She seems surprised by the brevity of my prayer.

"How does your hip feel?" I ask. "Can you check it out and try to do something you couldn't do before?"

The woman begins to twist and move. "I can't do this. I can't move like this," she tells me, shocked. "It doesn't hurt!"

"Well, it looks like you are doing it! God's really, really good, and he loves you so much. He just demonstrated how much he loves you."

Tears fill her eyes. "You know," she confesses in a whisper, "I always wanted to believe that was true. I always wanted to believe that God is good."

• • •

My life can be split into two parts pretty easily: before my heal-ing and after my healing. My before-healing years feel like a lifetime ago, distant memories from someone else's life. But memories from that past life occasionally sneak up on me: an antibiotic smell that transports me to a particular doctor's office, a conversation with an old friend that triggers forgotten details, or heating pads—I can't see a heating pad without thinking about the countless hours I spent getting IVs with a heating pad draped over my arm to help ease the constant ache. These memories used to come with pangs of regret for the years I tolerated illness in my life. Fortunately, God heals the whole person. He heals us physically, and he also restores time and memories. Instead of regret, my memories now cause me to shake my head in wonder at God's great grace in my life. The memories that once brought pain now bring praise.

Though my body and memories are now pain free, I'm grieved when I see others who aren't. The good news is that Jesus is incred-ible at bringing freedom to people. Healing memories and physical pain and restoring time are easy fixes for him. Joy, health, and free-dom are the fruit of biblical teaching and the accompanying permis-sion to wholeheartedly pursue healing as Scripture dictates and the Holy Spirit leads. Soon Christ's bride will step into her full authority to see all Jesus bought and paid for manifest on the earth.

It's said that if you can see a problem, you're probably part of the solution. I could see the problem caused by a lack of teaching about healing, and when I asked Jesus what he was doing about it, he gently asked me what I was going to do about it. "Well," I began cautiously, "I could teach what I've learned." There was no light-ning bolt or writing on the wall in answer to my tentative response, just a tender agreement from heaven and the grace to begin. For several days, I sat virtually unmoving as I wrote an outline for a proposed training. Given my personality, this was clearly divine grace at work.

A few weeks after I wrote my initial outline, I felt God speak to me about it, nonchalantly stating, "Looks like you've got yourself a book outline." His words caught me off guard. I was busy working on a different project and had tabled the healing training for the time being. But when God speaks, life flows into our spirits and gives us what we need to accomplish the task at hand. A deep confidence filled my heart. I knew in that moment that I would write a book about healing.

A funny thing happens when we put our thoughts on paper—we see how much and how little we know about the subject. As I looked over my newly expanded book outline, I saw that I possessed a solid basic understanding about healing, but I also saw the many holes that still needed filling. In other words, I knew enough to recognize what I didn't know. My years pursuing God and a lifestyle of healing had brought me into contact with some incredible men and women whose lives read like missing chapters from the book of Acts. I wondered if one of them wouldn't be better suited to write the book.

In my moment of self-doubt, I felt the Lord speak to me again. On this occasion, he quoted Proverbs 27:7: "To the hungry even what is bitter tastes sweet." I knew the Holy Spirit wasn't calling my efforts bitter. In fact, it was quite the opposite. Instead, he effectively told me that what I had to give, though it felt small and insignificant in my own eyes (bitter), would be readily welcomed by a church hungry for healing (it would taste sweet). Again, his words imparted something previously missing. Confidence in his faithfulness to see me through filled me as I meditated on his words. Later, he reminded me of the story of Noah. All Noah had to do was obediently bang boards together, and God supplied the rest. Likewise, all I had to do was bang sentences out on a keyboard and entrust the rain to God. He was faithful to Noah then, and he would be faithful to me now.

My task was to remain obedient to his voice and watch as his mighty hand opened doors no one could shut.

Roughly four years after my unassuming beginning, I'm finally approaching a finish line. Much like spectators cheering on tired runners at a race's end, images of the sick healed inspire my steps. My determination to see healing throughout the church grows as I imagine strength returning to withered frames, children released from hospitals and reunited with their families, and hope restored in places long filled with disappointment. However, it may come as a surprise to you that seeing people healed is not my primary reason for writing about healing. Sickness affronts the cross. It mocks our Lord as surely as the scoffers did at his crucifixion. So my greatest motivating factor in writing this book is to see Jesus receive the full reward of his suffering. Affliction, torment, disease, and even death are vanquished foes—it's high time they are forced to behave that way.

MEASURING GROWTH

I grew like a weed as a kid. Between my first day of fifth grade and the first day of sixth grade, I added ten inches to my height. Constantly hungry, I out-ate my dad many evenings (quite a feat for an eleven-year-old girl) and was convinced you could see my legs lengthen in real time. I, like so many kids, loved having my height measured and celebrated every quarter-inch gain. But even during my Goliath growth spurt, it was impossible to see the height accumulate overnight. Time is a necessary ingredient for measurable growth.

I hope you can see where this growth discussion is going—it's time for us to pull out the proverbial yardstick and measure our growth. It's important both to note and celebrate the changes that have occurred in our thinking regarding the goodness of our heavenly Father, our identity in him, and the topic of healing. To do so, let's revisit the expectations laid out way back in chapter 1. They were:

1. God will encounter you.
2. You will get hungrier for more of God.
3. Hearts will be set on fire.
4. People will be healed.

Take a moment to reflect on how those expectations were met. How did God encounter you as you read this book? What's your current hunger level for God? How has your desire to see God's kingdom come through you started to change? Does your heart burn with passion to see Jesus receive the full reward of his suffering, to see the will of God done here on earth as it's done in heaven? And finally, what do you expect will happen when you pray for healing?

I'm confident there has been measurable growth in your awareness of God's passion for you, your hunger for him, and your willingness to take risks based on your confidence in his nature. Recognizing our growth encourages us to continue our pursuit of God and healing, but it also reveals to us the places where we have been transformed. Radical growth occurs in our lives when we believe better. Our Christian walk begins when we believe *in* Jesus, but our journey progresses as we believe *like* Jesus.

All it takes for deception to lose its power is for us to recognize that we are deceived. It's only a matter of time before God's truth liberates us in every area of our lives, and because of the eternal life gifted us by Jesus, we have time in abundance. Where we were once bound by disappointment, past experiences, or wrong beliefs, Christ's light brilliantly shone and set us free. Gone are the days of working more or trying harder. Instead, we receive the necessary grace to become all that he created us to be and to do all that he prepared for us to do simply by believing his version of reality. Between the first page and now, there's been some seriously measurable growth in our lives.

LANDING THE PLANE

While I'm confident I could conclude this book without another word or punctuation mark and you'd still experience God do incredible things in and through you, abrupt endings cause whiplash. To know where we're headed, it helps to remember where we've been. The next few pages contain the highlights of the last fifteen chapters; they are keys to remember and refer to. But one last reminder: Even when we touch down and the seatbelt sign is turned off, we have yet to arrive at our final destination. This book is a jumping-off point, the start to a great adventure in God. This is the beginning, not the end.

Chapter 1: The Question of Beginnings

- Expect God to work in and through your life.
- Transformation comes through believing better, not trying harder.
- It is natural for a Christian's life to bear fruit that looks like Christ.

Chapter 2: The Question of Who He Is

- God is a ridiculously good Father.
- We cannot overestimate his goodness.
- We rely on God's love so we can live an empowered Christian life.
- The more our hearts encounter the Father's love, the more we become like Jesus.

- It's impossible to experience God apart from his goodness.

- The more we pursue God, the more he pursues us back.

Chapter 3: The Question of Who We Are

- We are the adored children of a really good Father.

- As his children, we have unlimited access to all he is and has.

- Our identity as his children is the foundation from which service flows—we work from love, not for love.

- Receiving what God has for us, including healing, brings him great joy.

- We are great and live impactful, world-changing lives because of who our heavenly Father is.

- We are saints, not sinners; we are adored children and holy ones.

- God wants to give us as much of his goodness as we can handle.

Chapters 4 and 5: The Question of Will: Parts 1 and 2

- Any investigation into God's character, nature, and will needs to start in Scripture.

- God revealed his will to heal in his name *Jehovah-Rapha.*

- God's will to heal is visible in the two places unaffected by sin: the garden of Eden and heaven.

- Jesus perfectly demonstrated God's will to heal by healing everyone who came to him.

- The Bible, not our experience, sets our expectation for healing.

- It is God's will to heal every person of every disease every time we pray for healing.

Chapter 6: The Question of Cost and Kingdom Come

- Jesus won the full healing of our bodies once and for all at Calvary.

- Sin is to the spirit what sickness is to the body. God "forgives all your sins and heals all your diseases" (Ps. 103:3).

- Healing is a demonstration of the presence, rule, and reign of the kingdom of God.

- Healing declares Jesus as the Messiah.

Chapter 7: The Question of Origin

- God's perfect will isn't always accomplished—yet.

- The kingdom of God is here and coming.

- Sin affected creation, which causes elements of the environment to harm us and make us sick.

- Our own choices can negatively affect our health.

- There is a very real enemy who actively seeks to harm us and cause us pain.

- Even in the midst of chaos, God is restoring all things.

Chapter 8: The Question of Punishment and Lessons

- Anything we tolerate has permission to remain.

- God is a good Father; he does not punish us with sickness.

- God does not send sickness for some "greater purpose" we can't or won't comprehend.

- God takes even the things expressly purposed for our harm and turns them into something better than we could imagine.

- The story isn't over until every pile of ashes is turned into a place of "beauty."

Chapter 9: The Question of Gifting

- Jesus is our model for the normal Christian life.

- Our mission is to make earth look like heaven and increase the boundaries of God's kingdom—the territory under his rule and reign.

- Healing is a normal part of Christian life and isn't just for the specially gifted.

- We are allowed to and encouraged to ask for a gift of healing.

- We make specific requests of the Lord and expect his answer to work in and through us.

- Small beginnings are worth celebrating.

- We step out and take risks without comparing ourselves to others.

Chapter 10: The Question of Failure

- Learning to do anything means inevitable mishaps and mistakes; this is completely okay and part of the process.

- We are always successful if the person we pray for feels valued, honored, and loved, whether he is healed on the spot or not.

- We have permission to begin at the beginning and set healthy expectations for ourselves as we grow in our giftings.

- Our heavenly Father is incredibly proud of us whenever we take a risk and step out in faith.

Chapter 11: The Question Without an Answer

- Even though it's God's will to heal everyone, not everyone is healed yet.

- Forgoing our right to understand leads to peace beyond our understanding in the midst of our pain.

- We humbly admit that we don't know why some people aren't healed, and we grieve our losses.

- Dealing with disappointment is a current reality that comes from living in the tension of the kingdom of God here and on the way.

- Even in the face of loss, the Bible, not our experience, sets our expectation for healing.

Chapter 12: The Questions That Limit Us

- Any belief that limits where and when God wants to heal has to go.
  - God heals in America *and* in the developing world.
  - God healed in the Bible and he heals today.

- Medical healings are not second-class healings.

- We follow God's voice as we pursue healing, understanding he can heal us through a miracle or through medicine.

- Health is greater than healing, and we are responsible for stewarding our health via:
  - Clean living
  - Expectant prayer
  - Medical care when appropriate

- Our own health does not disqualify us from praying for healing.

- God doesn't take back a healing. Recurring pain is frequently the enemy's attempt to induce fear and doubt.

- Persistence always pays off. Breakthrough is often just past the point where we feel like giving up the most.

Chapters 13 and 14: The Question of How: Parts 1 and 2

- Our public victories are won in secret, witnessed only by our heavenly Father.

- Faith enables us to act boldly.

- Conversely, lack of faith, or our "faith ceiling," limits our expectation for how God wants to move.

- We grow in faith by:

  - Asking for more faith

  - Prayer and fasting

  - Bible study

  - Reading/listening to healing testimonies

  - Studying the lives of healing revivalists

  - Thanking God before we see the breakthrough

  - Praying for the sick

- We fill ourselves with testimonies of what God is doing in expectation of what he will do.

- We stay focused on Jesus in spite of anything else that may happen.

- We pray from victory, not for victory.

- The credit and responsibility for healing rest on Jesus.

- If we don't see breakthrough, we pray again.

- Basic Healing Prayer Model:

  - Ask what hurts and how much

  - Stop and listen

  - Pray a ten-second prayer

- Ask a few more questions

- Pray again (if necessary)

- Have fun

- Stay positive

Chapter 15: The Question of Increase

- Thanksgiving and praise are cornerstones of our lives, both before and after we see the breakthrough.

- Tools that help us grow in healing:

  - Eating a steady diet of healing testimonies

  - Asking Jesus lots of questions

  - The laying on of hands for impartation

  - Spending time with others who move in healing

  - Using what we have

  - Expecting more

I hope you had your track shoes on because we covered a lot of ground. Like I said earlier, this book was never intended to be the final word on the subject of healing—but to open the topic for discussion and create an expectation for it in our lives. And as much as I hope you learned about healing, experienced it in your own life, and saw it come to others through you, above all I hope you encountered God in a way you had only dreamed of. He's good. He's powerful. He's intimately involved in our lives. If it's not too good to be true, it's not the end of the story.

• • •

BURN THE FLEET

Sticking with our transportation theme, we have one more task at hand: It's time to burn the fleet.

In ancient times, invading armies would set fire to their transports to remove the option of retreat. For soldier and general alike, the only direction available was forward into battle and the only way home was total victory. With this same forward-only mentality, Jesus came to earth and took on all our sin and sickness. He endured the horrors of the cross with a victory-only mindset foretold by the prophet Isaiah:

Because the Sovereign LORD helps me,
I will not be disgraced.
Therefore have I set my face like flint,
and I know I will not be put to shame.

ISAIAH 50:7

From his birth until the very moment of his death, Jesus did not waver or second-guess his goal. Retreat was not an option. Instead, he kept his eyes fixed on the promise (the joy set before him) and demonstrated unwavering confidence in the Father's faithfulness— even unto his own death.

There are certain points in our lives when we, too, must set fire to the ships and remove even the passing daydream of retreat from our minds. This is one of those moments. It's time to decide whether God heals today—and will heal through us—or not. If we don't do this now, self-doubt and double-mindedness disguised as logic and reason will quickly sink us and provide a tempting escape in places we are called to stand firm. Either God heals or he doesn't. Either he is good, personal, powerful, and actively involved in our lives, or he isn't. Either his Word or our past experiences are true—not both.

It's time to decide what we believe. It's time to burn the fleet and remove once and for all any question about God's desire or ability to heal the sick—and his desire and ability to do it through you.

A CALL TO BATTLE

When did I start believing God didn't desire to see me well? If my parents never stopped looking for a solution, taking me from doctor to doctor, putting me through numerous tests that were brutal for them to see—why did I assume my heavenly Father would settle for less? My parents paid an exorbitant price emotionally and financially to see me live a whole, healthy life. My Jesus paid a price far greater.

There are times when everything we experience is contrary to what we know is true. The Word of God will endure forever. He is unchanging. His heart for healing is clearly defined. I'm not naïve or unaware of the countless battles we face and the ones we lose. The more I pursue healing and the greater my desire to see it manifest, the more I'm exposed to the cruel suffering and loss that are reality for far too many people. Even so, in the midst of watching friends and family waste away to debilitating and downright demonic diseases, I know I cannot allow my view of God to change or my expectation, hope, and faith for healing to diminish.

I know how it's supposed to look: Our prayers plus God's unchanging will to heal equal complete healing for everyone. I know that's not our current reality—yet. But I also know that the lack is not on God's end of the equation. He completed his work. He wants to heal and does not withhold his healing grace from us. He cannot return what he already bought. His compassion for us is greater than we can comprehend. Every day that we get up and pray for his kingdom to come is one day closer to the full reality of his answer made manifest in all areas of our lives. The knowledge of the glory of God will cover the whole earth (Hab. 2:14), and we are part of making that happen.

It requires great courage to continue to hope in the face of loss, not to grow despondent when the facts fail to line up with God's glorious truth. A wise friend once told me that to live courageously, we need to feed on the courage of others. We can turn to the past to see what happens when someone dares to stand in the gap between what is right and pending darkness. As we study history, we gain perspective and realize that all it takes for the tide to turn is for someone to stand up in the face of evil and say, "This far and no farther."

One such courageous call to arms came on the heels of the British Expeditionary Force's retreat from Dunkirk in 1940. In the face of seemingly insurmountable loss that left continental Europe in Nazi control and Britain separated from her enemy by only a narrow channel, Prime Minister Winston Churchill gave one of history's greatest speeches that rallied a nation to fight and a world to hope:

> *Even though large tracts of Europe and many old and famous*
> *States have fallen or may fall into the grip of the Gestapo*
> *and all the odious apparatus of Nazi rule, we shall not flag*
> *or fail. We shall go on to the end, we shall fight in France, we*
> *shall fight on the seas and oceans, we shall fight with growing*
> *confidence and growing strength in the air, we shall defend our*
> *Island, whatever the cost may be, we shall fight on the beaches,*
> *we shall fight on the landing grounds, we shall fight in the*
> *fields and in the streets, we shall fight in the hills; we shall*
> *never surrender.*[40]

---

40. Winston Churchill, "We Shall Fight on the Beaches" (speech, London, June 4, 1940), *The Guardian*, https://www.theguardian.com/theguardian/2007/apr/20/greatspeeches3.

Likewise, we, the mighty army Christ envisioned, will fight. And we will win. We are the ones through whom the glory of heaven will be made known. We are the hands and feet of God on earth, the ones who expand and enforce his kingdom reign. We are unwavering in our faith and determination. We will not stop until every cancerous cell is removed, every genetic defect is reversed, and every life-stealing shred of sickness and disease is utterly destroyed, until even its memory is removed from the earth. We may lose a battle and suffer painful causalities, but we will not lower our hope to insulate ourselves from the agony of defeat. Instead, we will continue to raise our expectation to match that of Jesus. And even if disease attacks us or our loved ones, we will push forward. We will press on until earth looks like heaven. We will live an active faith that boldly declares, "My God is able." There is no alternative. God's perfect will shall be accomplished. The absolute fullness of Jesus' victory will be made manifest. We will look our enemy in the eye and fear not, for Christ has overcome the world.

CHAPTER KEYS

Revelation requires responsibility. Jesus spoke in parables in large part because he knew that not everyone had the desire or ability to live up to the responsibility that direct teaching would require of them (see Matt. 13:10–15). Fortunately, God's revelation comes with the necessary grace to live it out. We are now responsible for what we've learned about God's goodness and healing, but that doesn't mean he leaves us alone to figure out how to apply what we've learned. He is with us and he's not going anywhere. He continues to teach us and guide us as we mature as daughters and sons. The revelation of his goodness and healing is not a weight to carry but a spark to set you on fire. It's a starter's gun for a race fueled by joy into all that Christ won for you. It's the beginning of a life more exciting, more impactful, and more fun than you ever thought possible.

Passionate believers burning brightly for Jesus attract a crowd. The world is desperate to know the love of our good Father and the indescribable joy and peace that come with life in his kingdom. So light yourself on fire and burn brightly for all the world to see. Heal the sick wherever you go. And may the gospel be to you and through you the best news the world has ever heard.

MINISTRY

My benediction for you is the same offered by the apostle Paul in 2 Corinthians 13:14: "May the grace of the Lord Jesus Christ, and the love of God, and the fellowship of the Holy Spirit be with you all."

Father God, come with your fire. Burn up my option of retreat. Sear a resolute fortitude into my heart, mind, and spirit to stand unflinchingly on your Word in the face of hardships. Set me on fire with passion and love for you and for the world your Son came to save. And may Jesus receive the full reward of his suffering. All of this I pray in the mighty name of Jesus. Amen.

ACKNOWLEDGMENTS

...

When I began writing *HOPE,* I naively thought I could pound out a book in four months. I wasn't wrong, but I sure wasn't right. Transforming that initial rough draft into what you now hold in your hands required a legion of helpers—both those who assisted in the writing process with edits, proofreading, discussion, theology, and general feedback; and those who encouraged me to keep going when the finish line moved (again), who covered me and the book in prayer, and believed in me before I believed in myself. So many friends sent a text with just the right words, mailed a card brimming with belief, or simply asked about "the book" without being bored by my seemingly unchanging answer: "It's in process." I know everyone says this, but they say it because it's true—this book wouldn't have happened without these special people in my life.

Thank you to Mike and Cathy Wise. The Lord told me he'd send an editor and then you *asked me* to do it. Thank you for your invaluable theological knowledge and wisdom, for keeping me focused on one topic, for believing for me, with me, and beyond me. The first three or four drafts are all thanks to you.

Thank you also to my outstanding editor, Lauren. This is so. much. better. because of you. (And no, I'm not going to change how I wrote that "sentence." It's stylistic and on purpose.)

Thank you to Georgia for making *HOPE* come to life—a fun, beachy life.

Thank you to Judy, who is working to see everyone get a copy of *HOPE* (regardless of what language they speak).

Thank you to all of my beta and proofreaders for making me look good.

There are so many others who've been with me along the way: KK, love you deep; Jenny, remember those "before" days?; thank you to the Morrow Clan for housing me (literally), feeding me (again, literally), and always believing in me; Kate, you've known me, loved me, and encouraged me since before healing was part of my life; Jake and Kristin, for letting me walk the road alongside you and learn from your love, trust, and sense of fun; Amanda, for being my non-situational friend; Honja, for being a big sister, friend, validator, and design coach; Mark, for Club Yeshitla dinners, home groups, and helping shape something inside of me that wasn't there before; Carol, because sometimes those voicemail songs were just what the doctor ordered; and of course, Laura, my constant believer, with me from page one. Thank you!

Thank you to Steven and Chelsea. I'm glad you're stuck with me forever.

Thank you to my intercessors and prayer warriors—you've always been just an email away.

A huge thank you to Debbie Mac. You stepped into your calling and helped me break free into mine.

Thank you to those who have shaped me and my spiritual journey: Bill Johnson for his incredible revelation and ability to put it into words I can understand; Joaquin and Renee for leading by example and imparting troves of wisdom; Jason Chin—you've believed in me unlike any other and love does say go; Kristi, Gary, and the Dare to Believe crew for a space to learn, grow, and rest in God's presence; and Dr. Wright for countless cups of coffee, conversation, prayers, and encouragement over the years.

Finally, and most importantly, I want to thank my heavenly Father. You are always better than my last thought of you. What adventures we will have!